THE WEALTH OF NATURE

THE WEALTH OF NATURE

How Mainstream Economics Has Failed
the Environment

Robert L. Nadeau

 Columbia University Press   New York

COLUMBIA UNIVERSITY PRESS
Publishers Since 1893
New York   Chichester, West Sussex

Library of Congress Cataloging-
in-Publication Data
Nadeau, Robert, 1944–
The wealth of nature : how mainstream
economics has failed the environment /
Robert L. Nadeau.
p. cm.
Includes bibliographical references and index.
ISBN 0-231–12798–7
ISBN 0-231–12799–5 (pbk.)
1. Economic development—Environmental aspects.
2. Globalization—Economic aspects.
3. Globalization—Environmental aspects.
I. Title.

HD 75.6 .N34   2002
333.7—dc21   2002192651

♾

Columbia University Press books
are printed on permanent and
durable acid-free paper.

Printed in the United States of America
Designed by Audrey Smith

c 10 9 8 7 6 5 4 3 2 1
p 10 9 9 7 6 5 4 3 2 1

To my wife, Kathy Wax

with gratitude for all
her patience and understanding.

CONTENTS

CONTENTS

INTRODUCTION

Once, during a flight from San Francisco to Washington, D.C., I observed vast numbers of trucks and milelong strings of railroad cars moving along extensive networks of highways and tracks that threaded in all directions like a circulation system in some giant organism. Products from factories and farms were moving through these arteries toward distant cities and coastal ports, while raw or processed materials were flowing in the other direction to processing and manufacturing plants. I imagined that the web-like connections between electric power plants, transformers, cables, lines, phones, radios, televisions, and computers could be compared with the spine and branches of a central nervous system, and that centers of production, distribution, and exchange could be likened to tissues and organs. I enlarged this frame in my mind's eye to include all of the centers of production, distribution, and exchange and all of the connections between them in the global economy. This conjured up the image of a superorganism that feeds off the living system of the planet and continually extends its bodily organization and functions into every ecological niche.

I realized, of course, that the global economic system is not an organism. It is a vast network of technological products and processes that human beings created in an effort to enhance their material well-being by utilizing the resources of nature. Our species was able to create this system because our evolutionary history was, in one fundamental respect, unique. The evolution of the bodies and brains of our ancestors resulted, about sixty thousand years ago, in the capacity to acquire and use fully complex language systems. In these systems, a limited number of basic sounds, or phonemes, can be grouped together variously in word symbols within complex grammatical and syntactical structures to convey an infinite variety of meanings.

The ability to coordinate experience based on themes and narratives and to externalize ideas as artifacts allowed our ancestors to live in non-species-specific environments and to increase their numbers well beyond the limit that the usual dynamics of evolution would have allowed. Following the invention of a new narrative in the seventeenth century called science and the subsequent development of a host of new technologies, our ability to extend control over the processes of nature increased exponentially. This eventually resulted in the creation of a global economic system that does, in ecological terms at least, feed off the living system of the planet and extend its organization into virtually every ecological niche. And if this economic system continues to grow at the current rate based on existing technologies, it could easily undermine the capacity of the system of life to sustain our growing numbers.

Still ruminating on these matters as my plane was about to land at Washington's National Airport, I asked two large questions: Why do we coordinate our activities in the global economic system in ways that are so insensitive to the impacts of this system on the global environment? How can we begin to coordinate these activities in ways that could realize the goal of achieving a sustainable global environment? The answers to the first question that were eventually included in this discussion are complex and cannot be reasonably summarized here. It is, however, important to note at the outset that attempts to answer the second question led to a radical conclusion about the narrative that is almost universally used by economic planners in both business and government to manage the growth and expansion of the global market system—neoclassical economic theory. The radical conclusion is that fundamental assumptions about the character of economic reality implicit in the mathematical formalism of this theory are such that there is no basis for positing viable economic solutions to environmental problems within its framework.

The primary reason this is the case, which is not widely known or appreciated and which will be examined and explored throughout this discussion, is the following. The conception of the relationship between parts (economic actors and firms) and wholes (market systems) in neoclassical economics is completely different from and wholly incompatible with the actual dynamics of the relationship between parts (organisms) and whole (ecosystem or biosphere) in the global environment. This disjunction between part–whole relationships in an economic theory and the actual dynamics of part–whole relationships in physical reality is, as we shall see, no trivial matter. It explains why there is no basis in this theory for positing viable economic solutions to the crisis in the global environment and why the framework of the theory cannot be revised in ways that could provide these solutions.

If the framework of neoclassical economic theory could be enlarged in ways that could allow us to account realistically for the costs of doing business in a potentially sustainable global environment, there would be no need to question its usefulness. But if this is not "in principle" a possibility, it seems reasonable to conclude that students of economists should do what the best scholars have always done when an orthodox theory is incapable of coordinating experience with reality in ways that lead to the best or most desirable outcomes. They should develop a new theory that can serve as the basis for coordinating experience in economic reality in a potentially sustainable global environment and displace the neoclassical economic paradigm with that theory.

We have already witnessed some movement in this direction. Many well-known mainstream economists, including a number of Nobel laureates, have openly rejected assumptions about economic reality in neoclassical economics, and there is a growing awareness in the entire community of professional economists of the inherent limitations of this theory. Equally interesting, virtually all of the recent theoretical advances in mainstream economics, such as game theory and nonlinear analysis, challenge these assumptions and seek to model economic reality based on a marginally different set of assumptions. Yet most mainstream economists remain firmly attached to the neoclassical economic paradigm, and the vast majority of economic planners in both business and government are guided by predictions and analyses based on this paradigm.

The intent here is not to denigrate the virtues of the free market system or to argue that this system should be displaced by another system. It is to make the case that the only way in which we can hope to preserve most of the substantive benefits of free market economies is within the framework of an environmentally responsible economic theory. Recent studies in environmental science indicate that the time frame during which we can hope to obviate the prospect that large-scale changes in the global environment will become irreversible is a few decades at most. If we fail to meet this challenge, the existence of literally billions of human beings will be threatened, and conditions in geopolitical reality are likely to become quite chaotic.

In this situation, governments will probably feel obliged to impose massive command and control regulations to deal with this crisis, and most of the benefits of free market economies could be lost. What should become clear in the course of this discussion is that there is only one way in which we can hope to obviate this prospect. We must develop and implement an environmentally responsible economic theory that can realistically reflect in its price mechanisms the costs of doing business in a sustainable global environment.

There is, as I hope to demonstrate convincingly, no reason why an environmentally responsible economic theory cannot be developed fairly soon if sufficient resources are committed to this effort. It is, however, one thing to develop such a theory, and quite another to displace neoclassical economics with this theory. The large problem here is that assumptions about economic reality in neoclassical economics are deeply rooted in the Western metaphysical tradition and have a psychological and emotional appeal that is profoundly religious in character. Because understanding the metaphysical foundations of this appeal could be critically important in the effort to displace neoclassical economics with an environmentally responsible economic theory, this will be a subtext in all of the chapters on economics.

The business of confronting and dealing with the crisis in the global environment became much more challenging following the terrorist attacks on the World Trade Center and the Pentagon on September 11, 2001. If the war against terrorism lasts for several years, as President Bush now says it will, we must not only be concerned that a series of escalating attacks and counterattacks could result in more conventional wars between nation states, but we must also deal with the prospect that efforts to resolve environmental problems could be overshadowed by the seemingly more pressing need to protect public safety, conduct military strikes, and ensure military preparedness.

If the war on terrorism had been declared a few decades earlier, it would not have been entirely unreasonable to ignore the environmental crisis until the war had been won or became so routine and uneventful that it ceased to be a central preoccupation in the global community. Unfortunately, the state of the global environment is now such that it would be irrational, not to mention morally irresponsible, to postpone concerted international efforts to posit economic solutions to environmental problems for any extended period. One of the large challenges to those of us who care about the human future is to ensure that this does not occur.

I want to express my gratitude to the many experts in economics and environmental science who were kind enough to review and comment upon this book in manuscript form, particularly Richard Stefanik, Karim Ahmed, and Menas Kafatos. I also wish to give special thanks to Kirk Jensen, who provided consistent support and encouragement and offered a great number of helpful suggestions about ways in which this material could be organized and presented. This book could not have been completed without his assistance, and I am extremely grateful for his efforts.

THE WEALTH OF NATURE

CHAPTER 1

SPACESHIP EARTH

Homo economicus and
the Environmental Crisis

In July 1969 the Apollo 11 spacecraft emerged from the dark side of the moon and its on-board camera panned through the vast emptiness of outer space. Against the backdrop of interstellar night hung the great ball of earth, with the intense blue of its oceans and the delicate ochers of its landmasses shimmering beneath the vibrant and translucent layer of its atmosphere. The distances between us seemed suddenly contracted, the ecosystem vastly more fragile. But the impression that sent the adrenaline flowing through my veins was the overwhelming sense that the thing was alive! The teeming billions of organisms writhing about under the protective layer of the atmosphere ceased in the shock of that visual moment to be separate—they were interdependent, fluid, and interactive aspects of the one organic dance of the planet's life.

The preceding paragraph, an entry from my diary written a few days after images of the whole earth first appeared on American television, cannot, of course, be classed as scientific analysis. It does, however, reflect, in spite of the anthropomorphizing and rhetorical excesses, a new understanding of the dynamics of nature that in 1969 was occasioning a revolution in physics, biology, and the nascent discipline of environmental science. Those of us who saw the first televised pictures of the whole earth that year experienced the shock of the new. Many were awed by the delicate beauty of spaceship earth and felt a renewed sense of wonder and amazement at the fact of our existence in the vast cosmos. But what I found most overwhelming was the emotionally charged realization that earth is a single or unified living system and that all its life forms are interdependent and interactive "parts" of a self-perpetuating "whole."

In physics, in the years following 1969, attempts to understand the nonlinear dynamics of living systems would reveal a relationship between parts (organisms) and whole (ecosystem) in which the stability of the whole is mediated and sustained by interactions within and between the parts. In biology, the old mechanistic model of evolution as a linear progression from "lower" atomized organisms to more complex atomized organisms would be displaced by a model in which all parts (organisms) exist in interdependent and interactive relation to the whole (life). In environmental science, researchers would not only discover that all parts (organisms) exist in embedded relation to the whole (ecosystem or biosphere) and that the interactions within and between parts function as self-regulating properties of the whole. They would also reach the dire conclusion that continued disruptions of the complex web of interactions between these parts by human economic activity could eventually threaten the survival of our species.

In 1969, however, this new understanding of part–whole relationships in physical reality was not apparent in the commentary on the meaning of the whole earth image in print and electronic media. Many commentators perceived the image as eloquent testimony to the fact that America had made good on President Kennedy's 1961 pledge to beat the Soviet Union in the space race by putting a man on the moon by the end of the decade. And because the space race was also an arms race in disguise, some commentators interpreted the image as sign and symbol that the United States had overtaken the Soviet Union in the competition to develop superior intercontinental ballistic missiles and satellite surveillance systems. In this mechanistic understanding of the relationship between parts (nation-states) and whole (the planet), parts are separate and distinct entities that compete for domination of the whole, and the collection of unequal parts constitutes the whole.

An alternate but similar view of the whole as an economic entity emerged in the late 1960s, and its principal architects were neoclassical economists. The power and prestige of these economists derived in part from the conviction that they had been instrumental in winning World War II by effectively managing the American and British economies. Their privileged position was even more enhanced in the decades that followed because they appeared to be able to minimize unemployment, avoid slumps, and assure perpetual economic growth by making minor adjustments in fiscal and monetary policies. The new conception of an economic whole fashioned by the economists was a global market system in which parts (national economies and transnational corporations) compete for dominance or hegemony by perpetually enlarging markets and increasing profits. If neoclassical economists in 1969 had described the whole-earth image from their point of view, they would probably have conjured up a vision of an inexorable economic process that would eventually lead to a quite dramatic result—the emergence of a global economic system in which all economic actors would enjoy very high levels of material comfort and prosperity.

In 1969, however, a large and growing number of people in the nascent environmental movement were inclined, for reasons that were typically more philosophical than scientific, to privilege the welfare of the whole (the planet) over the competition between the parts (nation-states). From their point of view, the whole-earth image was a stark reminder that the ability of "little Spaceship Earth" (a phrase popularized by Buckminster Fuller) to sustain the growing number of our species could no longer be taken for granted. U Thant, secretary general of the United Nations, elaborated on this theme in an address to representatives of member nations in 1968:

> I do not with to seem overly dramatic, but I can only conclude . . . that the members of the United Nations have perhaps ten years left in which to subordinate their ancient quarrels and launch a global partnership to curb the arms race, to improve the human environment, to diffuse the population explosion, and to supply the required momentum to development efforts. If such a global partnership is not forged within the decade, then I have very much fear that the problems I have mentioned will have reached such staggering proportions that they will be beyond our capacity to control.[1]

The global partnership U Thant envisioned has yet to emerge, but environmentalism did become a political force to be reckoned with during the first Earth Week in April 1970. Growing concern about the state of the global environment was also reflected in the exponential increase in the number of books on the subject, ranging from popular manifestos such as Barry Commoner's *Closing Circle* (1971) to more technical studies such as the Club of Rome's *Limits to Growth* (1972). In 1973, the decision

3

by the Organization of Petroleum-Exporting Countries (OPEC) to increase oil prices by cutting production obliged leaders of industrialized nations to become more concerned about resource allocation and energy conservation. This resulted in the creation of new agencies, such as the U.S. Environmental Protection Agency, that were charged with protecting that part of the whole environment that existed within national boundaries.

During the 1970s, the country that was most willing to address environmental problems at the national level was the United States. But following the ideological crusade in the Reagan and Bush administrations (1981–88) to roll back or undermine environmental regulation, northern European countries and Japan engaged in more effective planning and created more innovative institutions. Meanwhile, new environmental concerns such as tropical deforestation, climate change, loss of species diversity, and the thinning ozone layer continued to fuel the growth of the environmental movement.

However, even after the first international conference on the environment in Stockholm (1972), international agreements that could coordinate the efforts of parts (nation-states) to improve the condition of the whole (global ecosystem) remained weak and largely ineffectual. In an effort to resolve this problem, the United Nations Environment Programme (UNEP) was created. One series of actions taken by this agency illustrated that international cooperation was capable of resolving a menacing environmental problem in a timely fashion. After scientists confirmed in 1984 that worldwide emissions of chlorofluorocarbons (CFCs) were damaging the ozone layer, UNEP organized the 1985 Vienna Convention. This resulted in the Montreal Protocol (1987) and a series of amendments at gatherings in London (1990), Copenhagen (1992), and Vienna (1995) in which member nations agreed to curtail production of CFCs sharply.

The environmental movement has been more successful on the local level, particularly in the rich nations. In these countries, some species on the verge of extinction have increased in number, and forests and wetlands that could have been exploited for economic reasons have been preserved. The cleanup of industrial wastewater improved the health and appearance of the Rhine River and the Great Lakes, and sulfur emissions were greatly reduced in virtually all advanced industrial countries. Leaded gasoline was eliminated in advanced industrialized countries, and municipal sewage plants were vastly improved. These local successes by the parts (nation-states) have not, however, even begun to slow, much less reverse, large-scale damage to the whole (global ecosystem), and we are rapidly moving toward the point where this damage could occasion human loss and suffering on a scale that is quite difficult to imagine.

Environmentalists have typically defined the whole as the entire planet or ecosystem, and they tend to privilege the welfare of this whole over the economic interests of parts (economic actors). Meanwhile, those who base their understanding of economic reality on neoclassical economics have been operating on a very different conception of the whole that privileges the economic interests of parts. In their view, the whole is a market system that exists in a domain separate and discrete from the natural environment; and the relationship of parts (economic actors and firms) to this whole is rigorously defined in terms of lawful or lawlike forces that govern the behavior and interaction of the parts.

From the perspective of environmentalists, those who adhere to the view of economic reality in mainstream economics fail to realize that the future welfare of the parts (economic actors) is intimately connected to the state of the whole (global ecosystem). But from the perspective of those who believe in this economic paradigm, environmentalists fail to realize that the stability of the whole (global market) is dependent on the perpetual growth and expansion of economically productive activities by the parts (economic actors). Although most members of the environmental movement view the resources of nature as literally priceless because their value cannot be reduced to or represented by units of money, most believers in mainstream economics take an entirely different view. From their vantage point, the value of natural resources can and should be represented in units of money, and this value can be determined only by the operation of price mechanisms within closed market economies.

In the debate over the environmental crisis, these very disparate conceptions of part–whole relationships manifest as competing and irreconcilable approaches that tend to divide the participants into two hostile camps with little or no sense of common purpose. Members of both groups realize, of course, that global economic activities are occasioning massive damage to the ecosystem and that we must begin to coordinate these activities in ways that will greatly mitigate this damage. But solutions to this problem that typically seem self-evident to those who endorse assumptions about the character of economic reality in neoclassical economics are normally perceived as rationalizations of the existing economic order by environmentalists. When environmentalists with backgrounds in economics propose solutions that are not commensurate with these assumptions, believers in the neoclassical economic paradigm tend to dismiss them out of hand.

One of the radical conclusions drawn in the course of this discussion is that assumptions about part–whole relationships in neoclassical economics are utterly different from and wholly incompatible with the actual dynamics of the relationship between parts (organic and inorganic processes) and whole (global ecosystem or biosphere) in physical reality. This fundamental disjunction between part–whole relationships in neoclassical economics and the actual dynamics of part–whole relationships in nature is not an esoteric matter with no real-world consequences. It explains why there is no basis for positing viable economic solutions to environmental problems within the framework of neoclassical economics and why this framework cannot be revised or expanded to provide these solutions. It also provides a more reasonable basis for understanding why those who believe in the neoclassical economic paradigm often have great difficulty comprehending, much less appreciating, the relationship between parts (economic activities) and whole (global ecosystem or biosphere) in environmental science.

HOMO ECONOMICUS

When economic conditions in Europe required a new understanding of economic reality in the eighteenth century, a number of metaphysically minded thinkers invented a narrative called classical economics. Markets as a means of exchanging goods had existed from the beginnings of recorded history, but the idea of a market system as a means of maintaining an entire society did not emerge until the seventeenth century. The creators of this system were moral philosophers who lived during a period in which new national economies emerged that were increasingly dependent on industrial production and international trade. This was a time when the old economic order, premised on custom and command, gave way to a new economic order that was sensitively dependent on the actions of profit-seeking individuals operating within the contexts of national market systems.[2]

But because the complex web of institutions, laws, policies, and processes that sustain and regulate production and exchange in modern markets did not exist, the new economic order more closely resembled a buzzing confusion than a rational process. The philosophers involved in the creation of classical economics believed that order lay beneath this chaos and that the ideal model for disclosing this order was Newtonian physics. In this physics, a universal force—gravity—acts outside or between parts (irreducible mass points or atoms), the collection of parts constitutes wholes, and physical systems are presumed to exist in separate and discrete dimensions in space and time.

The creators of classical economics (Adam Smith, Thomas Malthus, and David Ricardo) first posited the existence of a new set of laws, the natural laws of economics, and they assumed that these laws, like the laws of Newtonian physics, are preexisting and eternal. They then argued that the natural laws of economics act, like the universal force of gravity, in a causal and linear fashion between or outside atomized parts (economic actors) to maintain the stability of wholes (markets). This strategy allowed the classical economists to argue that the natural laws manifest as forces that govern the behavior of parts (economic actors) and perpetuate the orderly existence of wholes (markets), even if the parts are completely unaware that this is a consequence of their actions.

Adam Smith's term for the collective action of these forces was the "invisible hand," and this construct became the central legitimating principle in mainstream economics. As economists Kenneth J. Arrow and Frank H. Hahn put it, the "notion that a social system moved by independent actors in pursuit of different values is consistent with a final coherent state of balance . . . is surely the most important intellectual contribution that economic thought has made to the general understanding of social processes."[3] In *The Wealth of Nations*, Smith described the invisible hand as follows:

> As every individual, therefore, endeavors as much as he can to employ his capital in the support of domestic industry, and so to direct that industry that its produce may be of the greatest value; every individual necessarily labours to render the annual revenue of the society as great as he can. He generally, indeed, neither intends to promote the public interest, nor knows how much he is promoting it . . . and by directing that industry in such a manner as its produce may be of the greatest value, he intends only his own gain, and he is in this, as in many other cases, led by the invisible hand to promote an end which was no part of his intention.[4]

Smith argued that his invisible hand is analogous to the invisible force that causes a pendulum to oscillate around its center and move toward equilibrium or a liquid to flow between connecting chambers and find its own level. Based on this analogy, he claimed that the hand in economic reality was the force that moves independent actors in pursuit of different values toward the equalization of rates of return and that accounts for the tendency of markets to move from low to high returns. Obviously, Smith's invisible hand has no physical content and is an emblem for something postulated but completely unproven and unknown. Later in this discussion, it will be easy to appreciate why this is the case. Smith's invisible hand is premised on metaphysical assumptions, and his belief in its existence was an article of faith. Even more interesting, these metaphysical assumptions are also present in disguised form in neoclassical economics.

In textbooks on economics, the creators of neoclassical economics (William Stanley Jevons, Leon Walras, Francis Ysidro Edgeworth, and Vilfredo Pareto) are credited with transforming the study of economics into a rigorous scientific discipline with the use of higher mathematics. There are, however, no mentions in these textbooks, or in all but a few books on the history of economic thought, of a rather salient fact. The progenitors of neoclassical economics, all of whom were trained as engineers, developed their theories in a remarkably simple and direct way—they substituted economic constructs for physical variables in the equations of mid-nineteenth century physics.[5]

A number of well-known mid-nineteenth century mathematicians and physicists convincingly demonstrated that the economic constructs were utterly different from the physical variables and that there is no way in which one could assume that they were in any sense comparable. However, the economists refused or, more probably, failed to comprehend how devastating these arguments were, and they continued to claim that they had transformed economics into a science with much the same epistemological authority as the physical sciences. Eventually, the presumption that neoclassical economics is a science like the physical sciences was almost universally accepted, and this explains why we now award a Nobel Memorial Prize in economics that is viewed as comparable to those in physics and chemistry.

The result of this strange marriage between economic theory and mid-nineteenth century physics is a reified view of market systems and processes that features the following assumptions:

- The market is a closed circular flow between production and consumption with no inlets or outlets;
- Market systems exist in a domain that is separate and distinct from the external environment;
- The natural laws of economics act causally on atomized economic actors within closed market systems and these actors obey fixed decision-making rules;
- The natural laws of economics will, if left alone, ensure that closed market systems will perpetually grow and expand;
- The natural laws of economics will, if left alone, ensure that the global economy will perpetually expand;
- Environmental problems result from market failures or incomplete markets;
- The natural laws of economics can, if left alone, resolve most environmental problems via price mechanisms and more efficient technologies and production processes;
- Inputs of raw materials into the closed market system from the external environment are "free" unless or until costs associated with their use are internalized within the system;
- The external resources of nature are inexhaustible, or replaceable by other resources or by technologies that minimize the use of these resources or rely on other resources;
- The external environment is a bottomless sink for waste materials and pollutants;
- The costs of damage to the environment by economic activities must be treated as costs that lie outside the closed market system or are not included in the pricing mechanisms that operate within these systems;
- These costs can be incorporated or internalized within the closed market system with the use of shadow pricing and the establishment of property rights for environmental resources and amenities;
- There are no biophysical limits to the growth of closed market systems.

It will become abundantly clear in the course of this discussion that all of these assumptions are fundamentally wrong from a scientific point of view. Markets are open systems that exist in embedded and interactive relationship to the global environment, and there is a very definite relationship between economic activities and large-scale damage to this environment. Natural resources, particularly nonrenewable resources, are exhaustible, and our overreliance on some of these resources, particularly fossil fuels, is causing what may soon become irreparable damage to the ecosystem. The environment is not separate from economic processes, and wastes and pollutants from these processes are already at levels that threaten the stability and sustainability of ecosystems. Finally, the limits to the growth of the global economy in biophysical terms are real and inescapable, and the idea that market systems can perpetually expand and consume more scarce and nonrenewable natural resources is utterly false.

MAINSTREAM ECONOMICS AND THE ENVIRONMENTAL CRISIS

Much of the commentary in this discussion on the inherent flaws of the neoclassical economic paradigm derives from the work of a group of scholars who call themselves "ecological economists." Many of these scholars, as the name of their discipline implies, have background or training in both environmental science and neoclassical economic theory. The principal ambition of those who practice this discipline is to extend the framework of neoclassical economics to include scientifically valid measures of the damage done to the environment by economic activities. What the ecological economists have to say about the inherent flaws of neoclassical economic theory from an ecological perspective is, as we shall see, quite devastating, and many of their proposed economic solutions to environmental problems are carefully reasoned, beautifully conceived, and utterly appropriate. But if this is the case, why is there virtually no dialogue between the ecological economists and the mainstream economists who sit at the right hand of global economic planners?

Some have blamed the usual culprits—the greed or power of corporations, the resistance of the established economic order to change, or the inability of economic planners and mainstream economists to understand and appreciate the impact of economic activities on the global environment in scientific terms. But there is, as a number of ecological economists seem to appreciate fully, a much more fundamental reason why these economists have not been successful in their efforts to expand the framework of neoclassical economics to include environmental costs of economic activities—assumptions about relationships between parts (economic actors and firms) and wholes (markets) in neoclassical economics are completely incompatible with the actual dynamics of part–whole relationships in physical reality.

If we could posit viable economic solutions to environmental problems within the framework of neoclassical economics, the prospects that we could begin very soon to coordinate our experience in the global economy in ways that would allow for the emergence of a sustainable environment would be greatly improved. There would be no need to engage in the arduous business of developing and implementing an environmentally responsible economic theory. As I hope to demonstrate, however, those who have attempted to extend the framework of neoclassical economics in an effort to deal effectively with the environmental crisis face an insuperable barrier. Assumptions about part–whole relationships embedded in the mathematical formalism of neoclassical economics are such that there is no basis for realistically assessing the costs of doing business in the global environment.

The intent here is not, however, to launch an ill-mannered attack on mainstream economists or to deny the many virtues of the free market system. This system tends to enhance individual initiatives, promote creative endeavors, and encourage rapid economic development. And if one also concedes that neoclassical economic theory is a useful tool in managing market economies, why does it matter that the theory is premised on a conception of part–whole relationships that is not accord with biophysical reality and cannot be viewed as scientific?

One answer is that the conception of part–whole relationships in neoclassical economics results in assumptions about market economies that effectively undermine efforts to deal with the environmental crisis in economic terms. Another is that the belief that mainstream economics is a science has frustrated the ability of economic planners to recognize the paramount importance of the physical sciences in positing effective solutions to environmental problems. There is, however, another major reason why we must develop an environmentally responsible economic theory and displace neoclassical economics with this theory.

If we continue to chart the future of the global economy based on assumptions about economic reality in neoclassical economics, conditions in the global environment are likely to deteriorate to the point where threats to human populations will require massive manipulation of the global economy by governments and international agencies. In this situation, the idea that the alleged "forces" of the free market system will resolve the crisis in a timely fashion would seem rather absurd and terribly callous. Leaders would quickly realize that the only effective way to impose order on this chaos would be to implement a system that it the very antithesis of the free market—a command-and-control regulation economy. If, however, we develop and implement an economic theory that can realistically assess the costs of doing business in the global environment, this dire situation can be avoided and the substantive virtues of the free market economies preserved.

THE REAL ECONOMY

For reasons that will soon become obvious, economic reality as it is conceived in neoclassical economics does not describe the actual character of this reality in empirical or scientific terms. The "real" economy, as the current ecological crisis reveals in no uncertain terms, encompasses all human activities associated with the production, distribution, and exchange of tangible goods and commodities and the consumption and use of natural resources, such as arable land and water.

As E. O. Wilson points out, our species is the "greatest destroyer of life since the ten-kilometer-wide meteorite landed near the Yucatan and ended the Age of Reptiles sixty-five million years ago."[6] The claim that human impacts on the global ecological system are leading us down the path to large-scale disruptions of this system is accurate. And the inference that our species, like that of the great dinosaurs, may become extinct in the process should be taken quite seriously. If the cold war is in fact over and we manage to prevent any future use of nuclear weapons, the three menacing and interrelated problems that must be resolved in the interest of human survival are overpopulation, global warming, and loss of species diversity. The following is Wilson's overview of the population problem:

> The global population is precariously large, and will become much more so before peaking some time around 2050. Humanity overall is improving per capital production, health, and longevity. But it is doing so by eating up the planet's capital, including natural resources and biological diversity millions of years old. *Homo sapiens* is approaching the limit of its food and water supply. Unlike any species that lived before, it is also changing the world's atmosphere and climate, lowering and polluting water tables, shrinking forests, and spreading deserts. Most of the stress originates directly or indirectly from a handful of industrialized countries. Their proven formulas for prosperity are being eagerly adopted by

the rest of the world. The emulation cannot be sustained, not with the same levels of consumption and waste. Even if the industrialization of developing countries is only partly successful, the environmental after-shock will dwarf the population explosion that preceded it.[7]

In 1600 the global human population was roughly half a billion, in 1940 our numbers had grown to two billion, and in 1999 the count was six bil-lion and increasing at the rate of 200,000 each day. This exponential increase means that people born in 1950 were the first to witness a dou-bling of the human population in their own lifetime, from 2.5 billion to more than six billion. The problem faced in predicting future increases in the global human population is that the estimates are extremely sen-sitive to the replacement number or the average number of children born to each woman. In 1963 each woman bore an average of 4.1 chil-dren, but by 2000 that number had declined to 2.6. If this number declined to 2.1, it is estimated that there would be 7.7 billion people on earth in 2050 and a leveling off of the human population at 8.5 billion in 2150. If the number decreased slightly to 2.0, the population would peak at 7.8 billion and then decline to 5.6 billion by 2150. But if the number of these births is 2.2, estimates are that the global human pop-ulation would be 12.5 billion in 2050 and 20.8 billion in 2150. Even if the human birth rate were to decrease to one child per woman, the global human population would not peak for one or two generations. Because estimates of the number of people that can be sustained in the biosphere over an indefinite period tend to fall between five and sixteen billion, most experts agree that what is required is not merely zero population growth but negative population growth.[8]

This problem becomes even more menacing when the increases are viewed within the context of the real economy as opposed to the abstrac-tions of the economists. Suppose, for example, that the population levels off at ten billion by 2050 and that this entire population enjoys the same level of material prosperity as those in the middle classes of North Amer-ica, Western Europe, and Japan. Although most economists seem to believe that this can and will happen, the realities of the real economy indicate that it cannot.

One measure of the interaction between people and the global envi-ronment is based on a formula developed by Paul Ehrlich and John Hol-dren.[9] This formula yields a complex number when population size times per capita affluence (consumption) times a measure of the energy used in sustaining consumption is computed. The results of these computations can be illustrated in terms of the "ecological footprint" of the productive land required to support each member of society with existing technology. If the entire world were to achieve the five hectare per person figure that exists in the United States (one hectare is 2.5 acres), this would require the use of an amount of land represented by two additional planet earths.[10] The dream that the standard of living in the entire world can be raised to that in prosperous countries based on existing technologies and allowing for current levels of consumption and waste may seem laudable. But when we examine the biophysical limits of economic growth based on existing resources and technologies and the impacts of this growth on the environment, this dream begins to look like a program for ecological disaster.

About 11 percent of the world's land surface is under cultivation; the remaining 89 percent has marginal value in these terms or no use at all. We could clear and plant what remains of tropical rain forests and savannas, but this would result in the loss of most species of plants and animals on earth. The price paid here for a marginal increase in agricultural production would be to undermine further the ability of the biosphere to maintain the relative abundance of atmospheric gases that maintain the earth's temperature at levels suitable for life. We have managed thus far to sustain the human population, in many cases marginally, with the use of pesticides and other technologies. But this had not been without cost in the real economy. By 1989, 11 percent of global cropland was severely degraded, and the area of global cropland available per person decreased by about a quarter of an acre from 1950 to 1995.[11]

We could seek to alleviate this problem by irrigating deserts and nonarable croplands, but there are already too many people competing for too little water. The aquifers of the world, which are critical to crop growth in drier regions, are being drained of water faster than the reserves can be replaced by rainfall and runoff. The Ogallala aquifer, a principal source of water in the central United States, dropped three meters in a fifth of its area in the 1980s and is now half depleted in Kansas, Texas, and New Mexico. Even more dramatic, the water table under Beijing fell thirty-seven meters from 1965 to 1995, and the groundwater reserves in the Arabian Peninsula are expected to be exhausted by 2050. Meanwhile, all seventeen of the world's oceanic fisheries have been harvested beyond capacity, and some fisheries, such as those in the Atlantic banks and Black Sea, have suffered a commercial collapse.[12]

Most Americans are becoming increasingly concerned about the prospect of global warming, but they do not seem to appreciate the enormity of this problem fully. However, the two thousand scientists associated with the United Nations Intergovernmental Panel on Climate Control (IPCC), who work worldwide to gather and assess climate data with the use of supercomputers, are most aware of how large this problem has become. These scientists, in the most comprehensive study on this subject to date, predict that average earth temperature over the next hundred years could rise by 10.4 degrees Fahrenheit, 60 percent higher than the same group estimated six years ago. They also made it clear that this projected increase, which would be the direct result of human economic activities, would result in the most rapid and dramatic change in conditions that sustain life on this planet in the last ten millennia.[13]

The IPCC scientists predict that this rise in temperature would cause brutal draughts, massive floods, and violent storms around the planet. Sea levels would rise by as much as thirty-four inches because of the expansion of marine waters resulting in part from the breakup and melting of the Antarctic and Greenland ice shelves. Tens of millions of people would be displaced in low-lying regions in China, Bangladesh, and Egypt. Some coastal nations, such as Kiribati and the Marshall Islands, and the small atoll countries in the Western Pacific would be completely submerged. The IPCC scientists also predict that there will be large increases in precipitation patterns in North Africa, in the temperate regions of Eurasia and North America, and in Southeast Asia and the Pacific coast of South America. The amount of precipitation in Australia, most of South America, and southern Africa is expected to drop correspondingly, with disastrous consequences for people living in these regions.

Inasmuch as minor perturbations in the globally interactive ecosystem can have large effects, the rise in marine water temperature above twenty-six degrees centigrade in areas where clouds and storms are generated would dramatically increase the frequency of tropical cyclones. People living in the highly populated region of the eastern seaboard of the United States would experience more heat waves in the spring and more hurricanes in summer. Tundra ecosystems could disappear entirely, and projected decreases in agriculture production would impact many more people in developing countries than in industrialized northern countries. The IPCC scientists also claim that many species of microorganisms, plants, and animals will be unable to adapt to changes in their environment or to emigrate to more habitable areas. Because this would result in the extinction of large numbers of species and a dramatic decline in species diversity, the long-term consequences in the real economy of the global environment could be devastating.

One of the largest contributors to the loss in biodiversity has been the clearing of forests through the almost universal spread of agricultural into even the most marginally productive areas. This process has destroyed about half the forest cover that reached its maximum six to eight thousand years ago following the retreat of continental glaciers. At present over 60 percent of temperate hardwood and mixed forests, 30 percent of conifer forests, 45 percent of tropical rainforests, and 70 percent of tropical dry forest have been lost, and the remainder is being cut at an accelerating rate.[14] The precise rate of extinction caused by the wholesale destruction of species habitats by global economic activities is not known. But most researchers in the field generally agree that it is somewhere between one thousand and ten thousand times the rate before the expanding global economic system began to exert significant pressure on the global environment.[15]

According to mainstream economists, one of the major justifications for continuing to expand the global economic system based on current theory and practice is that the process will necessarily extend the benefits of this system to poor people living in third world countries. However, a recent report by the United Nations Conference on Trade and Development not only indicates that extreme poverty in the world's least developed forty-nine countries has doubled over the last thirty years. It also estimates that, if current trends persist, the number of people living on less than $1 a day will rise from the current figure of 307 million to 420 million by 2015. Even more sobering, the report convincingly makes the case that most of these countries are trapped in a cycle of poverty that they cannot escape and that the usual dynamics of international markets will not relieve the terrible suffering of the hundreds of millions that live within their borders.[16]

MAPPING THE JOURNEY

Economic planners who are committed to doing business as usual also typically dismiss the concerns of environmental scientists by claiming that science has not progressed to the point where it can predict with a high degree of certainty the state of the global environment over extended periods. In the absence of such predictions, the planners typically assume that the scientists are merely offering opinions about a situation that is poorly understood or largely unknown. This is not, however, the case. We know a great deal about the present state of the global environment, and our ability to predict its future within an increasingly reduced range of probabilities has become more refined. The totality of this knowledge clearly indicates that if we continue to coordinate our economic activities based on assumptions from mainstream economics, the ability of this planet to sustain human life could be greatly compromised.

The claim that economics is a science was not terribly problematic until the last few decades because the numbers of economic actors had not grown to the point where large-scale negative impacts on the real economy of the global environment could threaten human survival. Now that we have reached that point, we must not only recognize that the theory that legislates over the human future in economic terms is not clothed in the raiment of scientific knowledge. We must also understand the manner in which unscientific assumptions in neoclassical economics frustrate our ability to understand, much less resolve, the environmental crisis.

Environmental scientists must obviously play a vital role in our dealings with the environmental crisis, but the vast majority of these scientists realize that their proper role is to provide the best scientific description of the present and future state of the environment and not to engage in policy decisions. Those who are most empowered to make those decisions are elected representatives in government and board members and chief executives in the business community. The real power behind these thrones lies, however, in the concerted action of the electorate and the consumer, and it is only this power, in my view, that can effectively resolve environmental problems and create a sustainable environment.

One of the large ambitions here is to provide those who are willing to engage in this formidable enterprise with in-depth understanding of why neoclassical economic theory cannot in principle realistically account for the costs of doing business in the global environment. In the chapters on the origins and history of classical and neoclassical economics that follow, my intent is to communicate what is largely unknown outside a small community of scholars about these subjects as opposed to what is widely known. For example, there are no mentions in textbooks on economics of the fact that Smith's invisible hand is a metaphysical construct or that the natural laws of economics as he conceived them rest on metaphysical foundations. Conspicuously absent in these textbooks, too, is any mention of the fact that these metaphysical foundations were perpetuated in disguised form by the creators of neoclassical economics in a mathematical formalism borrowed wholesale from a soon-to-be-outmoded mid-nineteenth century physics. For our purposes, however, these unknowns, which some might regard as mere curiosities in the history of Western thought, are very significant because they clearly indicate that the central legitimating principle in neoclassical economics, the invisible hand, exists only in the minds of those who believe in its existence.

CHAPTER 2

THE NOT SO WORLDLY PHILOSOPHERS

Metaphysics, Newtonian Physics, and Classical Economics

> It is not from the benevolence of the butcher, the brewer, or the baker, that we expect our dinner, but from their regard to their interest. We address ourselves, not to their humanity but to their self-love, and never talk to them of our own necessities but of their advantages.
>
> —Adam Smith, *The Wealth of Nations*

The ground on which the entire elaborate structure of neoclassical economics stands is the assumption that Adam Smith uncovered the lawful workings of market economies. In this chapter I will demonstrate that this assumption is false, and in the next I will disclose that the creators of neoclassical economics misused and manipulated mid-nineteenth physics in a failed attempt to ground metaphysical assumptions about the invisible hand in physical reality. After these economists wed the natural laws of economics to the mathematical formalism of mid-nineteenth century physics, the metaphysical foundations of these laws took on a new disguise. The form of this disguise was an increasingly more complex maze of mathematical equations that allegedly chart the movement of the invisible hand in general equilibrium theory.

Smith derived his understanding of the character of the natural laws of economics from Newtonian physics and developed a view of market systems predicated on the understanding of the relationship between parts (economic actors) and wholes (market systems) in this physics. The

French moral philosophers who originally articulated these ideas argued that the natural laws of economics govern the movement and interaction of atomized individuals, much as the law of gravity governs the movement and interaction of atoms, or mass points, in Newtonian physics. They also presumed that putative natural laws exist in a domain separate from and superior to sensible objects and movements, and they derived this idea from an understanding of physical laws that was a product of the seventeenth-century assumption of metaphysical dualism.

The most fundamental aspect of the Western intellectual tradition is the idea that there is a fundamental division between material and immaterial worlds, or between the realm of matter and the realm of pure mind or spirit. The metaphysical framework that is consistent with this idea is known as ontological dualism. As the word "dual" implies, the framework is predicated on an ontology, or a conception of the nature of God or Being, that assumes reality has two distinct and separable dimensions. Copernicus, Galileo, Kepler, and Newton were inheritors of a cultural tradition in which ontological dualism was a primary article of faith, and they were all convinced that doing physics was a form of communion with the geometrical and mathematical forms resident in the perfect mind of God. This idealization of the mathematical ideal as a source of communion with God provided a metaphysical foundation for the emerging natural sciences. It also served as the metaphysical foundation for a view of the natural laws of economics that Smith would later use to legitimate the existence of the invisible hand.

The French natural philosophers who first developed this view assumed that any hidden laws that order human society must, like the laws of Newtonian physics, exist in an immaterial realm that is separate and distinct from physical reality. They also assumed that the natural laws, like the laws of classical physics, are preexisting and eternal, and they identified the realm in which the alleged natural laws exist with the mind of God. The conspicuous absence of any such claims in *The Wealth of Nations* (1776) is the basis for the orthodox view that Smith purged economic theory of all metaphysical concerns and uncovered the lawful workings of market economies. This, however, is simply not the case.

The French moral philosophers who influenced Smith argued that the ideal model for disclosing the existence of these natural laws was Newtonian physics. Charles-Louis de Secondat, baron de Montesquieu (1689–1755), appealed to this physics to create sociology, a new field of study premised on the idea that observation of empirical data could uncover laws that govern complex social phenomena. In a study of the institutions of monarchy, republic, and despotism, Montesquieu posits the existence of an equilibrium between competing forces analogous to that in Newtonian physics. As R. Aron puts it, "Montesquieu's essential idea is not the separation of powers in the judicial sense but what might be called the *equilibrium of social forces* as a condition of political freedom."[1]

A similar view of natural laws appears in the work of Francois Quesnay (1694–1774), the founder of the French Physiocratic movement. Quesnay was a physician who included among his clients madame de Pompadour, mistress to Louis XV. Quesnay's primary interest, however, was to make rational sense out of the chaotic economic system of France in the years before the French revolution. He and his followers sought to disclose the existence of an order of nature, or Physiocracy, in which only land yields a surplus because machines merely reshape material taken from nature with no net increase in the amount of material.

In the absence of the abstract assumptions about land, labor, and capital that lend credence to the modern notion of excess value, the idea that the only source of this value is the generative powers of nature is not as strange as it might now appear. If, for example, 50 bushels of wheat yields a crop of 200 bushels, the Physiocrats would argue that the additional 150 bushels is a gift from nature with surplus value. But if men in a small factory use clay to make pots, the argument would be that the clay in the pots is no greater than that used to make the pots, and therefore there is no increase in value.

Quesnay claimed that the natural laws that determine excess value, like the laws of Newtonian physics, are created by God and operate on atomized individuals to perpetuate and sustain the whole of human society in universal harmony. Both sets of laws, those that operate on the human intellect and those that govern the behavior of matter, constitute, said Quesnay, "the general order of the formation of the universe, where everything is foreseen and arranged by the Supreme Wisdom."[2] The order that results from the action of the natural laws is apparent, he claimed, in the continuous production and distribution of food and other goods essential to human survival. Quesnay was also convinced that these laws, like those of Newtonian physics, act with a precision that lends itself to description and analysis in geometrical and arithmetical terms: "The natural laws of the order of society, are precisely the physical laws of the perpetual reproduction of the goods necessary for man's subsistence, conservation and well-being."[3]

Quesnay's most celebrated attempt to disclose the existence of the "order of nature" took the form of a *Tableau économique* that was intended to provide a rigorous calculation of the effects of measures taken by the sovereign to ensure the economic well-being of the nation. Hypothetical production and distribution figures for the national product were factored into an "arithmetical formula," and the resulting political arithmetic allegedly provides a basis for the correct administration of the national economy based on rigorous calculation and measurement of relevant quantities.[4] It is also worth noting that Quesnay was among the first of a long line of economic theorists who did not understand the physics on which his economic theory is based and that the mathematics used in the *Tableau* was limited to arithmetic and geometry.

Anne-Robert-Jacques Turgot (1727–1781) is recognized for articulating a view of a mechanistic economic system based on the metaphor of the circulation of blood. In this system, there is an alleged resemblance between the workings of a market and the dynamics of fluids. In contrast with the other Physiocrats, Turgot did not use mathematical formalism to develop a systematic treatment of the market. But he did manage to introduce the concept of equilibrium in a loose exposition in which the workings of the market economy are linked to the equilibrium of fluids in a system of interconnected vessels:

> The different employments of capital produce, therefore, very unequal products; but this inequality does not prevent the exercise of a reciprocal influence on one upon the other or the establishment between them of a sort of equilibrium, as between two liquids of unequal gravity that communicate with one another at the bottom of a reversed siphon of which they occupy the two branches: they will not be on a level, but the height of one cannot increase without the other also rising in the opposite branch.[5]

In a celebrated letter to David Hume, Turgot elaborated upon his definition of the term equilibrium. The term, he said, mirrors that in Newtonian dynamics and denotes levels of production, employment, and remuneration that tend to remain in equilibrium.

The marquis de Condorcet (1743–1794), who died after spending several months in hiding as a fugitive from the Terror during the French Revolution, was a skilled mathematician who possessed a more refined understanding of Newtonian physics than his friend and mentor Turgot's. Condorcet's formidable ambition was to create a *mathématique sociale* that could objectively disclose the lawful dynamics governing human choice with the use of probability calculus. Because careful observation and the collection of large amounts of empirical data had previously disclosed hidden lawful dynamics in astronomy, Condorcet argued that the same methods could uncover the hidden lawful dynamics of social and economic systems. This served as the basis for his now famous claim that the social sciences would eventually be grounded on solid empirical foundations and display all of the mathematical rigor of the physical sciences:

> These sciences, whose object is man himself and whose direct end is man's happiness, are now almost established and their development will be as certain as that of the physical sciences. The cherished idea that our grandchildren will surpass us in wisdom is no longer an illusion. Whoever reflects upon the nature of the moral sciences cannot, in fact, but see that, supported by factual observation like the physical sciences, they must follow the same method, acquire an equally precise language, and attain the same degree of certainty.[6]

Condorcet held that the mathematical tool that can yield results comparable to those in the physical sciences is probability calculus, and he used this tool in an effort to uncover the hidden dynamics of social and political realities. In a study on the democratically elected assemblies, Condorcet isolates and examines the behavior of a voter as *homo suffragans*—an atomized participant in the electoral process. In the probability calculus that allegedly predicts the behavior of voters, the atomized participant is represented as the rough equivalent of the Newtonian constructs of the material point, the line without extension, and the frictionless surface. The resulting mathematical abstraction, a dimensionless material point, possesses only one real quantity—a mass expressed in completely formal and quantitative terms. Hence *homo suffragans* is a social atom that has been divested of all human qualities other than the social faculty of voting.[7]

THE NOT SO WORLDLY PHILOSOPHER: ADAM SMITH

Adam Smith (1723–1790), who was notoriously absent-minded, lectured much of his life on problems in moral philosophy at the University of Glasgow. The discipline of moral philosophy, which was much more broadly defined than it is today, covered natural philosophy, ethics, jurisprudence, and political economy.[8] It was on this broad canvas that Smith attempted to depict the inner workings of the cosmic machine and the place of human beings within its systems, wheels, and chains.

Understanding the work of Adam Smith as a whole is recognized as notoriously difficult owing to what an earlier generation of German scholars termed the "Adam Smith Problem." The problem concerns the glaring contradiction between the themes in Smith's two books—self-interest in *The Wealth of Nations* (1776) and sympathy in *The Theory of Moral Sentiments* (1759). Some have argued that these contradictions result from some radical change in the worldview of Smith during the seventeen-year period between the first publications of the two books. The problem with this thesis is that both books were consistently revised and edited for five or more editions in Smith's lifetime, and the final edition of *The Theory of Moral Sentiments* was published in the year of his death (1790). More important, Smith viewed both books as part of a single corpus, and his reasons for doing so become clear when they are read in this way.

Those who have struggled with the Adam Smith problem have apparently failed to recognize that the problem can be resolved based on an improved understanding of the central role played by metaphysics in all of Smith's published work. Smith embraced a new understanding of the nature and function of God, known as Deism, that grew out of attempts to reconcile the existence of God with the implications of Newtonian physics. Because this physics assumes that physical laws completely determine the future state of physical systems, the Deists concluded that the universe does not require, or even permit, active intervention by God after the first moment of creation. They then imaged God as a clockmaker and the universe as a clockwork regulated and maintained after its creation by physical laws alone. Smith's understanding of the relationship between the clockmaker and the clockwork accounts in part for his extensive use of mechanical metaphors and analogies. It was also the foundation for his belief that two disembodied sets of natural laws regulate and maintain the orderly machinations of the clockwork—the laws of Newtonian physics and the natural laws of the market system.

Although the construct of the invisible hand is the ghost in the machine in virtually all of Smith's writings, it is explicitly mentioned only three times in three very different theological contexts. In the essays, the invisible hand is that of Jupiter and the construct is used to illustrate how primitive or "savage" people dealt with the irregular phenomena of nature.

In *The Theory of Moral Sentiments*, the hand belongs to a Deistic providence which ensures that the less fortunate are fed in spite of the greed of the rich. In *The Wealth of Nations*, the hand is the metaphor for the natural laws that act to maintain harmony and stability in market systems with the same impersonal force as the laws of physics. Taken together, the essays and *The Theory of Moral Sentiments* constitute a critique of the history, sociology, and psychology of religion. This critique is designed to demonstrate that during the course of civilization polytheism is replaced by theism and human beings eventually came to realize that nature is a system or machine that obeys both physical and natural laws.[9]

In the long essay on astronomy, the invisible hand of Jupiter symbolizes the "principles that lead and direct philosophical inquiries," which Smith defines as the passions of wonder, surprise, and admiration.[10] In the section entitled "Of the Origin of Philosophy," he claims that polytheism originated among primitive people and was a product of the "vulgar superstition which ascribes all the irregular events of nature to the favour or displeasure of intelligent, though invisible beings, to gods, daemons, witches, genii, fairies."[11] These primitive people, who were not aware of the existence of nature's "hidden chains," were awed, says Smith, by "magnificent" irregularities such as thunder, lightning, and comets. He then mentions the invisible hand in an effort to explain why such people responded differently to regular and irregular phenomena: "It is the irregular events of nature only that are ascribed to the agency and power of the gods. Fire burns, and water refreshes; heavenly bodies descend, and lighter substances fly upwards, by the necessity of their own nature; nor was the invisible hand of Jupiter ever apprehended to be employed in those matters."[12]

The reason these savage people associated the activities of the gods with irregular events, says Smith, is that man was the only "designing" power they knew, and man "never acts but either to stop, or to alter the course, which natural events take, if left to themselves." As Smith sees it, the fundamental problem with the "lowest and most pusillanimous superstition" of these savages is that it prevented them from realizing that "hidden chains" link all events to the invisible causes of physical and natural laws.

Smith frequently identifies nature with the way things operate on their own accord, and the goal of philosophy, he said, is to "lay open" the "invisible chains which bind together" the natural world.[13] It is, therefore, no accident that the argument for the system of natural liberty in *The Wealth of Nations* is designed to promote trust in the "natural course of things."

This trust is warranted, says Smith, because the "hidden chains" of the invisible hand regulate the "system of natural liberty" and constrict the sphere of human "intention and foresight."[14] His argument for the existence of this system is premised on the assumption that "no human wisdom or knowledge could ever be sufficient" to provide the sovereign with the ability to manage effectively the "industry of private people" and direct it "toward the employments most suitable to the interests of society." Given that human beings, both individually and collectively, cannot effectively manage market economies or predict their futures, the only alternative, argues Smith, is for each individual "to pursue his interests in his own way" within "the laws of justice."[15]

The usual interpretation of Smith's system of natural liberty is that it legitimates the idea that each of us should have the freedom to pursue our livelihood and self-interest in the absence of traditional political, religious, and moral constraints. And because this system requires that the role of government be limited, it is also widely assumed that Smith makes government the servant of individualism. The problem with these interpretations, which are typically used to support the claim that Smith was a libertarian, is that the system of natural liberty is embedded in larger systems and all these systems obey natural laws.

In the section on education in *The Wealth of Nations*, Smith first endorses the idea from the ancient Greeks that philosophy should be divided into natural philosophy, which would later be called "physics," moral philosophy, and logic. He then argues that this division requires that the study of both the human mind and "the Deity" must fall under the province of physics, which investigates "the origin and the revolutions of the great system of the universe." Smith then concludes that the human mind and the Deity "in whatever their essence might be supposed to consist, were parts of the great system of the universe."[16]

In the physics essay, Smith criticizes those who attempt to explain nature's "seeming incoherence" by appealing "to the arbitrary will of some designing, though invisible beings, who produced it for some private and particular purposes." He then proceeds to fault the superstitious for their inability to conceive of the "idea of a universal mind, of a God of all, who originally formed the whole, and who governs the whole by general laws, directed to the conservation and prosperity of the whole, without regard to that of any private individual."[17] But as our ancestors progressed in knowledge, says Smith, they achieved a higher understanding of the relationship between parts and wholes and realized that nature is "a complete machine . . . a coherent system, governed by general laws, and directed to general ends, viz., its own preservation and prosperity."[18]

Clearly, Smith believed that the universal mind of God served as a template for the creation of a world that is entirely governed following its creation by general laws. His phrase "general laws" refers to both physical and natural laws, and he implies that they have the same ontological status—both originate from the universal mind of a Deistic God, exist in a realm separate and discrete from the material world, and act on atomized parts to maintain the stability of the whole.

The special character of Smith's metaphysics allows us to answer a question that has perplexed most experts on the history of economic thought: Why does Smith appeal to God to legitimate the existence of the invisible hand in his other major work, *The Theory of Moral Sentiments*, and yet refrain from doing so in *The Wealth of Nations*? The answer is that the understanding of the character of natural laws in *The Wealth of Nations* is more narrowly predicated on the assumption that these laws have equal status with physical laws. The omission of any appeals to God serves to reinforce the seeming validity of this assumption. It also implies that the real existence of the natural laws is self-evident, and, therefore, that any appeal to metaphysics is ad hoc and unnecessary.

Smith's metaphysics also allows us to understand why he had no difficulty arriving at the conclusion that natural laws act to preserve the whole (human population) without regard for the well-being of particular parts (individuals). In his view, mind and nature are both systems or machines that do not require any "personal" intervention because the orderly relation between parts is entirely maintained by general laws. This also explains why the biblical God, who disrupts the orderly workings of nature by staging miracles and singles out individuals or groups for covenants, revelations, rewards, and punishments, is conspicuously absent in virtually all of Smith's work. From his perspective, this God is a product of the frenzied imagination of those who did not realize that nature is "a complete machine" in which "hidden chains" govern the orderly interaction of parts to preserve the existence of the whole.

These views are apparent in Smith's descriptions of the workings of the invisible hand in *The Theory of Moral Sentiments*. Here the hand is part of the "regular" workings of nature and ensures that social benefits result as an unintended outcome of selfish actions. Smith argues, for example, that the invisible hand increases the fertility of the earth and benefits the whole of mankind despite inequality in capital resources and ownership of land. But because the landlord, writes Smith, can eat only a portion of the produce of his land, the remainder is consumed by those who provide him with luxuries.[19] Hence the rich, despite their "natural selfishness and rapacity," are "led by an invisible hand to make nearly the same distribution of the necessities of life which would have been made had the earth been divided into equal portions among all its inhabitants; and thus without intending it, without knowing it, advance the best interests of society, and afford means to the multiplication of the species."[20]

It is also worth noting that Smith consistently views ideas as systems and emphasizes the basic similarity between systems and machines. A machine, wrote Smith, "is a little system created to perform, as well as to connect together, in reality, those different movements and effects which the artist has occasion for." He goes on to say that a system "is an imaginary machine invented to connect together in the fancy those different movements and effects which are already in reality performed."[21] This linkage between a machine as a system that performs and connects together parts "in reality" and ideas as a system that describes the connections and interactions of parts "in reality" reveals a fundamental bias. For Smith, natural laws govern the mechanisms of human choice and the mechanisms of production and exchange to maintain the orderly workings of the whole.

If the behavior of atomized economic actors is controlled by the "invisible chains" of natural law in the system of the universe, what does this imply about the system of natural liberty? Smith claims that a natural order emerges when conscious interference with an economic system is minimized and that the system of natural liberty contributes to the maintenance of this order. Yet his argument for the existence of the system of natural liberty, as noted earlier, is predicated on the assumption that "no human wisdom or knowledge could ever be sufficient" to create or sustain this order. Some have attempted to resolve this paradox by arguing that Smith distinguishes between a macro-level where natural laws govern the state of the whole (market system) and a micro-level where the parts (economic actors) enjoy a radical freedom to pursue their self-interests.[22] For Smith, however, macro-level order and micro-level actors are intimately connected.

In *The Theory of Moral Sentiments*, Smith makes this connection clear in his commentary on the Stoic philosophers: "A wise man does not look upon himself as a whole, separated and detached from every other part of nature, to be taken care of by itself and for itself." He rather considers himself as "an atom, a particle, of an immense and infinite system, which must and ought to be disposed of according to the convenience of the whole."[23] The basic argument here is that natural laws act on the parts (atomized individuals) to enhance the welfare of the whole (human population) as a collection of parts, and the freedom of the parts is utterly constrained by these laws. In the "great machine of the universe" with its "secret wheels and springs,"[24] the system of natural liberty may allow the atomized individual to live with the illusion that his or her actions are freely taken. But as the wise man knows, this freedom does not, in fact, exist because the "connecting chains" of the invisible hand sustain the whole (economy) in the absence of conscious intervention by parts (economic actors).

It is this understanding of the relationship between the whole and its parts that informs Smith's commentary on the "prudent man" in *The Wealth of Nations*. The prudent man is praised for his "industry and frugality" and for "steadily sacrificing the ease and enjoyment of the present moment." The reward for this virtue, says Smith, is that the "situation" of this man grows "better and better every day."[25] In addition to celebrating the economic virtues of the prudent man, Smith also stresses his apolitical character. The prudent man "has no taste for that foolish importance which many people wish to derive from appearing to have some influence in the management" of public policy. Such a man prefers "that the public business were well managed by some other person" so that he is left to "the undisturbed enjoyment of secure tranquility."[26] The clear inference is that this tranquility derives from the recognition that public affairs are managed in ways that sustain order and stability by natural laws and that the actions of atomized individuals only serve to frustrate the proper functioning of these laws.

Smith's understanding of natural laws also explains why he consistently denigrates the power of human choice and alleges that human planning, intention, and foresight have had little or no impact on the course of history. Smith talks a great deal about great moments in history, but he never suggests that these moments are due to the actions of great men. The driving force that inexorably moves the whole of humanity toward greater wealth and progress with something like the precision of a linear equation is that of natural laws. This view is apparent in *The Theory of Moral Sentiments* in the beginning of the paragraph on the invisible hand:

And it is well that nature imposes upon us in this manner. It is this deception that rouses and keeps in continual motion the industry of mankind. It is this which first prompted them to cultivate the ground, to build houses, to found cities and commonwealths, and to invent and improve all the sciences and the arts, which ennoble and embellish human life; which have entirely changed the whole face of the globe, have turned the rude forests of nature into agreeable and fertile plains, and made the trackless and barren ocean a new fund of subsistence, and the great high road of communication to the different nations of the world. The earth by these labours of mankind has been obliged to redouble her natural fertility, and to maintain a greater multitude of inhabitants.[27]

The natural laws that impose on atomized human beings and keep them in motion within evolving systems and machines are not dependent in their operation on the intelligence and creativity of individuals, even in the sciences and the arts. Even more interesting for our purposes, the laws that govern the ever-expanding market systems obliged "earth" to "redouble her natural fertility" to maintain the growing human population.

TIGHTENING THE CHAINS: THOMAS MALTHUS AND DAVID RICARDO

Thomas Malthus (1766–1834) and David Ricardo (1772–1823) endorsed Smith's understanding of natural laws and attempted to tighten the "invisible chains" that "connect" parts in the machine of the market system in a more rigidly deterministic way. Malthus's "An Essay on the Principle of Population As It Affects the Future Improvement of Society" was written in response to the views of a utopian thinker named William Godwin. In Godwin's teleological account of the human future, the sexual passions that lead to increases in birth rate would somehow diminish after a universal harmony in social and political reality is achieved. When that occurs, wrote Godwin, "there will be no war, no crime, no administration of justice, as it is called, and no government. Besides there will be no disease, anguish, melancholy, or resentment."[28]

Malthus's dissenting views were published anonymously in 1798. The usual interpretation of his principle of population is straightforward—because population increases geometrically and food supply increases arithmetically, population growth tends to outrun the means of subsistence. Note, however, the manner in which this argument is actually made:

> I think I may fairly make two postulata.
>
> First, That food is necessary to the existence of man.
>
> Secondly, That the passion between the sexes is necessary and will remain nearly in its present state.
>
> These two laws, even since we have had any knowledge of mankind, appear to have been fixed laws of nature, and, as we have not hitherto seen any alteration of them, we have no right to conclude that they will ever cease to be what they now are, without an immediate act of power in that Being who first arranged the system of the universe, and for the advantage of his creatures, still executes, according to fixed laws, all its various operations.[29]

Although Malthus, an ordained clergyman, allows for the prospect that the "laws of nature" could be altered by an "immediate act of power in that Being who first arranged the system of the universe," his conception of this Being closely resembles the Deistic God of Smith. For example, the claim that "fixed natural laws," like the laws of physics, govern the "various operations" of the "system of the universe" in a causal and deterministic fashion clearly implies that the system does not need or require any intervention from God or any other "external" agency.

While Smith argued that the natural laws that determine the future of markets are essentially benevolent, Malthus concluded that the laws of population could ultimately threaten the very existence of humanity:

> Assuming then, my postulata as granted, I say that the power of population is indefinitely greater than the power in the earth to produce subsistence for man.
>
> Population, when unchecked, increases in a geometrical ratio. Subsistence increases only in an arithmetical ratio. A slight acquaintance with numbers will show the immensity of the first power in comparison of the second.
>
> By that law of our nature which makes food necessary to the life of man, the effects of these two unequal powers must be kept equal.
>
> This implies a strong constantly operating check on population from the difficulty of subsistence. This difficulty must fall some where and must necessarily be severely felt by a large portion of mankind.[30]

Although the inequality between the powers associated with these natural laws could have disastrous consequences for all of mankind, Malthus claims that this will not occur because the interplay between them results in "a strong constantly operating check" on population growth that affects only a "portion" of mankind. Assuming, like Smith, that impersonal and deterministic natural laws govern the interaction between parts (individuals) to perpetuate the existence of the whole (species), Malthus concludes that we should not interfere with the operation of the laws. In his view, the deaths of large numbers of the working poor are the unfortunate but inevitable result of the operation of the lawful mechanisms of an essentially benevolent nature. But as his biographer, James Bonar notes, the logic that led Malthus to this conclusion was apparently lost on his contemporaries: "He was the best abused man of his age. Bonaparte himself was not a greater enemy of the species. Here was a man who defended small-pox, slavery and child-murder—a man who denounced soup-kitchens, early marriages and parish allowances. . . . From the first Malthus was not ignored. For thirty years it rained refutations."[31]

Why, then, was Malthus eventually elevated to the pantheon of great economists? Studies on population growth lent some credence to his prediction that the human population would double every twenty-five years, but mainstream economists have not, in general, been troubled by the long-term impacts of this phenomenon on the economy or the environment. It was not, therefore, the principle of population that elevated Malthus to his present status, but the gradual acceptance by mainstream economists of the real or actual existence of the invisible hand.

The natural laws of Smith may be more benevolent and less menacing than those of Malthus, but there is no difference between them in ontological terms. The natural laws of both Smith and Malthus are created by a God who withdraws from the universe after the first moment of creation, exist in a realm prior to and separate from physical reality, and act causally and deterministically on atomized parts (individuals) to sustain the whole (species). The assumption that the "unseen chains" of the laws of population, like those of the natural laws that collectively constitute the invisible hand, cannot be broken also served to reinforce the view that social-political problems do not lie within the domain of economic theory. This premise allowed subsequent generations of economists to more effectively argue that the business of economists is to describe the lawful workings of the free market system and not to concern themselves with problems that exist in "other" domains of reality.

David Ricardo (1772–1823) was the son of Jewish merchant banker who emigrated from Holland, and his expertise as a stockbroker allowed him to retire with a large fortune at the age of forty-two. The system or machine of the market in Ricardo's *On the Principles of Political Economy* (1817) is as abstract and unadorned as a linear equation, and the atomized entities within this system are "forced" to obey the "laws of behavior." Workers appear, as Robert Heilbroner puts it, as "undifferentiated units of economic energy, whose only human aspect is a hopeless addiction to what is euphemistically called 'the delights of domestic society.' " And capitalists are depicted as "a gray and uniform lot, whose entire purpose on earth is to accumulate—that is, to save profits and to reinvest them by hiring more men to work for them; and this they do with unvarying dependability."[32]

One of Ricardo's burning ambitions was to repeal a set of laws passed by a majority of landowners in Parliament that were designed to prevent cheap grain from being imported into Britain. In his view, the so-called Corn Laws were an obvious impediment to improving national welfare, and most of his economic theory is intended to demonstrate that this is the case. Like Smith, Ricardo believed that the market system constantly tends to expand and that the resulting new shops and factories create more demand for labor. As the population increases, the increased demand for grain would, he says, result in higher prices and in the cultivation of more marginal land.

What is not revealed in the standard textbook definition of the Ricardian theory of rents is the uses made of the assumption of the Physiocrats that only land yields surplus value and the view of the resources of nature that results. The following is from the chapter "On Rent" in *On the Principles of Political Economy*:

Rent is the portion of the produce of the earth, which is paid to the landlord for the use of the original and indestructible powers of the soil. It is often, however, confounded with the interest and profit of capital, and, in the popular language, the term is applied to whatever is annually paid by a farmer to his landlord. . . . But it is evident, that a portion only of the money annually to be paid for the improved farm, would be given for the original and indestructible powers of the soil; the other portion would be paid for the use of the capital which had been employed in ameliorating the quality of the land, and in erecting such buildings as were necessary to secure and preserve the produce.

On the first settling of a country, in which there is an abundance of rich and fertile land, a very small proportion of which is required to be cultivated for the support of the actual population, or indeed can be cultivated with the capital which the population can command, there will be no rent; for no one would pay for the use of the land, when there is an abundant quantity not yet appropriated, and therefore, at the disposal of whosoever might cultivate it.

On the common principles of supply and demand, no rent would be paid for such land, for the reason stated why nothing is given for the use of air and water, or for any of the gifts which exist in nature in boundless quantity.[33]

For the Physiocrats, only land can produce surplus value, and capital investments do not increase this value. Ricardo argues, however, that whereas fertile land in earlier times was a gift of nature that existed in such abundance that it was regarded as free, progress has resulted in a situation in which fertile land is scarcer and capital investment is required to increase production. He then argues that the cultivation of the more marginal land necessarily increases the overall costs of production and that this is reflected in higher prices for grain and increases in rent for the landlord who owns the best land.

Rent as Ricardo defines it is the difference in profits that results when the costs of growing crops on fecund land are less than those of growing crops on less fecund land. In both instances, landlords must pay the same wages and bear the same capital expenses. However, the landlord who owns the more fertile land reaps more profits than do his competitors. The problem with this picture, says Ricardo, is that those who are responsible for this progress, the capitalists, are obliged to pay higher subsistence-level wages to workers while the rising aggregate of rents increases the profits of landlords.

What is significant here for our purposes is the assumption that the "laws" of supply and demand determine which quantities in nature are free and which are included within the system of the market. When land is plentiful, there is no rent because land has no market value and no one would elect to use his "capital" to buy and cultivate what exists in abundance. The following passage further illustrates this point:

If air, water, the elasticity of steam, and the pressure of the atmosphere, were of various quantities; if they could be appropriated, and each quality existed in only moderate abundance, they, as well as the land, would afford a rent, as the successive qualities were brought into use. With every worse quality employed, the value of the commodities in the manufacture of which they were used, would rise because equal quantities of labor would be less productive. Man would do more by the sweat of his brow, and nature perform less; and the land would no longer be imminent for its limited powers.[34]

Based on the assumption that the only natural resources that have value are those that are subject to the law of supply and demand, Ricardo argues that the resources of nature are free unless, or until, they become sufficiently scarce to warrant the capital investment that would allow for their appropriation and sale. Although he implies that more of these resources will have value owing to the inevitable expansion of markets and the associated emergence of new manufacturing techniques, the assumption that lies at the core of his argument is that the powers of nature are, in general, inexhaustible. It is this assumption that allows Ricardo to argue that there are no limits on the growth and expansion of markets.

Ricardo also formulated another idea that is predicated on the assumption that the resources of nature are unlimited, which has assumed increasingly more importance during the present era of globalization. He argued that because costs of production in countries with different technologies, resources, and customs vary, a country that produces goods at costs comparatively lower than in other countries and trades with these countries has a comparative advantage. And if all countries specialize in production where they have comparative advantages and trade with each other, Ricardo concluded, total production would be maximized and there would be more wealth to share. He also assumed, however, that investment capital is immobile and confined within national boundaries. If this were not the case, then investment capital would flow to the country with the absolute advantage in production and other nations would suffer. The irony here is that proponents of globalization endorse a policy of capital mobility between nations as a development strategy in spite of the fact that their understanding of the advantages of globalization is premised on a theory developed by Ricardo that assumes that this mobility does not exist.

At this point, it should be clear that the existence of the natural laws that serve to legitimate all of the major assumptions in classical economics is predicated on a belief in Deism and the seventeenth-century assumption of metaphysical dualism. Some historians of mainstream economics recognize that the French moral philosophers who influenced Smith's conception of natural laws made overt appeals to metaphysics to legitimate the existence of these laws. Nevertheless, most avoid confronting the Adam Smith problem by extracting well-known passages from *The Wealth of Nations* and treating them as pieces of revisionist history. Others seek to avoid the problem by arguing that *The Wealth of Nations*, given the absence of appeals to the Judeo-Christian God, is an entirely secular study of economic reality that is different in kind from Smith's other works.

One large explanation for this failure to recognize that the invisible hand was and is a metaphysical construct is that these historians are viewing Smith's conception of the hand through the conceptual lenses of neoclassical economic theory. In the next chapter, we will examine in some detail the manner in which the creators of neoclassical economics abused mid-nineteenth physics to substantiate the claim that mainstream economics is a science and to perpetuate the notion that the central construct in this economics, the invisible hand, actually exists.

CHAPTER 3

THE EMPEROR HAS NO CLOTHES

The Neoclassical Economists and
Mid-Nineteenth Century Physics

> A feat is made for laughter, and wine maketh merry, but money answereth all things.
>
> —Ecclesiastes

The nineteenth-century economists who attempted to clothe economic theory in the raiment of scientific knowledge made no overt appeals to metaphysics. But they did embrace the view of the classical economists that natural laws have a prior existence in an immaterial realm and act outside or between atomized parts (economic actors and firms) via a chain of causation to maintain the stability of wholes (market systems). The fact that the creators of neoclassical economics translated this conception of natural laws into some mathematical formalism from mid-nineteenth physics and that this resulted in an economic theory that would soon be widely regarded as comparable to theories in the physical sciences does not, in itself, seem problematic. If we also consider that subsequent refinements in this theory allowed neoclassical economists to describe tendencies to occur in market systems that provided a more reasonable basis for managing these systems, perhaps this alleged problem is not really a problem at all.

For reasons that will soon become more apparent, however, the neoclassical economic paradigm is an enormous problem because it is premised on assumptions about the character of economic reality that effectively undermine the prospect that the crisis in the global environment can be resolved in economic terms. The creators of this theory were obliged to make these assumptions in order to make the case that economic variables could be substituted for physical variables in the equations of mid-nineteenth century physics. These economists failed to realize that there was no absolutely no basis for making these substitutions in scientific terms, and the reasons they gave for doing so are logically inconsistent and absurd. And yet the originators of neoclassical economics still managed to promulgate the fiction that they had transformed the study of economics into a rigorously mathematical discipline comparable to the physical sciences. This eventually resulted in the almost universal acceptance of an economic paradigm in which there is no basis for realistically assessing the affects of global economic activities on the state of the global environment or for realistically accounting for the costs of doing business in this environment.

The intent in this chapter is to demonstrate the manner in which this misalliance between economic theory and mid-nineteenth physics allowed the metaphysical origins and foundations of the construct of the invisible hand to be disguised under an increasingly complex maze of mathematical formalism. For those interested in a more complete discussion of the manner in which the creators of neoclassical economics abused mid-nineteenth century physics in developing their theories, two books by Philip Mirowski, a professor of economics and historian of science at Notre Dame University, are highly recommended.[1] Another required text for those who wish to explore this aspect of the history of economic thought in more detail is a book by Bruno Ingrao, a professor of economics at the University of Sassari, and Giorgio Israel, a professor of mathematics at the University of Rome.[2]

The physics that the creators of neoclassical economics used as the template for their theories was developed from the 1840s to the 1860s. During this period, physicists responded to the inability of Newtonian mechanics to account for the phenomena of heat, light and electricity with a profusion of hypotheses about matter and forces. In 1847, in a paper titled "On the Conservation of Force," Hermann-Ludwig Ferdinand von Helmholtz, one of the best-known and most widely respected physicists of the time, posited the existence of some vague and ill-defined energy that could unify these phenomena. This served as a catalyst for a movement in which physicists attempted to explain very diverse physical phenomena in terms of a unified and protean field of energy.

Because the physicists were unable to specify the actual character of energy and could not be precise about what was actually being measured, their theories were not subject to repeatable experiments under controlled conditions. This not only violated one of the cardinal rules of the scientific method—the predictions of any potentially valid theory must be testable and potentially falsifiable in repeatable experiments under controlled conditions—but it also forced the physicists to take the very weak position that the usefulness of the model was, in itself, a form of scientific proof. The amorphous character of energy in the physical theories also obliged the physicists to appeal to the law of the conservation of energy, which states that kinetic and potential energy in a closed system is conserved. This appeal was necessary because it was the only means of asserting that the vaguely defined system somehow remains the "same" as it undergoes changes and transformations.[3]

The originators of neoclassical economics began with the assumption that a particle or mass point could be viewed as the equivalent of an atomized economic actor that moves along a path in accordance with the principle of least action. Aware that energy in the equations of mid-nineteenth century physics is a force that pervades all space, they concluded that this space could also be filled by a postulated form of energy called utility. None of these figures appears to have seriously considered the fact that utility, assumed to be synonymous with economic satisfaction and well-being, cannot be directly known or measured and is in no way comparable to energy as that term is used in mid-nineteenth century physics. What is equally remarkable, they also dismissed or rationalized away issues of integration and invariance that are critically important to the proper application of the conservation principle.

The strategy of the creators of neoclassical economics was as simple as it was absurd—they took the equations from the mid-nineteenth century physics and changed the names of the variables. The economists substituted utility for energy, the sum of utility for potential energy, and expenditure for kinetic energy. Although there was no basis for claiming that the natural laws of economics are in any sense the equivalent of the physical variables, the strategy allowed utility to be treated as a field of vector potentials in which the sum of income and utility is conserved. None of these now famous people seemed to realize that the sum of income and utility in neoclassical economics, much less in economic reality, is not conserved and that the conservation principle is quite meaningless in any real economic process. Nevertheless, the assumption that income and utility are conserved legitimates the real or actual existence of the invisible hand in its current form—constrained maximization in general equilibrium theory.

In the resulting formalism, the mind of atomized economic actors was presumed to operate within a field of force identified, in both figurative and literal terms, with energy. The forces associated with this energy were represented as prices and spatial coordinates describe quantities of goods. Because utility in the formalism is conserved, the first neoclassical economists were obliged to view production and consumption of goods and commodities as physically neutral processes that do not alter the sum of utility. They did so by arriving at a very strange interpretation of the implications of what was then regarded as a self-evident truth in the physical sciences—the law of the conservation of matter, or the idea that matter cannot be created or destroyed. If matter, they argued, is immutable, then the production of goods and commodities cannot alter or change the stuff out of which goods or commodities are made, and any value that accrues as a result of production can only reside in the mental space of economic actors. Similarly, they argued that if the immutable stuff out of which goods or commodities are made cannot be changed by consumption, any value associated with consumption must also reside in the minds of economic actors.

After this strange view of substance in economic reality was incorporated into the equations borrowed from mid-nineteenth century physics, it served as part of the rationale for the theory of value in neoclassical economic theory. In the formalism of this theory, the atomized immaterial minds of economic actors operate within a field of force (utility) in which the natural laws of economics legislate over the choices made by the actors. And this became the basis for the claim that the value assigned to all the immutable unchanging stuff that circulates in a closed loop from production to consumption in a market system is the direct result of the operation of the natural laws.

THE CREATORS OF NEOCLASSICAL ECONOMICS

William Stanley Jevons (1835–1882), after being encouraged by his father to become an engineer, studied chemistry and mathematics in London and attended some of Michael Faraday's lectures at the Royal Institution. In these lectures, Faraday attempted to demonstrate that magnetic forces did not obey the Newtonian force rule and argued that other forces were at work. Jevons was also familiar with the work of Thompson and Joule on the interconvertibility of heat and mechanical energy that laid the foundations for the law of the conservation of energy. But because Jevons was not a skilled mathematician, his understanding of matters scientific was crude at best and completely distorted at worst.

In order to appreciate why Jevons appeared to have no difficulty identifying mind or consciousness in economic reality with a point particle moving in a field of energy, consider the following passage from his major work, *The Principles of Science*:

> Life seems to be nothing but a special form of energy which is manifested in heat and electricity and mechanical force. The time may come, it almost seems, when the tender mechanism of the brain will be traced out, and every thought reduced to the expenditure of a determinate weight of nitrogen and phosphorous. No apparent limit exists to the success of the scientific method in weighing and measuring, and reducing beneath the sway of law, the phenomena of matter and mind. . . . Must not the same inexorable reign of law which is apparent in the motions of brute matter be extended to the human heart?[4]

Mind, suggests Jevons, is a manifestation of energy, the physical substrate of mind can be reduced to a measurable quantity, such as the "weight of nitrogen and phosphorous," and the "phenomena" of mind are potentially explainable in terms of collections of particles subject to the "inexorable reign" of deterministic physical laws. If one actually believed, as Jevons apparently did, that this is the case, it would not require a great leap of faith to arrive at what is in retrospect a very strange conclusion. If mind in economic reality is a manifestation of energy that is similar to or the same as the protean field of amorphous energy described in mid-nineteenth century physics, utility can be substituted for energy in the equations of this physics.

Perhaps the best way to illustrate Jevons's understanding of the linkage between the alleged natural laws of economics and the laws of physics is to examine his sunspot theory. The basic argument was that if sunspot activity causes fluctuations in temperature that result in fluctuations in grain production, this should result in corresponding fluctuations in the share price index and in microeconomic expansions and contractions via a chain of causation. Knowing that some astronomers had concluded that sunspot activity occurred in regular cycles of 11.1 years, Jevons first tried to make the case that English grain prices from 1254 to 1400 followed a cycle of eleven years. He then concluded that the resemblance between the lengths of the two cycles indicates that sunspot activity is causally linked to grain production.

When critics pointed out that there were no records of sunspot activity in the Middle Ages, Jevons decided to look for correlations between existing data on sunspot activity since 1749 and figures on European grain production. When this effort failed, he claimed that the resemblance between the eleven-year period between English credit crises and the cycles of sunspot activity clearly indicated that there was a causal connection. But after compiling a list of English credit crises from 1777 to 1878, Jevons was unpleasantly surprised to discover that astronomers had revised their previous estimates on the periodicity of sunspot cycles to 10.5 years. Undaunted, Jevons massaged the data a bit and announced that the average interval between the credit crises was actually 10.5 years.[5] At this point, a number of detractors pointed out that his definition of a credit crisis, which was directly related to the choice of dates, was sufficiently vague to allow for a broad range of interpretations.[6]

Jevons's work on sunspot theory was part of a larger effort to demonstrate that market processes necessarily maximize utility in a regime of free competition and that any conscious intervention frustrates this lawful process. But if markets lawfully maximize utility, or individual happiness and well-being, how does one explain the misery and suffering occasioned by periodic depressions? Jevons's answer was that depressions must be caused by natural forces that act on the closed market system from the outside and periodically disrupt its proper workings.

Subsequent generations of neoclassical economists did not try to establish a direct linkage between the natural laws of the market and lawful physical events. Nevertheless, they did embrace Jevons's view that market processes are inherently stable and self-correcting and that fluctuations in "closed" markets are caused by "outside" forces. Although one must credit Jevons for realizing that the forces of nature could be directly related to economic activities, his abstract and wholly unrealistic view of market systems was anything but natural. Yet this view would serve to legitimate the idea that continued growth and expansion of markets is an inevitable consequence of the operation of "natural" market forces and that anything that lies outside these closed systems, including the global ecosystem, must be viewed as exogenous.

Jevons was quite convinced that his appropriation of the equations of mid-nineteenth century physics had transformed economics into a science. Yet his understanding of the ontological status of the natural laws that allegedly act between or outside the parts (economic actors) to maintain the stability of the whole (market system) was the same as that of Adam Smith. Both predicated the existence of these laws on the seventeenth-century assumption of metaphysical dualism and both believed that natural laws have equal status with physical laws. The following passages from Jevons's *Theory of Political Economy* illustrate these points:

> Repeated reflection and inquiry have led me to the somewhat novel opinion, that value depends entirely upon utility. Prevailing opinions make labour rather than utility the origin of value; and there are even those who distinctly assert that labour is the cause of value. I show, on the contrary, that we have only to trace out carefully the natural laws of the variation of utility, as depending upon the quantity of the commodity in our possession, in order to arrive at a satisfactory theory of exchange, of which the ordinary laws of supply and demand are a necessary consequence.[7]

Jevons first posits the existence of a new set of invisible natural laws that allegedly describe the quantity of scarce goods in our possession and encompass the ordinary laws of supply and demand. The hidden metaphysical assumption is that these natural laws, like the laws of classical physics, exist in an immaterial domain and produce measurable results via a chain of causation. Jevons next explains why his theory is scientific or "in harmony with the facts":

> It is clear that Economics, if it is to be a science at all, must be a mathematical science. There exists much prejudice against attempts to introduce the methods and language of mathematics into any branch of the moral sciences. Many people seem to think that the physical sciences form the proper sphere of mathematical method, and that the moral sciences demand some other method—I know not what. My theory of Economics, however, is purely mathematical in character. Nay, believing that the quantities with which we deal must be subject to continuous variation, I do not hesitate to use the appropriate branch of mathematical science, involving though it does the fearless consideration of infinitely small quantities. The theory consists of applying differential calculus to the familiar notions of wealth, utility, value, demand, supply, capital, interest, labour, and all the other quantitative notions belonging to the daily operations of industry. . . . To me it seems that our science must be mathematical, simply because it deals in quantities.

> Whenever things treated are capable of being greater or less, there the
> laws and relations must be mathematical in nature.[8]

Jevons argues that because his theory deals in quantities that are subject to
continuous variation, this justifies the translation of nebulous constructs
in economic theory into well-defined quantities with the use of the differential calculus. In physics, the differential calculus was invented to
describe the movement of point particles in vector space in terms of continuous functions that result in infinitely small differentials in accordance
with the classical laws of motion. Jevons, however, seems quite oblivious
to the fact that economic actors cannot be described in this fashion. One
does not have to be a trained logician to appreciate the absurdity of this
circular argument—the theory must be scientific because it is mathematical and the theory must be mathematical because it is scientific.

Leon Walras (1834–1910), who was encouraged by his father to study
engineering, enrolled in the École des Mines in 1845. Dissatisfied with
the study of engineering, Walras read philosophy, history, literary criti-
cism, and political economy. During this period, he also read a popular
account of the philosophy of Kant and embraced a confused monism
that was a synthesis of materialism and spiritualism.[9] In spite of his lack
of training in either mathematics or physics, Walras viewed Newtonian
astronomy and classical mechanics as the unequaled models of scientific
knowledge, and his grand ambition was to use these models to create
"the science of economic forces, analogous to the science of astronomical forces."[10]

Like Jevons, Walras posited an additive utility function in which the
utility of a good is solely the function of the quantity of the good consumed. The additive utility function allowed the utility of a bundle of
goods to be expressed as the sum of the single utility functions that
allegedly expresses the pleasure derived by the consumer in his or her consumption of each good in the bundle. Walras's *rareté*, which is the equivalent to Jevons's marginal utility, refers to the last increment of utility
(pleasure) derived by a consumer from an infinitesimal increment in the
consumption of a particular good. He also claimed that whereas the marginal utility of a good is positive, the added utility for the consumer of
successive amounts of a particular good gradually diminishes. For example, the first piece of bread consumed by a hungry man would have the
most added utility and the amount of utility associated with consuming
subsequent pieces would gradually diminish.

In *Elements of Pure Economics*, Walras makes a stark distinction between forces associated with the natural laws of economics and the force of free will:

> We may divide the facts of our universe into two categories: those which result from the play of blind and ineluctable forces of nature and those which result from the exercise of free will, a force that is free and cognitive. Facts of the first category are found in nature, and that is why we call them natural phenomena. Facts of the second category are found in man, and that is why we call them human phenomena. . . . The operations of the forces of nature constitute the subject matter of what is called pure natural science or science properly speaking. The operation of the human will constitute, in the first place, the subject matter of what is called pure moral science or history, and in the second place, as will be seen presently, the subject matter of a study to which another name, either art or ethics, is attached.[11]

Walras claims that all natural forces that operate outside the atomized human mind are "blind and ineluctable," and he includes in these forces those associated with the natural laws of economics. Later in this same discussion, the distinction between the natural and the human becomes a distinction between things and persons, and this distinction becomes the basis for yet another distinction between the relations of persons and things in industry and the relations between persons and other persons in institutions. Walras then concludes, "The theory of industry is called applied science or art; the theory of institutions moral science or ethics."[12]

This categorical distinction between the domain of economics and all other human domains, including institutions, soon became one of the central dogmas of mainstream economics. But how does Walras justify its existence? He does so by claiming that there is only one natural phenomenon in economic reality—the single relation between two things represented by the value or price of a good. "Thus," he argues, "any value in exchange, once established, partakes of the character of a natural phenomenon, natural in origins, natural in its manifestations and natural in essence."[13]

Assuming that "natural" means "from or pertaining to nature," on what basis does Walras conclude that an established value in exchange can be viewed as natural in its origins, manifestations, and essence? Markets are human inventions that have taken a wide range of different forms, the value of any commodity is normally a function of a staggering array of variables, and prices paid are invariably tied to individual tastes and preferences. For Walras, however, none of this matters because he assumes that natural prices are governed by deterministic "natural" laws, and this assumption allows him to argue that these prices are therefore "natural" in origins, manifestations, and essence. When contemporary mainstream economists use the term *natural*, as in "natural rates of unemployment," they rarely comment on its meaning. Their use of the word implies, however, that there is a natural or lawful order in market systems and that whatever is natural must be good. And this serves to reinforce the view that outside intervention by government or other agency on closed market systems will disrupt the otherwise inevitable progress toward the good.

Although Walras's natural economic order is very rigid and highly mechanistic, he does not claim that human will has absolutely no influence on prices. But he does say that the forces that regulate comparative prices are comparable to the law of gravity, and this becomes the basis for the following argument. Just as the force of human will can resist the force of gravity, it can also resist the forces that regulate competitive prices. Yet one cannot, says Walras, fundamentally alter the manner in which economic forces govern the interaction of atomized economic actors any more than one can alter the manner in which gravity governs the interactions between point particles. And because the force of gravity tends to move physical systems toward equilibrium, Walras concludes that economic forces tend to move competitive prices toward equilibrium. It is this more restricted view of determinism that allegedly legitimates his "theory of the determination of prices under a hypothetical regime of perfect competition."[14]

In *Elements*, Walras says that the real forms from which the ideal competitive market can be derived are found in auctions, such as the stock exchange and the commodities exchange. In Walras's ideal market, initial resources are given, distribution is known, there is no production of new goods, and the preferences of individual traders are represented by utility functions that determine the amount of goods held by each. It is these otherworldly conditions that allow utility to be maximized in rigid linear equations in which the demand and supply of each good owned by each trader is precisely defined in an auction as a function of the prices cried by the auctioneer.

The auctioneer, which is an algorithm and not a person, automatically increases the price if demand exceeds supply and decreases the price if supply exceeds demand. In this system, price is at equilibrium only when it is a "stationary price," and the entire market reaches equilibrium only when demand is equal to supply on all individual markets. The general equilibrium of the market is derived through the interaction of economic variables that Walras substituted for physical variables in equations borrowed from mid-nineteenth century physics. This substitution obliged Walras to assume that conditions of equality between supply and demand of all goods can be rigidly defined at the point at which the individual trader obtains maximal satisfaction of needs compatible with initial resources.

The unknowns in these equations are expressed in terms of a *numéraire*, and exchange values are the solutions to the equations. Walras termed the abstract disembodied mechanism that the auctioneer uses to adjust gaps between supply and demand *tâtonnement*. This mechanism represents the spontaneous workings of competitive markets in a sphere where indeterminate human thoughts and behaviors do not exist. The radical departure from the real world is also apparent in the assumption that *tâtonnement* can function in the absence of exchange and that exchange occurs only when prices are at equilibrium.

Another disembodied abstract mechanism in Walras's economic universe is an intermediary figure, the *arbitrageur* or entrepreneur, that automatically purchases productive services and combines them to facilitate more production. When Walras introduced this algorithm into the equations that yield competitive equilibrium, he discovered that equilibrium could be reached only if the amount earned by the entrepreneur is zero. Although the idea that entrepreneurs do not seek to maximize profits is, of course, absurd, Walras is obliged to claim otherwise to save the appearances of an economic theory that is embedded in equations from mid-nineteenth century physics. Given that Walras's mechanism bears no resemblance to the motivations and behavior of actual entrepreneurs, how does he justify its existence? He does so by appealing to the natural laws that allegedly manifest in spontaneous adjustments and cause firms in competitive markets to switch to more profitable production processes and to abandon those that incur losses.

Walras also appealed to an ad hoc assumption to save appearances in his theory in an effort to reconcile fundamental differences between pure exchange and productive processes. He was obliged to view the pure exchange of the auction as timeless and reversible in order to wed this construct to the mathematical formalism of mid-nineteenth physics. But because productive processes obviously exist in time and are irreversible, Walras invented *tâtonnement sur bons*, or contingent contracts, to maintain the illusion that pure exchange takes place only at equilibrium prices.

The idea of contingent contracts serves this purpose because it allows the sale of new goods from production to be treated as hypothetical orders that are translated into prices by *tâtonnement* only at the point at which prices on all markets are at equilibrium. Note what Walras has to say about this matter: "Equilibrium in production, like equilibrium in exchange, is an ideal and not a real state. It never happens in the real world that the selling price of any given product is absolutely the cost of the productive services that enter into that product, or that the effective demand and supply are absolutely equal. Yet equilibrium is the normal state, in the sense that it is the state towards which things spontaneously tend under a regime of free competition in exchange and production."[15]

If equilibrium in production and exchange is a condition that does not exist in the real world, how does Walras possibly conclude that this is the "normal state"? He does so by alleging that the natural laws of economics manifest as forces that move the atomized parts of the closed market system toward equilibrium under ideal free market conditions. And he also suggests that the ideal state could become the real state if the natural laws were allowed to operate without interference.

In an article titled "Economique et mécanique," Walras claims that the "physico-mathematical science" outlined in *Elements of Pure Economics* uses the same mathematical formulae used to describe the mechanics of the equilibrium of the lever and the relations between celestial bodies.[16] In this article, Walras criticizes physicists who argue that the mathematics of physical theories cannot be applied in economics because utility is not a measurable quantity. He claims what these physicists have failed to realize is that they have also been vague about the quantification of basic variables such as "mass" and "force." Walras then concludes that *raretés* are the equivalent of forces in the physical equations and that utility is the equivalent of energy because both function as scalar quantities.[17] Obviously, this entire argument is absurd. There is no equivalence between the economic concepts and the physical variables, and the only basis for comparison is that the concepts have been substituted for the variables in the equations of mid-nineteenth century physics. The substitution of utility for energy may allow utility to be represented as a scalar function, but this clearly does not mean that the two quantities are in any sense the same.

The fact that the neoclassical model in mainstream economics was derived from this incredibly inept manipulation of a soon to be outmoded physics would soon be forgotten. What would survive, however, is the assumption that the usefulness of economic models in neoclassical economics is a form of scientific proof. Note how Walras exploits this idea in an attempt to reinforce his claim that economics is a science in the following commentary on the relationship between geometry and prices:

> Force and velocity are also measurable magnitudes, but the mathematical theory of force and velocity is not the whole of mechanics. Nevertheless, pure mechanics surely ought to precede applied mechanics. Similarly, given the pure theory of economics, it must be applied economics; and this pure theory of economics is a science which resembles the physico-mathematical sciences in every respect. This assertion is new and will seem strange; but I have proven it to be true, and I shall elaborate the proof in what follows.
>
> If the pure theory of economics or the theory of exchange and value in exchange, that is, the theory of social wealth considered by itself, is a physico-mathematical science like mechanics or hydrodynamics, then economists should not be afraid to use the methods and language of mathematics.[18]

Walras argues that because pure mathematics precedes applied science, it follows that pure economics should precede applied economics. The only basis for the claim that his economics is "pure" is that it represents vague economic concepts in the mathematical equations of mid-nineteenth century physics. Yet this is the basis for his "proof" that the resulting economic theory "resembles the physico-mathematical sciences in every respect" and should be viewed as a science "like mechanics or hydrodynamics."

Like the classical economists, Walras also appealed to the seventeenth-century assumption of metaphysical dualism to legitimate the claim that the natural laws of economics exist in an immaterial realm and are ontologically equivalent to laws of physics:

> Everyone who has studied any geometry at all knows perfectly well that only in an abstract, ideal circumference are the radii all equal to each other and that only in an abstract, ideal triangle is the sum of these angles equal to the sum of two right angles. Reality confirms these definitions and demonstrations only approximately, and yet reality admits to a very wide and fruitful application of these propositions. Following these same procedures, the pure theory of economics ought to take over from experience certain type concepts, like those of exchange, supply, demand, market, capital, income, productive services and products. From these

real-type concepts the pure science of economics should then abstract and define the ideal-type concepts in terms of which it carries on its reasoning. The return to reality should not take place until the science is completed and then only with a view to practical applications.[19]

The "science of economics" can, says Walras, disclose the "real-type concepts" by disclosing the "ideal-type concepts" that exist in purely mathematical form and govern the mechanisms of a market. The correspondence between the "real" and "ideal" will be complete, Walras suggests, when the "science is completed," and his belief in that prospect is premised on the real existence of natural laws that can be completely described in "purely" mathematical terms. He also implies that the immaterial realm in which the natural laws exist is the same as that where physical laws exist.

Walras's tendency to conflate the real and the ideal is particularly apparent when he draws comparisons between physical and economic forces. He not only claims that the forces regulating market prices operate like the forces of attraction that govern the movement of stars and planets, but he also alleges that lawful character of market forces can be reduced, like the force of gravity, to a few basic laws that explain a myriad of particular facts:

> Maximum effective utility, on the one hand; uniformity of price, on the other—be it the price of a consumer's good on the final products market, or the price of a service on the services market, or the price of net income on the capital goods market—these always constitute the double condition by which the universe of economic interests is automatically governed, just as the universe of astronomical motions is automatically governed by the double condition of gravitation which acts in direct proportion to the square of the distances. In one case as in the other, the whole science is contained in a formula two lines in length which serves to explain a countless multitude of particular phenomena.[20]

Obviously, there is no scientific basis for alleging that the "universe of economic interests" operates in the same manner as the "universe of astronomical motions," and the inverse square law does not apply to the relationship between utility and prices. These comments also suggest that Walras did not realize that energy is a vague concept in the equations of mid-nineteenth physics. He exploited this vagueness in making the claim that energy is the equivalent of utility, but he obviously did not understand that the physics on which his theory was based was quite different from classical dynamics. It is also interesting that Maxwell published his theory of electromagnetism and articulated the second law of dynamics during a period in which neoclassical economists were elaborating upon Walras's "pure" economic theory. If the creators of neoclassical economics had used the physics of electromagnetism as the basis for their theories, the fundamental flaws in their models would have been quite apparent.

In the cryptic discussions of the origins of neoclassical economic theory found in most introductory textbooks, the claim is normally made that this theory was independently and simultaneously "discovered" in the 1870s by the Englishman Jevons, the Frenchman Walras, and the Austrian economist Carl Menger (1840–1921). The implication is that any theory that emerges independently and simultaneously in very different cultural contexts must be empirically valid. As Mirowski has demonstrated in exhaustive detail, however, this discovery was not simultaneous, and the inclusion of Menger in the pantheon of the first neoclassical economics was a historical accident.[21]

Menger did claim that he was one of the originators of neoclassical economic theory, but he rejected the unifying principle of the theory, the construct of utility, and made no use of the new mathematical techniques borrowed from mid-nineteenth century physics. Mirowski agues that the primary reason why Menger's false claim was taken seriously is that one of his illustrious students, Friedrich von Wieser, managed to promote it during a period in which the work of his former teacher was largely unavailable outside of the German-speaking world. In any event, the argument that general equilibrium theory must reveal truths about economic reality because of the manner in which it was "discovered" has no foundations whatsoever.

Francis Ysidro Edgeworth and Vilfredo Pareto embraced Walras's claim that utility was the equivalent of energy in the equations of mid-nineteenth century physics along with his conclusion that economics had become a rigorously scientific discipline. The enthusiasm with which Edgeworth preached this gospel is apparent in the following passage:

The application of mathematics to the world of the soul is countenanced by the hypothesis (agreeable to the general hypothesis that every psychical phenomena is the concomitant, and in some the sense the other side of a physical phenomena), the particular hypothesis, adopted in these pages, that Pleasure is the concomitant of Energy. Energy may be regarded as the central idea of Mathematical Physics: maximum energy the object of the principle investigations in that science. . . . 'Mécanique Sociale' may one day take her place along with 'Mécanique Celeste,' throned each upon the double-sided height of one maximal principle, the supreme principle of moral as of physical science. As the movements of each particle, constrained or loose, in a material cosmos are continually subjugated to one maximum sub-total of accumulated energy, so the movements of each soul whether selfishly isolated or linked sympathetically, may continually be realizing the maximum of pleasure.[22]

Pareto's position, although more pugnacious, is essentially the same as that of Edgeworth:

Strange disputes about predestination, about the efficacy of grace, etc., and in our own day incoherent ramblings on solidarity show that men have not freed themselves from these daydreams which have been gotten rid of in the physical sciences, but which still burden the social sciences. . . . Thanks to the use of mathematics, this entire theory, as we develop it in the Appendix, rests on no more than a fact of experience, that is, on the determination of the quantities of goods which constitute combinations between which the individual is indifferent. The theory of economic science thus acquires the rigor of rational mechanics.[23]

MORE RECENT DEVELOPMENTS IN NEOCLASSICAL ECONOMICS

Alfred Marshall (1842–1924), the dominant figure in mainstream economics from 1890 to the beginning of World War I, popularized neoclassical economic theory and altered some of the work he promoted. Many historians of economics have cited Marshall's claim that the "Mecca of the economist lies in economic biology" and concluded that he preferred the biology metaphor to the physics metaphor. In the next sentence, however, Marshall writes, "But biological conceptions are more complex than those of mechanics; a volume on Foundations must therefore give a relatively large place to mechanical analogies."[24] Similarly, those who frequently quote Marshall's pronouncement "burn the mathematics" should read the following passage from the eighth edition of his *Principles of Economics*:

The new analysis is endeavoring gradually and tentatively to bring over into economics, as far as the widely different nature of the material allow, those methods of the science of small increments (commonly called the differential calculus) to which man owes directly or indirectly the greater part of the control that he has obtained in recent times over physical nature. It is still in its infancy; it has no dogmas, and there is no standard orthodoxy. . . . There is a remarkable harmony and agreement on essentials among those who are working constructively by the new method; and especially among such of them as have served an apprenticeship in the simpler and more definite, and therefore more advanced, problems of physics.[25]

When Marshall made this comment, the physics used by the creators of neoclassical economics was outmoded, and yet he appears to have been completely unaware that this was the case.

John Maynard Keynes (1883–1946), a student of Marshall's, wrote his most seminal work during a period in which the Great Depression was challenging neoclassical assumptions about the lawful mechanisms of market systems. In 1935, Keynes wrote in a letter to playwright George Bernard Shaw, "You have to know that I am writing a book on economic theory which will largely revolutionize—not as I suppose at once, but in the course of the next ten years—the way the world thinks about economic problems."[26] What was most radical about the book that Keynes felt would occasion this revolution, *The General Theory of Employment, Interest and Money*, is that it grounds economic processes in historical time, or in a more experiential sense of time where the future cannot be known and the past cannot be changed.

As we have seen, the mathematical formalism of mid-nineteenth century physics obliged Walras to view economic actors as imbued with prodigious knowledge of economic variables and existing in a wholly abstract realm where time in all of its real or actual dimensions does not exist. Keynes's more recognizably human economic actor is quite different. He or she is motivated in part by "animal spirits" and irrational desires and inhabits an economic reality in which knowledge is always proximate and future outcomes are essentially indeterminate.

In *The General Theory*, Keynes first makes the case that there is nothing inherent in the mechanisms of a free market system to prevent a situation in which surplus savings does not decrease interest rates and investment spending plummets due to expectations of future low sales. In the absence of borrowing and investment spending, he concluded, there is no economic impetus to expand or grow the economy. And this, as the worldwide depression in the 1930s had shown, could lead to some very unfortunate results—massive unemployment, a spiral of contraction due to lack of spending on capital equipment, and a climate of uncertainty in which private investment was not sufficient to reverse the economic decline. Keynes's well-known solution to this problem is that government should take up the slack by funding projects that employ the unemployed. The monies earned by these individuals would, said Keynes, increase the buying power that fuels consumption and lead to resumption of private investment in business expansion.

Much was troubling, then and now, about *The General Theory* from the perspective of neoclassical economists. Keynes's claim that the unimpeded operations of the natural laws of economics can result in a situation in which an economy not only fails to grow but even contracts suggested that the laws of economics were fallible. And because the prescribed remedy for this situation was large-scale intervention by government, or by an agency "outside" the closed market system, this not only suggested that the system cannot under all conditions be viewed as closed, but also indicated that there were situations where the natural laws of economics, if left alone, could not sustain the economic well-being of even the majority of economic actors.

The realization that led Keynes to develop a theory that would later be dubbed the "Keynesian heresy" is apparent a letter he wrote in 1934 to economist John Hicks: "I shall hope to convince you some day that Walras's theory and all the others along these lines are little better than nonsense."[27] If Keynes had been able to convince other neoclassical economists that Walrasian general equilibrium theory is "nonsense," then the revolution he had in mind might have actually occurred. This did not happen, however, because Keynes wed new assumptions about economic reality to a mathematical formalism that was essentially the same as what Walras derived from mid-nineteenth physics. This resulted in some "logical" contradictions within the formalism that John Hicks would later claim to have eliminated in a mathematical framework for analyzing the factors determining the aggregate level of demand. The framework essentially buries the indeterminate aspects of Keynes's analysis under two deterministic and independent lines that represent equilibria in investment and savings (IS) and equilibria in liquidity money supply (LM), which, taken together, translate into a general equilibrium level of demand.

Strangely enough, the essential incompatibility of the IS-LM model and the Keynesian process model did not become fully apparent until the 1960s. By this time, however, a fundamentally static vision of a market economy as a closed circular flow in which the level of aggregate demand could be regulated by consciously determined public policy, such as that of the Federal Reserve Board in the United States, was firmly in place. The curious result of this wayward course of events was that Keynes's heresies were rendered impotent in mainstream economics, and the "revolution" that he thought would occur was undermined by appeals to a construct that was, in his view, utter nonsense—Walrasian general equilibrium theory.

Keynes's suggestion that the behavior or parts (economic actors and firms) cannot under certain conditions prevent the whole (market system) from moving toward a state of general equilibrium resulted in the development of macroeconomics. Based largely on the broadly homogenous categories of economic activity developed by Keynes, macroeconomists attempt to study the whole of the economy by representing the economic behavior of the parts within these categories as lawfully determined based on deductions from general equilibrium theory. The resulting mathematical models are used to assess macroeconomic issues such as the effects of government policies on inflation and unemployment, the impacts of changes in the overnight interest rates by the central bank on stock markets, and the overall costs associated with increases in the minimum wage. But because virtually all of these macroeconomic models are extensions of the means and methods of the microeconomic models in general equilibrium theory, they are predicated on the same assumptions about the relationships between parts (economic actors and firms) and wholes (market systems).

In the 1930s and 1940s, the foundations were laid for the axiomatization of general equilibrium theory, or for reformulating it within a framework of hypotheses perfectly delineated and rigorously expressed in mathematical language. The impulse toward axiomatization came from two gifted mathematicians, John von Neumann and Oskar Morgenstern, who were highly critical of the conversational and imprecise language used by neoclassical economists and their apparent unwillingness to develop more sophisticated mathematical models. In conversation with Morgenstern, von Neumann said the following about the state of research in this discipline at the end of the 1930s: "You know, Oskar, if those books are unearthed sometime a hundred years hence, people will not believe they were written in our time. Rather they will think that they are contemporary with Newton, so primitive is their mathematics. Economics is simply still a million miles away from the state in which an advanced science is, such as physics."[28]

Morgenstern was similarly disdainful of the state of economic theory. In a review of John Hicks's *Value and Capital* (1939), Morgenstern dismissed the value of this well-received and widely read attempt to develop a more comprehensive economic theory based on Walrasian analysis by concluding that it was "outdated and lacking in rigor."[29]

The rigor that von Neumann and Morgenstern wished to introduce into economic theory was predicated on the belief, popular in intellectual circles at the time, that more sophisticated mathematical techniques could disclose the underlying dynamics of human consciousness and decision-making. As Morgenstern put it, "It suffices to be familiar with the present state of the investigations of the foundations of mathematics to realize that all mathematical theorems are derived without exception from logic and solely from logic. From this follows that the potential use of mathematics in the social sciences means nothing else but that their problems can be formulated and treated in an exact manner."[30]

The notion that timeless, universal truths govern the dynamics of human thought and behavior and that the essence of these truths consists of immaterial ideas, or preexisting logics, that can be uncovered by advances in mathematical theory is everywhere present in the work of von Neumann and Morgenstern. Both figures may have very much aware that the mathematical clothes worn by the emperor of neoclassical economics in the 1930s were largely imaginary, but they firmly believed that a real or actual garment could be woven from the thread of higher mathematics.

One irony here is that their attempts to create this garment served to perpetuate the fiction that the invisible hand actually exists by disguising the metaphysical assumptions upon which its existence is predicated under increasingly elaborate layers of mathematical formalism. Another is that von Neumann and Morgenstern attempted to do so during a period in which their conception of the relationship between mathematical theory and physical reality was completely undermined, for reasons we will discuss later, by developments in quantum physics. This conception was also undermined in a somewhat different way by Gödel's demonstration in his incompleteness theorem that no finite system of mathematics can be used to derive all true mathematical statements, and, therefore, that no algorithm, or calculation procedure, can prove its own validity.

Most of the research in neoclassical economics since the 1940s, particularly in general equilibrium theory, has been based on extensions and refinements of the work of von Neumann and Morgenstern. In *Foundations of Economic Analysis* (1947), Paul Samuelson attempted to systematize general equilibrium theory with the use of organic methodologies and mathematical techniques that were less rigorous than those used by von Neumann and Morgenstern. This is, however, the first treatise in economic theory in which the formal mathematical apparatus is embedded in the main argument and not placed in appendices, and Samuelson clearly implies that the transcendent truths that lie at the core of economic behavior can be described and decoded by the apparatus.

In *Foundations*, Samuelson assumes that any problem in economic theory can be reduced to a system of equations and that general equilibrium is the solution of all the equations that represent the lawful dynamics of a free market system. He defines a meaningful mathematical theorem as "simply a hypothesis about empirical data which could conceivably be refuted, if only under ideal conditions."[31] Samuelson then goes on to specify that a theorem "may be indeterminate and practically difficult, or impossible to determine. . . . But it is meaningful because under ideal circumstances an experiment could be devised whereby one could hope to refute the hypothesis."[32]

The curious presumption that a system of idealized representations of economic activity in mathematical theorems could somehow be proven if an ideal experiment could somehow be conducted would soon become the primary justification for the real existence of the invisible hand in neoclassical economic theory. However, the mathematical formalism in this theory is such that it is not possible to define the specific roles or behavior of economics actors based on the functional form of the equations. Hence hypotheses normally refer to some qualitative properties of the functions that allegedly emerge from the formalism, such as convexity or monotony.

Aware of this problem, Samuelson rationalizes away the fact that experimental verification of general equilibrium is impossible by claiming that this is an indispensable aspect of theoretical economics: "It is precisely because theoretical economics does not confine itself to specific narrow types of functions that it is able to achieve wide generality in its initial formulation."[33] If a scientist claimed that a scientific theory is useful because it is sufficiently general to disallow any prospect that its predictions can be subjected to experimental proof, he or she would be the laughingstock of the profession. Mainstream economists, however, have rather consistently used this argument to justify the claim that neoclassical economics is a sci-

THE EMPEROR HAS NO CLOTHES

ence comparable to the physical sciences and has much the same status as a theory in the physical sciences.

Convinced that neoclassical economics was, or would soon become, a rigorously scientific discipline like physics, Samuelson concluded that the task of economics is to develop empirically valid mathematical descriptions of decisions made by economic actors in free market systems. This was, in his view, a possibility because he believed, like von Neumann and Morgenstern, that immaterial logics condition and control economic decisions in ordinary language and that their pristine and universal structures and dynamics could be decoded and represented in mathematical language. This belief explains why Samuelson was willing to make the totally unsubstantiated claim that the science of economics is based, like physics, on the "observation of physical facts" and that those who practice this science "have the common task of describing and summarizing empirical reality."[34]

In the equations of physical theories, variables typically have a counterpart in physical reality that is observable or potentially observable and new physical theories are deemed valid only if they make predictions that can be confirmed in repeatable experiments under controlled conditions. The primary reason why the predictions of general equilibrium theory cannot be confirmed in this manner is that the variables in the mathematical formalism are self-referential functions that have no real or actual counterpart in physical reality. Given that these predictions are the product of a system of equations that refers only to itself, there is no basis in principle for confirming or denying them. This leads to the obvious conclusion that that there is simply no way in which to prove that the theory is valid or invalid in scientific terms.

Gerald Debreu, who sought to complete the work begun by von Neumann and Morgenstern, published a complete axiomatization of general equilibrium theory in *Theory of Value* (1959) in which the emphasis is shifted from the mathematical techniques of infinitesimal calculus to those of algebra and typology.[35] He extends this mathematical apparatus to include a broad new range of quantitative and qualitative analysis with the aim of creating a formal structure that clearly reveals "all the assumptions and the logical structure of analysis."[36] This approach represents a major shift in neoclassical economic thought because it attempts to account for the formation of exchange values in pure mathematical language and without references to the interpretive value of the concepts. As Debreu puts it, "Allegiance to rigor dictates the axiomatic form of the analysis where the theory, in the strict sense, is logically disconnected from its interpretations."[37]

The presumption behind this analysis is that a purely mathematical economic theory can disclose previously hidden lawful dynamics in economic reality, just as purely mathematical theories in physics have disclosed hidden dynamics of physical reality. And because the mathematical constructs in physics can be understood mathematically without any reference to their meaning in ordinary language, Debreu claims that this should also be the case for constructs in an axiomized mathematical treatment of general equilibrium theory. The problem with these assumptions is not merely that there is no one-to-one correspondence between the variables in this theory and the actual behavior of economic systems. It is also that the constructs on which the theory is based are the same as those in Walrasian general equilibrium theory, and this fact is only thinly disguised by a mathematical formalism that differs in form and content from that used by Walras.

Debreu may have been successful in representing these constructs in a framework of hypotheses that are perfectly delineated and rigorously expressed in mathematical language. But this does not, in any sense, prove the validity of the assumptions and only serves to disguise their metaphysical foundations under another complex set of mathematical idealizations that says nothing in ordinary language about the actual character of the assumptions. Yet Debreu assumes that a self-referential mathematical system that has no real or actual counterpart in economic reality can disclose hidden lawful dynamics in this reality. For example, he claims that "uncertainties" about the future of market economies are "due to the unknown choice that nature will make from the set of possible states in the world" and that these uncertainties can be eliminated based on future extensions of axiomatization in neoclassical economic theory.[38]

Another neoclassical economist with a talent for higher mathematics, Kenneth Arrow, collaborated with Debreu to develop the Arrow-Debreu model for general equilibrium theory (1954).[39] This mathematical model describes a hypothetical perpetually expanding market system in which idealized economic actors possess an unlimited understanding of the consequences of their economic choices and engage in perfect competition without any transmission and information costs. In this model, general equilibrium theory is rigorously expressed in mathematical terms as a set of ideal conditions in an idealized economic system characterized by an equilibrium of perfect competition. The mechanism in the model that allegedly confirms that these actors have made the mutually compatible decisions that result in this equilibrium is a set of signals, or market prices, that operates automatically even though the vast majority of actors are totally unaware of its existence.

The history of general equilibrium theory is much more complex and detailed than this brief account suggests, and a complete history would require several volumes. What is most important about this history for our purposes, however, is that the theory is now and always has been predicated on assumptions about the relationship between parts (economic actors and firms) and wholes (market systems) articulated by the creators of neoclassical economics. It should now be clear that these assumptions were metaphysical in origins and assumed the guise of scientific truths after the creators of neoclassical economics incorporated them into a mathematical formalism based on a bastardized version of mid-nineteenth century physics. It should also be clear that this myth was perpetuated in theories that disguised the metaphysical foundations of the assumptions under an increasingly complex maze of mathematical formalism.

From its origins to the present, the primary theoretical justification for general equilibrium theory has been the claim that complex mathematical analysis can disclose the lawful dynamics of human choices in economic reality. This may have allowed for large degrees of freedom in the extension of the mathematical analysis. It has also resulted, however, in a situation in which there is little or no concern about how realistic the model might be in its description of actual economic behavior or the ability of the model to accurately predict the future consequences of that behavior. There is, therefore, a simple reason why neoclassical economists who specialize in general equilibrium theory have not chosen to dirty their hands with the messy business of empirical verification and interpretation. The theory is such that it cannot be examined, much less confirmed, in this manner.

GAME THEORY

A fair number of economists over the past two decades, including luminaries such as Arrow and Hand, have expressed doubt about the efficacy of general equilibrium theory, but it is still the central legitimating construct in mainstream economics. Within the community of mainstream economists, the most serious objections have been raised by proponents of game theory. Game theory in economics originated in 1944 with the publication of *The Theory of Games and Economic Behavior* by John von Neumann and Oskar Morgenstern. A game, explained the authors, is a set of rules and objectives and a ranking of objectives by a set of players. Assuming that the sets are discrete and well defined, von Neumann and Morgenstern argued that they can be expressed in mathematical equations and manipulated by mathematical symbols to predict outcomes.

Martin Shubik, perhaps the best known and most influential of the game theorists, has been consistently critical of Walrasian general equilibrium theory because it assumes that economic actors have no freedom to make mistakes or even to make choices about the economic process. He claims that an alternate and more realistic description of the behavior of economic actors can be disclosed in noncooperative game theory. "Noncooperative game theory," writes Shubik, "appears to be particularly useful for the study of mass phenomena in which the communication between individuals must be relatively low and individuals interact with a more or less faceless economy, polity or society."[40]

These impersonal forces can be represented, says Shubik, "through the construction of mathematical models in which the 'rules of the game' derive not only from the economics and technology of the situation, but from the sociological and legal structure as well."[41] In Shubik's mathematical models, the basic features of an economy (tastes, technologies, and endowments) are essentially the same as those in conventional Walrasian models, and sociological, political, and legal forces are represented mathematically as the rules that act arbitrarily on the closed economy from the outside. These rules do not, claims Shubik, lie within the sphere of the closed economy because they are not "natural" or do not operate in accordance the natural laws of economics. Although Shubik recognizes that the natural laws of economics are not the single determinate of economic behavior, these laws function as the prime determinant of such behavior in his theory. The economic actor in his mathematical models may be buffeted by arbitrary variables that operate outside the closed market system, but this actor is still represented as a point particle subject to the influence of natural laws.

In a recently published two-volume work, *The Theory of Money and Financial Institutions*, Shubik attempts to reconcile microeconomic and macroeconomic theory by constructing a process-oriented theory of money and financial institutions based on a theory of games. He claims that it is possible to "construct process models of the economy that are as rigorous as general equilibrium theory but explain more phenomena."[42] Shubik then suggests that the essential problem with general equilibrium theory is that it is predicated on an absurdly reductive and restrictive view of economic actors: "The rational, economic, institution-free individual assumed in its models is an overly simplistic abstraction of a subtle and complex creature who must function with high constraints on perception and ability to calculate, who uses both internal and external memory, and whose goals can hardly be well defined outside the context of the society in which the individual functions."[43]

Shubik then notes that in the absence of "well-defined models of politico-economic and socio-economic behavior," he is obliged to make the "usual assumptions concerning the existence of well-defined preferences and utility functions, not because I believe in them, but because I want to show that even with these assumptions we can go beyond the results of general equilibrium theory."[44] This effort to transcend the limits of general equilibrium theory is predicated on an interesting view of the "institutions of society in general, and the financial institutions in particular." These institutions, writes Shubik, are the "neural network of the sensors of the body economic, guiding the flows of funds, credits, and other financial paper that guide the real goods and services of the economy." He then proceeds to demonstrate that the process of setting up playable games "forces us" to invent minimal financial and governmental institutions even if we do not invoke the maximization of utility or use equilibrium as a general solution.[45]

Based on the assumption that the "neural network" of financial institutions "emerges" as a logical necessity of decision making in market economies, Shubik claims that game theory can disclose the "emergent" logics that structure this network, and this becomes the basis for two large claims—"minimal financial institutions" emerge as a "logical, technological, and institutional necessity when economic activity is described as a playable game," and "both game theoretic and general-equilibrium models often predict the same apparently general, noninstitutional outcome."[46]

In the conclusion of this densely mathematical treatise, Shubik cautions that his game theoretic "process models that can be solved for general equilibrium solutions" are not meant to closely approximate reality. "They are meant to be well-defined playable games where details (money, credit, the rate of interest, and so forth) are clearly defined and causality can be considered."[47] Yet he also claims that the models can demystify the lawful dynamics of market economies, such as perfect insight, rational expectations and the laws of Walras and Say.[48]

Like most theoreticians in neoclassical economics, Shubik is a very gifted mathematician, and his analysis is staggeringly complex in these terms. However, the alleged symmetries between the outcomes of the playable games and those of general equilibrium theory are not emergent properties of a neural network of institutions that direct the future of a market economy in causal terms. They are simply artifacts of a mathematical analysis predicated on assumptions about the relationships between parts (economic actors and firms) and wholes (market systems) in general equilibrium theory. What is most important to realize here is that game theory, even in its most sophisticated forms, perpetuates belief in the real or actual existence of the invisible hand by disguising the natural laws of economics under a maze of different mathematical formalism. It does so by alleging that causal mechanisms in market economies are emergent properties of human decision making within the lawful constraints of market processes as opposed to the transcendent godlike agencies that lurk behind the equations of general equilibrium theory.

Another fundamental problem faced by the game theorists is that because economic transactions in the real world are also serial and multiple, any accurate depiction of the results of such transactions requires that games be repeated. However, repetition in noncooperative games leads to the addition of more ad hoc assumptions about how each player will interpret the sequence of moves of other players. And this, as many game theorists have discovered, undermines the prospect that the outcome will be either fixed or determinant.

The work of the game theorists has proved very unsettling for many mainstream economists. In Walrasian general equilibrium theory, the natural laws of economics allegedly determine the optimal outcome of an economic process and economic actors are devoid of all distinctly human characteristics and obey fixed decision-making rules. In this theory, the realm of the economy is also stable and unchanging and economic actors are viewed as supremely rational entities who do not talk back. In opening the box of human subjectivity, game theorists have been obliged to posit an increasing number of ad hoc variables to account for the decision making of individual economic actors. This explains why the history of game theory is marked by a continual regression into the staggering complexities of language and culture.

Bargaining games led to cooperative games to noncooperative games and to games where players are free to interpret the meaning of economic variables and the intentions of other players. More than half of a typical textbook on game theory is devoted to describing a staggering array of variants on particular games based on quite different conceptions of uncertainty, and there is no sense of generality or unity. It now seems clear that the complexities of language and culture cannot be reduced to deterministic mathematical models and that attempts to do so have begun to undermine the validity of mechanistic rationality in general equilibrium theory. As R. Sugden puts it, "There was a time, not long ago, when the foundations of rational-choice theory appeared firm, and when the job of the economic theorist seemed to be one of drawing out the often complex implications of a fairly simple and uncontroversial system of axioms. But it is increasingly becoming clear that these foundations are less secure than we thought, and that they need to be examined and perhaps rebuilt. Economic theorists may have to become as much philosophers as mathematicians."[49]

Wassily Leontief, a Nobel laureate in economics, has also expressed doubts about the efficacy of the orthodox neoclassical paradigm:

> Page after page of professional journals are filled with mathematical formulas leading the reader from sets of more or less plausible but entirely arbitrary assumptions to precisely stated but irrelevant conclusions. . . . Year after year economic theorists continue to produce scores of mathematical models to explore in great detail their formal properties; and the econometrics fit algebraic functions of all possible shapes to essentially the same sets of data without being able to advance, in any perceptible way, a systematic understanding of the structure and the operations of a real economic system.[50]

The decision to award the 2001 Nobel Memorial Prize in Economic Science to economists who have done pioneering research on the imperfections of market systems is another indicator that mainstream economists have begun to question the validity of assumptions about the character of economic reality in the neoclassical economic paradigm. The winners, Joseph Stiglitz, George Akerlof, and Michael Spence, were chosen because they have demonstrated that "imperfect information" in actual economic processes challenges the assumption that atomized economic actors are fully aware of complex economic variables in every transaction. According to these economists, these imperfections result in situations where the alleged lawful dynamics of closed market systems cannot allocate resources in the most efficient way and government must, therefore, intervene and make the necessary adjustments. For example, Stiglitz has shown that if the Securities and Exchange Commission did not enforce full disclosure in financial markets, investors would not have sufficient information to determine a proper value for stocks and some sectors of the market would have more information than others.

These criticisms and revisions of assumptions about the character of economic reality in neoclassical economic theory do not mean, however, that mainstream economists are in the process of developing a new theory predicated on a different set of assumptions. Virtually all of the most advanced theoretical work in mainstream economics is premised on the assumptions that market systems are, by varying degrees, closed, self-correcting, and self-sustaining. And the primary impulse in most of these theories is to disclose the hidden dynamics that move market systems toward optimal states of equilibria with the use of increasingly more sophisticated mathematical techniques. For example, nonlinear analysis, particularly convex analysis, has been used to buttress the theoretical claims of the game theorists and the resulting mathematical formalism, as the work of Jeanne-Pierre Aubin illustrates, is staggeringly complex. But as the title of Aubin's best-known book, *Optima and Equilibria: An Introduction to Nonlinear Analysis*,[51] attests, the ghost in the machine is still the natural laws of economics and the primary impulse is to uncover the immaterial logics that allegedly sustain the orderly workings of market systems.

More important for our purposes, the vast majority of mainstream economists who work in business and government, including those at the International Monetary Fund and the World Bank, are not terribly concerned with the most advanced theoretical work in their discipline. Legions of these economists are engaged on a daily basis in developing analyses and making predictions that guide the decision making of global economic planners and that serve to legitimate assumptions about economic reality in the neoclassical economic paradigm. Many of these planners are aware of the negative impacts of their decisions on the global environment and seek to minimize these impacts as long as profit margins can be maintained. These good intentions are, however, typically defeated by our now familiar culprit—blatantly unscientific assumptions about economic reality that make it virtually impossible to resolve environmental problems in economic terms.

THE POLITICS OF THIS EXPERIENCE

Because the predictions of neoclassical economic theory are not subject to empirical verification, the primary determinant of which theories are used to coordinate economic activities in particular market economies is the political process. Some theories may have more predictive value than others in dealing with specific sets of initial conditions, but the predictions themselves are merely useful approximations of tendencies to occur that point toward directions in which an economy may move under relative stable conditions. When the predictions are grossly inaccurate, as they almost invariably are under unstable market conditions, neoclassical economists typically attempt to explain, or explain away, the discrepancies by attributing the causes to market failures that can be potentially corrected or to events that occur "outside" the closed market system and interfere with its operation.

In countries with functional democracies, large-scale changes in the organization of market systems typically occur after a political party that closely identifies itself with a particular understanding of the character of economic reality wins a general election during a period of economic crisis and manages to implement an alternate economic program. In the vast majority of cases, the economic crisis can be directly attributed to, or has been massively aggravated by, what mainstream economists call "nonmarket variables," or events that are presumable not subject to the lawful mechanisms of the closed market system. The alternate economic program is normally based on the views of economists that are most consistent with the ideological commitments of the victorious candidate for president or prime minister, with the ideological agenda that distinguishes the party of this candidate from that of other parties, and with the ideologically driven solutions to economic problems that appeal to large numbers of dissatisfied voters.

Perhaps the best way to illustrate these dynamics is to examine briefly the large role played by the competition between Keynesian and anti-Keynesian economic theory in the electoral process in Britain and the United States. In the aftermath of World War II, there was no private sector capable of mobilizing the investment, capital goods, and skills required to rebuild economies devastated by this conflict and international trade was massively disrupted. Only governments seemed capable of marshaling the resources needed to deal with these large problems, and the economic model used in most industrial nations in the West and in large parts of the developing world was based on Keynes's vision of a reformed and managed national economy. In these so-called mixed economies, state ownership, industrial policy, and fiscal management were used in various combinations in an effort to protect capitalism from its own excesses and to save capitalism from the lure of socialism.

Until the late 1970s, Keynesian "new economics," with its emphasis on managing the overall economy with the fiscal tools of taxation and spending, appeared for the most part to have fulfilled its promise of sustained economic growth and full employment. Many economists during this period challenged Keynes's vision, but the most fervent anti-Keynesians, whose names would become household words during the Thatcher-Reagan era, were Friedrich Hayek and Milton Friedman. What is most interesting about the work of Hayek and Friedman for our purposes is that their theories are narrowly predicated on assumptions about part–whole relationships in closed market systems that the creators of neoclassical economics embedded in a mathematical formalism borrowed from mid-nineteenth century physics. Both economists extended and refined this formalism with their own original contributions, and each received the Nobel Memorial Prize in economics in recognition of these contributions. But their understanding of the lawful dynamics of the economic process closely resembles that of Jevons, Walras, Edgeworth, and Pareto and is premised on the same metaphysical assumptions.

The legacy of Hayek, the most influential proponent of the Austrian free-market school of economics, can best be summarized by the response of Larry Summers, former secretary of the treasury in the second Clinton administration, to the question, "What's the single most important thing to learn from an economics course today?" Summers replied, "What I leave my students with is the view that the invisible hand is more powerful than the hidden hand. Things will happen in well-organized efforts without direction, control, plans. That's the consensus among economists."[52] This view is everywhere present in a book that became the "bible of economics" for Margaret Thatcher and the blueprint and rationale for the changes in the structure of the British economy that occurred during her tenure as prime minister—Hayek's *Road to Serfdom*.[53]

Originally published in 1944, this extremely conservative rendering of the truths of neoclassical economics denounces the welfare state, the mixed economy, and all forms of collectivism. The book was published in the United States by the University of Chicago Press and achieved much wider fame after *Reader's Digest* released a condensed version. Keith Joseph, who had been elected to Parliament as a Conservative in 1956 and who served as minister in charge of social services after Edward Heath become prime minister in 1970, read *The Road to Serfdom* and experienced what he later described as a "conversion to conservatism."[54] This conversion took place during a period in which the British economy was severely disrupted by a wholly unanticipated consequence of the Yon Kippur War, the 1973 oil crisis, and a prolonged coal miners' strike.

Following his conversion, Joseph joined a right-of-center think tank called the Institute of Economic Affairs that would, under his leadership, promote Hayek's views and popularize the economic agenda that eventually became the basis for the "Thatcherite revolution." Always impatient with the pace of change, Joseph next established the Centre for Policy Studies with the professed aim of converting the Conservative Party to belief in the "more pristine" understanding of the lawful workings of the market system championed by Hayek. He recruited Margaret Thatcher, a member of Parliament who had previously served as minister of education in the Heath government, to serve as his vice chairman, and the Centre began to promote its understanding of the actual character of the market system by sponsoring a flood of books, pamphlets, seminars, dinners, and luncheons.

At the top of the reading list Joseph distributed to his vice chairman and to other Tory politicians was Hayek's *Road to Serfdom*, which Thatcher had first read as an undergraduate student at Oxford. After rereading the book, she had her own conversion experience and became a true believer in the notion that the unimpeded operations of the invisible hand could resolve virtually all economic and social problems.[55] During the two years before Thatcher became prime minister, the British economy had performed badly and alternate economic solutions were high on the political agenda. The British government was forced to borrow money from the International Monetary Fund to protect the pound and the conditions of the loans required sizable cuts in public expenditures. These cuts sparked a rebellion within the ranks of the Labour Party, and Labour Prime Minister James Callaghan added more fuel to this flame by supporting plant closures and a reduction in the labor force at state-owned companies. The economic situation reached crisis proportions after a strike by public-sector employees resulted in the rationing of medical care in hospitals and mounds of uncollected garbage in city streets. To make matters even worse, another strike by truck drivers brought the entire British economy to the point of virtual collapse. On a day when even the catering staff at the House of Commons was on strike, the Labour government lost a vote of no confidence and Callaghan was obliged to call the general election that made Thatcher prime minister in 1979.

Thatcher made it quite clear that she wished to chart a future for the British economy based on a distinctly un-Keynesian view of the market system in which the "Nanny State" would be replaced by the risks and rewards of "enterprise culture."[56] But during her first three years in office, Thatcher was not successful in translating this vision into reality, and the planned Thatcherite revolution was a failure or, more accurately, a non-event. Interest rates rose to 16 percent, inflation was anticipated to reach 20 percent, and government deficits continued to climb.

Keith Joseph, who remained Thatcher's unofficial minister of thought and who served officially as secretary of state for industry in her government, was eager to privatize state-owned industries and to confront the politically powerful trade unions. To prepare for this struggle, he presented senior civil servants in his ministry with a reading list containing Hayek's *Road to Serfdom*, Adam Smith's *The Wealth of Nations* and *The Theory of Moral Sentiments*, and eight pamphlets written by himself.[57] Meanwhile, the Tory government was embroiled in an effort to displace Keynesian monetary policy with monetarism by attempting to ensure that increases in the money supply would be commensurate with economic growth. When economic conditions failed to improve and the political unrest increased, Thatcher's support in the poles dropped to 23 percent, making her the most unpopular prime minister since the advent of modern polling in Britain.

What saved the Thatcher government from almost certain defeat in the 1983 general election was the decision to respond to the invasion by Argentine troops of islands eight thousand miles from England with an impressive display of military force. After several naval battles, a full-scale landing, and three weeks of fierce fighting, Britain emerged victorious in the Falklands War, and the nationalistic fervor that accompanied this victory changed Thatcher's political fortunes dramatically. She won the general election with a 144-seat majority, and her government suddenly had the political clout to implement a legislative agenda designed to create a market system in Britain consistent with that envisioned by Hayek.

The other confrontation that enhanced Thatcher's standing in the polls took the form of a standoff with the National Union of Coal Miners, led by Marxist Arthur Scargill, that began 1984. When Scargill and other union leaders refused to allow some mine pits to be closed, the Thatcher government anticipated a strike and asked the Central Electricity Generating Board to stockpile enough coal inventories to prevent the blackouts and power cuts that had crippled the British economy during the 1974 strike. After a year, the strike was broken, and the relationship between labor, management, and government fundamentally altered.

This new relationship allowed the Thatcher government to privatize state-owned industries, such as British Gas, British Airways, British Steel, British Coal, and British Rail, and to sell off government shares in North Sea oil and British Petroleum. By 1992, two thirds of the state-owned industries, forty-six businesses employing roughly 900,000 employees, were privately owned.[58]

These changes did not occur without a great deal of social unrest and political opposition, and this accounted in large part for the overwhelming 179-seat majority won by Tony Blair's "New Labour Party" in the 1997 general election. Although Blair rejected the emphasis in the "Old Labour Party" on government intervention and state ownership, his vision of the free market, premised on compassion, social democracy, and inclusiveness, was more Keynesian and quite different from that of Hayek. A devout Christian since his undergraduate years at Oxford, Blair is committed to what he terms an "ethical socialism" that is more rooted in the ideals of Christian community and personal responsibility and that places less emphasis on the class struggle and dependence on the state.[59]

The intimate connection between the competition between Keynesian and anti-Keynesian economics and the political process is also apparent in the more market-oriented United States during the post–World War II era. The United States, in contrast with most other industrialized economies, has consistently favored a regulatory approach to solving economic problems, with the use of a web of regulatory agencies and antitrust legislation enforced by a powerful judiciary. And because America emerged from World War II with an intact and greatly strengthened economic system, it was not necessary, as it was in Europe, for government to play a large and central role in the management of the postwar economy.

Economic planners in Washington first began to apply Keynesian fiscal policies in 1938, and subsequent planners were heavily influenced by the work of Keynesian "new economists" at Harvard through the Johnson and Kennedy administrations. Richard Nixon, who attributed his 1960 defeat by John Kennedy to the recession of that year, declared, "Now, I am a Keynesian" shortly after winning the presidency in 1970.[60] He then proceeded to implement a Keynesian full employment budget in which deficit spending was used to reduce unemployment and inflation-unemployment tradeoffs were addressed with an income policy in which government intervention was used to control wages.

Against the advice of Federal Reserve Chairman Arthur Burns, a conservative anti-Keynesian economist, Nixon took the nation off the gold standard, which weakened the dollar against other currencies and added to inflation by driving up the costs of imported goods. This action created a situation in which mainstream economists at central banks were obliged to take on the role of seeking to protect the stability of international commerce in the currency markets by buying or selling national currencies in response to sudden swings in their relative values. The Nixon administration also extended government regulation into new areas with the creation of the Environmental Protection Agency, the Occupational Safety and Health Administration, and the Equal Opportunity Commission. What is remarkable here is that the influence of Keynesian economics explains, in large part, why the administration of one of America's most conservative politicians instituted more liberal economic reforms than any other administration, with the exception of that of Franklin Roosevelt.

During the 1970s, the American economy did not perform well owing to the large-scale impacts of the 1973 oil boycott that massively contributed to the breakdown of the Britain economy. In 1974, inflation was at its highest level since World War I and unemployment reached 9.2 percent, or two points greater than any time in the years since that war. Another nonmarket variable entered the picture when the Shah of Iran was toppled from power in 1979, and a second major drop in the supply of oil raised the price from thirteen to thirty-four dollars a barrel.

As lines at gas stations grew progressively longer and inflation hit 13.2 percent, President Jimmy Carter was desperate for ways in which to slay the inflationary dragon and remain in office. Several of his advisors told him that economist Paul Volcker, who was exposed in graduate school at Princeton to professors from the Austrian university where Hayek did his doctoral work, might be able to deal with the problem of inflation as chairman of the Federal Reserve. After Carter appointed Volcker to this office, the chairman chose to fight inflation with a blunt instrument that produced dramatic results. Rather than explicitly set the prime rates that affected the price of money, Volcker elected to control the actual supply or quantity of money by managing bank reserves. As the Fed restricted the money supply, interest rates climbed to 20 percent, unemployment hit 10 percent, and the economy entered the worst recession since the Great Depression.[61] The sad state of the economy and the Iran hostage crisis were the major factors contributing to Carter's defeat by Ronald Reagan in the 1980 election.

Friedrich Hayek's more direct influence on the American political process and on an economist who would serve as the minister of economic thought for Ronald Reagan, Milton Friedman, began in 1950. In that year, Hayek left the London School of Economics and accepted an appointment at the University of Chicago. By the end of the 1950s, economists in the "Chicago School" had distinguished themselves as the most vocal opponents of Keynesian new economics and its influential proponents at Harvard. Their central argument was that government intervention disturbs the lawful mechanisms of closed market systems and that these mechanisms, if left alone, could resolve both social and economic problems more effectively and efficiently. The Chicago economists also believed that a small number of mathematical theorems could predict the manner in which decision makers would allocate resources and how these allocations would result in prices.

Milton Friedman, who did his graduate work at the University of Chicago and became a professor there in 1946, launched a direct assault on virtually every aspect of Keynesian economics in the late 1950s. In response to charges that the Chicago School was dogmatic, rigid, and given to a simple-minded reductionism, Friedman set out to demonstrate that there was a direct and explicit connection between free-market capitalism and democracy. In *Capitalism and Freedom,* published in 1962, he argued that the mechanisms of the market system cannot function properly in the absence of economic freedom and that this freedom cannot exist in the absence of political liberty.[62] This marked the beginning of Friedman's celebrity status among conservatives, and that status was considerably enhanced when he served as the principal economic advisor to Republican presidential candidate Barry Goldwater in 1964. After receiving the Nobel Memorial Prize in economics in 1976, Friedman further popularized his views in a mass-market bestseller, *Free to Chose,* which became the basis for a series of programs on public television.[63] He soon retired from teaching, joined the Hoover Institution at Stanford, and established direct contact with Ronald Reagan and his advisors.

When Reagan defeated Carter in the 1980 presidential election, economic problems during the 1970s caused many to question the efficacy of Keynesian new economics, and this greatly enhanced the influence of the Chicago economists who claimed that government intervention was the primary source of these problems. In this climate, there also emerged a group of economists, known as "supply-siders," who firmly believed that the best way to fight inflation was to control the money supply and that the international currency should be based on fixed rates, preferably the fixed rate of gold. But the concept of the supply-siders that had the largest impact on the Reagan administration was the notion that revenues lost as a result of tax cuts would be more than made up by the additional tax revenues resulting from higher growth rates.

Based on appeals to the claim of the Chicago economists that the market system would perform better with less interference by government and to the argument of the supply-siders that economic growth would be enhanced by cutting taxes, the Reagan administration managed to cut the top marginal rates for federal incomes taxes from 70 percent to 28 percent. But because the increases in tax revenues predicted by the supply-siders did not materialize and the large tax cut was accompanied by massive increases in defense expenditures, the gross national debt during the Reagan presidency rose from $995 billion to $2.9 trillion and the annual deficit tripled.[64] It is also worth noting that between 1979 and 1989, the portion of the national wealth held by Americans in the top 1 percent increased from 22 percent to 39 percent, and some experts have estimated that by the mid 1990s the top 1 percent had captured 70 percent of all earnings since the mid-1970s.[65]

When George H. W. Bush took office in 1989, his "Read my lips, no new taxes" campaign slogan made tax increases politically undesirable, and his administration elected to confront the problem of the ballooning deficits by containing government spending. Fortunately for the Bush administration, two nonmarket variables, the fall of the Berlin Wall and the collapse of the Soviet Union, made it politically feasible to reduce defense spending. But after the Reagan tax cuts for affluent Americans failed to generate the anticipated additional tax revenues and overall revenues fell during the recession of the early 1990s, the annual deficit by the end of Bush's term in 1992 had climbed to $290 billion.

The successful campaign against big government and excessive government spending during the late 1990s coincided with a heady period of economic growth fueled by lower interest rates, cheap oil, expanding global markets, high tech innovations, and dot-com mania. These developments not only serve to explain why fiscal conservatives gained ground in both parties and why the anti-Keynesian pro-market "New Democrats" became power brokers after Bill Clinton was elected president in 1993. They are also the principal reasons why Newt Gingrich and his Contract with America took center stage in American domestic politics after the Republicans captured both houses of Congress in 1994.

The goal of the Gingrich Republicans was to enact a budget that would eliminate federal deficits in seven years by curbing the growth of

Medicare, Medicaid, and various welfare programs, and by turning over the administration of most of these programs to the states. They also called for very large tax cuts for high-income Americans based on the presumption that this would encourage investment and stimulate the economy. When Clinton vetoed this budget, the Gingrich Republicans refused to pass the continuing resolution that would provide the temporary funds to keep the federal government going, and this resulted in shutdowns in November and December 1995. As it turned out, the American public was more frightened than pleased by this action, Gingrich and his followers fell out of favor, and the primary source of this conflict, the federal deficit, ceased to be a burning issue in 1997.

The remarkable speed with which the federal deficit came down, from 5 percent of gross domestic product in 1992 to less than 1 percent in 1997, was not anticipated by any economists and those who attempted to explain it have done so after the fact. In 1993, economists working for the Clinton administration and at the Congressional Budget Office predicted that the 1997 deficit would be more than $200 billion, and there were absolutely no indications that the actual deficit in that year could be about a tenth of that figure, $22.6 billion.[66] The economists who proffered the after-the-fact explanations said that the turnaround resulted from reductions in government spending, particularly on defense, slightly higher taxes, and a dramatic increase in the flow of additional tax revenues generated by a strong economy.

The tensions between the vestiges of Keynesian new economics, which allows for prudent government spending to sustain a safety net of social services and programs, and the anti-Keynesian economics of the sort promulgated by the Chicago School, which calls for displacing or augmenting government activities with the mechanisms of the closed market system, was quite apparent in the 2000 presidential campaign. While Democrat Al Gore argued for increased federal spending to sustain the Social Security Retirement System and the Medicare and Medicaid programs, Republican George W. Bush claimed that market mechanisms could reduce government spending and provide more beneficial outcomes for already overburdened taxpayers. And while Gore made the case that increased governmental regulations and more government spending were required to deal with problems in the global environment, Bush took the position that these measures would adversely affect the U.S. economy and that market mechanisms would resolve the problems in the absence of such impacts.

In the American two-party system, the outcomes of presidential elections in which the Democratic and Republican candidates endorse disparate solutions to economic and social problems have often been determined by very narrow margins. These margins were so close in the 2000 election that most analysts concluded that the outcome would have been different if a third party candidate, Ralph Nader, had withdrawn and thrown his support to Gore. And given that the outcome was finally determined by a Supreme Court ruling that gave Bush a majority of votes in the Electoral College even though Gore had won the popular vote by a margin of roughly 500,000, this victory could hardly be construed as a mandate for change.

Polls taken during and after this election indicated the American public was deeply divided on virtually every issue, including that of the environment. Gore, who has systematically studied the linkage between global economic activities and the crisis in the global environment and who even published a best-selling book on the subject, *Earth in the Balance*, in 1993, was clearly more informed on this issue than Bush.[67] In one of the televised debates, Bush even suggested that there was no valid scientific evidence indicating that global warming is a problem.

From our perspective, the fact that Bush did not feel that there was any great need for government to play a substantive role in resolving environmental problems makes a curious kind of sense. Virtually everything he said about this matter during the campaign was based on the presumption that the lawful mechanisms of market systems will resolve environmental problems even if individual economic actors are not aware that this is the case. This rather pristine belief that the invisible hand, will, if left alone, produce this remarkable result and still promote maximal economic growth is profoundly religious in character. But because this metaphysical construct is embedded in assumptions about the dynamics of part–whole relationships in neoclassical economic theory and arrayed in the garment of scientific knowledge, it has some real-world consequences. Some of these consequences during the current Bush administration are economic initiatives that have massively contributed to the crisis in the global environment, a refusal to cooperate with other industrialized countries in dealing with this crisis, and an environmental policy, if it can be called that, that is little more than a thinly veiled attempt to serve the economic interests of corporate America.

It is not my intention to denigrate the intellectual ability of neoclassical economists or to claim that the work done by these economists is not useful in coordinating our experience with market economies. Those who are expert in this discipline are typically very gifted analytical thinkers with a penchant for higher mathematics, and their analyses of tendencies to occur in market systems are critically important to the efficient management and regulation of these systems. If we do manage to develop an environmentally responsible economic theory that is capable of realistically assessing the costs of doing business in the global environment, the concerted efforts of these talented individuals will certainly be required.

However, mainstream economists who wish to become involved in this effort must abandon assumptions about the relationship between parts (economic actors and firms) and whole (market system) embedded in the mathematical formalism of neoclassical economics. There is no doubt that these assumptions function in mathematically complex theories as a reasonable approximate basis for coordinating our experience with market systems. But that does not mean that the assumptions accurately reflect or mirror actual dynamics in market processes or that the theory is a valid depiction or description of these processes. It means that the theories are capable of modeling market processes in proximate terms because they consist of mathematically sophisticated descriptions of previously observed tendencies that have been perpetually revised to achieve greater approximations of these tendencies. The next chapter will examine the manner in which metaphysically based assumptions in neoclassical economics frustrate or, in most cases, effectively undermine, efforts by global economic planners to posit economic solutions to environmental problems.

CHAPTER 4

NO FREE LUNCH
Mainstream Economics and Globalization

> Free trade is the religion of our age. With its heaven as the global economy, free trade comes complete with comprehensive analytical and philosophical underpinnings. Higher mathematics are used in stating the theorems. But in the final analysis, free trade is less an economic strategy than a moral degree. Although it pretends to be value-free, it is fundamentally value-driven.
>
> —David Morris

Economic planners who attempt to chart the future of the global economy are increasingly aware of the damage being done to the global environment by economic activities. But virtually all efforts by these planners to understand, much less effectively deal with, the environmental impacts of globalization have been frustrated or undermined by assumptions from neoclassical economics. The most insidious of these assumptions in environmental terms is that market systems are closed and that natural resources have no monetary value unless or until such a value is established by price mechanisms that operate within these systems. The creators of neoclassical economics did not arrive at this assumption based on any systematic study of actual or real economic processes. They were obliged to view market processes as existing in an immaterial domain separate and discrete from material reality to make the case that the sum of income and utility is conserved in equations borrowed from mid-nineteenth physics. The presumption that environmental resources that exist outside of this domain are a free lunch also served to reinforce another fundamental credo in neoclassical economics—markets will necessarily grow if the natural laws of economics are allowed to operate within the closed market system without outside interference by government or some other agency.

The seeds of the global market economy were planted in Bretton Woods, New Hampshire, during the United Nations Monetary and Financial Conference in July 1944. The representatives of the U.S. corporate and foreign policy establishments gathered at this conference were looking forward to the end of World War II with the hope that a world united in peace and growing prosperity would soon emerge. Most of those present assumed that protecting the national interests of the United States required free access to markets and raw materials of the Western Hemisphere, the Far East, and the British Empire. With this aim in mind, the conference recommended that worldwide financial institutions be created for "stabilizing currencies and facilitating programs of capital investment for constructive undertakings in backward and underdeveloped nations."[1]

The opening session of the 1947 Bretton Woods meeting was chaired by U.S. Secretary of the Treasury Henry Morgenthau, whose keynote address envisioned "the creation of a dynamic world economy in which the peoples of every nation will be able to realize their potentialities in peace and enjoy the fruits of material progress on an earth infinitely blessed with natural riches." He then called on all participants to accept the "elementary axiom . . . that prosperity has no limits. It is not a substance to be diminished by division."[2] The assumptions from mainstream economics that inform these comments and that would later guide the decision making of the architects of the Bretton Woods system are: (1) growth and expansion of market systems is inevitable if barriers to the operation of the natural laws of economics are removed; (2) this growth and expansion will necessarily benefit members of every nation that eliminates such barriers; and (3) the expansion of market systems will not be constrained by limits in natural materials and resources.

At the end of this historic meeting, the World Bank and the International Monetary Fund (IMF) were established and the groundwork was laid for what would later be called the General Agreement on Tariffs and Trades (GATT). The IMF was designed to function as a sort of international credit union that would lend money to member countries in financial difficulty so that they might have more time to put their economic house in order. The World Bank was created to make loans that would promote the reconstruction of economies devastated by World War II and to lend money to poorer nations to finance development projects. Since

1947, the World Bank and IMF have fulfilled their mandate to promote economic growth in a global economy with considerable success. Global economic growth has expanded by a factor of four and international trade by a factor of five, and direct foreign investment has increased at roughly three times the rate of trade expansion.[3] These economic gains are widely celebrated by mainstream economists, but the impacts of the associated economic activities on the global environment are rarely recognized in their theories or included in their accounting practices.

The North American Free Trade Agreement (NAFTA), which came into existence in January 1994, was designed to transform national economies in North America into a single market economy. NAFTA confers on the companies of member nations national treatment rights, meaning that international companies must be given the same treatment as domestic companies. The agreement also extends to international companies procurement rights that allow them to bid against domestic companies on public and government contracts. As a result, virtually all control over foreign investments in countries such as Canada and Mexico has been lost, and thousands of enterprises have been taken over by transnational corporations.

During the first forty years of its existence, GATT was primarily concerned with the rules for tariffs and quotas, and members would periodically meet and discuss these rules for trade in various products. But after the Uruguay Round of Negotiations in 1996, GATT was expanded to include a set of comprehensive international rules about which policy objectives member nations could pursue and the means by which they could do so. The agreement also provided that all participating nations must abide by the rules, regardless of cultural differences and the enormous disparity between economic infrastructures and production capacities.

A new governing structure for the World Trade Organization (WTO) was established to enforce these rules with sanctions and to provide the legislative capacity to revise and expand the rules. Among the qualifications for membership on this body, which has legal powers not unlike those of the UN, the World Bank, and the IMF, is experience on national trade delegations or as a lawyer dealing in national trade disputes. Responding to pressure to provide broader representation, then-President Clinton created the Trade and Environmental Policy Committee and appointed an equal number of representatives from corporations and citizen groups. This broader representation did not, however, effectively speak to the concerns of environmentalists because the advisory committees on timber, chemicals, and other environmentally sensitive products are composed exclusively of representatives from the international business community.

The absurd idea that market systems exist in a domain that is separate and discrete from all other aspects of human reality and that nonmarket processes exist outside these systems also explains why environmental, health, labor, and human rights concerns have never been high on the agenda of the WTO. Canadian cigarette packaging requirements, Thai cigarette sales limitations, and Danish bottle recycling laws have been challenged as nontariff barriers to the GATT free trade rules. Similarly, the U.S. government has challenged European bans on bovine growth hormone and transgenic crops, while some European nations have challenged U.S. fuel consumption standards for automobiles and U.S. food labeling laws.[4]

This makes for an interesting situation. Appeals to blatantly unscientific assumptions about part–whole relationships in mainstream economics served to legitimate the existence of the WTO and to empower this body to legislate over the future of the global economy based on these assumptions. Those who serve on the WTO are appointed by governments committed to the process of globalization as it is understood and defined by neoclassical economists, and the rules of membership are such that this paradigm informs all their decisions. This does not mean that the members of the WTO are unaware of the results of scientific studies on the state of the global ecosystem. Yet this has little impact on their decision making because assumptions from mainstream economics typically frustrate the ability of the members to understand these results, and environmental concerns tend to be almost entirely ignored or greatly diminished by the mandate to create a global economy.

NEOCLASSICAL ECONOMICS AND THE CORPORATIONS

Most mainstream economists, including those employed by governments and universities, serve, in one fashion or another, the interests of corporations. Forty-seven of the hundred largest economies in the world are transnational corporations, and 70 percent of global trade is controlled by five hundred of the largest corporations.[5] Corporate law requires that the management of publicly held companies act primarily in the interests of stockholders, and the primary business of any such company is to make a profit on services or products that reach increasing numbers of clients or consumers. If a publicly held company fails to increase profits via growth and expansion, its shares on the stock market will be devalued and its economic existence imperiled.

It is therefore easy to appreciate why corporate executives and board members are drawn to the neoclassical assumptions that closed market systems will lawfully expand in the absence of outside interference and that nonmarket environmental resources and impacts exist outside these systems. These assumptions sanction the view that the growth of markets and the realization of more profits is a lawful or natural condition and that outside intervention by government or some other agency is an impediment to economic progress. Let us also not forget that this argument carries great currency because of the widely held belief that mainstream economics is a science with something like the same epistemological authority as the physical sciences.

Many managers of corporations are concerned about environmental problems, and some, such as those in the insurance industry, base their economic planning on scientific studies of climatic changes that could be occasioned by global warming. It is, however, normally impossible for executives of public companies to privilege environmental concerns over corporate profit. Because these individuals are obligated under corporate law to make a profit, other considerations, including the state of the global environment, must be secondary. An individual executive might prefer to "do something for the environment," but acting on this impulse could expose the company to damaging lawsuits by stockholders or other parties whose economic interests are compromised. Also consider that the obligation by corporate managers to translate subjective concerns into numbers used by mainstream economists to assess the worth of company assets and stocks tends to exclude from the decision-making process anything that cannot be represented in these terms. Forests, for example, are numerically represented as board feet, and the pollution, toxic waste, and carcinogens generated in a manufacturing or production process are numerically represented in cost-benefit ratios and trade-off analyses.

My intent is not to attack the integrity of corporate managers and investors or to denigrate the idea of the corporation. It is to demonstrate that assumptions about part–whole relationships in economic reality that are alleged to be actual or real in mainstream economics largely define the structure and mission of corporations and the ways in which they are obliged to do business. The problem is not merely that these assumptions preclude the prospect of realistically assessing the costs of doing business in the real economy of the global environment. It is also that they serve as the guidelines and integrative structures for the creation of a global economy in which short-term benefits are grandly outweighed by present and future environmental costs.

Many supporters of globalization have argued that although the capacity of the earth to absorb wastes and to provide raw materials and energy is limited, advances in technology will greatly ease these constraints. For example, the revolution in biotechnology could dramatically increase food production, and fossil fuels could be displaced by renewable energy sources and controlled fusion reactors. Similarly, advances in nanotechnology could allow goods and commodities to be assembled on the molecular level and greatly reduce energy use and the amounts of raw materials processed and used in the manufacturing process. Obviously, advances in technology are critically important to the timely resolution of the environmental crisis. But those who believe that this crisis can be eliminated by a technological fix typically fail to appreciate that continued growth in the human population offsets productivity gains occasioned by new technologies. For example, the productivity gains associated with the green revolution in Indian agriculture have not kept pace with the increase in demand for agricultural products resulting from dramatic increases in population.

Some of those who believe that technological advances will resolve the environmental crisis claim that we are witnessing the emergence of a "dematerialized economy" in which the value of services based on technologies such as the computer increases and the amount of matter-energy required for these services diminishes. These technological optimists argue that because value in this situation is measured in immaterial "value" units instead of "physical" units, this new economy can grow forever without encountering physical limits. But as economist and ecologist Herman Daly notes, the "notion that we can save the 'growth forever' paradigm by dematerializing the economy, or 'decoupling' it from resources, or substituting information for resources, is fantasy. We can surely eat lower on the food chain, but we cannot eat recipes."[6] Also keep in mind that there are few economic incentives to encourage the large-scale development and implementation of new green technologies, that current plans for the future of the global economy are heavily reliant on existing technologies, and that economic development in the third world is almost entirely dependent on old, inefficient, and highly polluting technologies.

THE BUSINESS OF ENRON: GLOBAL MARKETS
FOR SCARCE NATURAL RESOURCES

After the collapse of Enron in December 2001, most analysts were quick to blame this colossal business failure on a corporate culture of greed and arrogance that bred excessive secrecy. But as the Justice Department, the Securities and Exchange Commission, and Congress engaged in the arduous task of unraveling the tangled web of Enron's business practices, there was the growing recognition that the responsibility for this massive corporate train wreck extended well beyond actions taken by chief executives of the company. The directors of Enron were blamed for failing to question closely decisions made by management, the accounting firm of Arthur Anderson was accused of ignoring financial irregularities and destroying records, the lawyers were chastised for concealing the financial plight of the company, and the ratings agencies were faulted for their reluctance to downgrade credit ratings.[7] All these groups undoubtedly share responsibility for Enron's problems. But there is another, much more fundamental, reason why the company failed.

The largest contributor to Enron's success and the ultimate cause of its failure was a business plan and a corporate ethic narrowly predicated on belief in the inherent efficacy of four fundamental assumptions in the neoclassical economic paradigm: (1) the lawful mechanisms of closed market systems can, if freed from the constraints of government regulation and oversight, expand the availability of natural resources, lower their costs, and resolve production and distribution problems; (2) the resources of nature are unlimited or alternate resources and/or technological improvements can be substituted for scarce resources; (3) capital is substitutable for natural resources, and the trading of these resources is no different in kind from the trading of any goods, commodities, and services; and (4) the only economic value that can be conferred on natural resources is exchange value, or the amount of capital that buyers are willing to pay sellers to secure rights to the use or further sale of these resources.

Voted the "most innovative" on *Fortune* magazine's list of the most-admired companies for six years, Enron pioneered the business of trading energy on a commodities exchange market and managed to do so by largely deregulating this market. As Kurt Eichenwald put it in the *New York Times*, "The company's financial successes were in no small part the byproduct of its political and regulatory campaigns to deregulate the marketplace. It created what one executive last year referred to as 'a regulatory black hole.' "[8]

Before founding Enron in 1985, Kenneth Lay earned a Ph.D. in economics at the University of Missouri, served as a navy officer at the Pentagon, and worked as an aide to a federal regulator for the natural gas industry.[9] Known for his almost religious belief in the inherent ability of free market systems to resolve complex human problems, Lay began almost immediately after becoming president of Enron to mastermind what would eventually become the most well-funded and highly coordinated attempt to deregulate markets for electricity and natural gas in U.S. history.

Lay was a major fundraiser for the George H. W. Bush 1992 presidential reelection campaign and chairman of the Houston host committee for the GOP convention where Bush was nominated. After the elder Bush lost the election, Lay made a number of senior members in the previous Bush administration, including former Secretary of State James Baker and former Secretary of Commerce Robert Mosbacher, directors or consultants of Enron. When Bill Clinton became president, Lay increased Enron's political contributions to the Democrats and continued to maintain a close friendship with Clinton's first chief of staff, Thomas "Mack" McLarty. The Enron chief also cultivated a relationship with George W. Bush long before he was a serious national candidate, contributed to his campaign to become governor of Texas, and became head of then-Governor Bush's Business Council in 1994. When Bush was inaugurated president in January 2001, Lay and other Enron executives had contributed more to his political career than any other group, in excess of $550,000. Enron then contributed an additional $100,000 to Bush's inaugural committee, and Lay made a personal contribution of another $100,000.[10]

Since 1997, Enron's political action committees donated $1.9 million to seven hundred candidates in twenty-eight states and contributed $1.1 million to state and local candidates in the 2000 election cycle alone.[11] By the late 1990s, Enron's directory listed more than 150 staffers working on state and government affairs, and the company developed a complicated computer program, called "the matrix," that was intended to calculate how much a change in regulation would cost. If the figure seemed too high, executives typically interpreted this as a signal to mobilize its lobbyists and to put additional pressure on politicians who had received significant campaign contributions from the company.[12] The goal of this enterprise was to break up monopoly control of energy markets by local utilities and to change the rules so that energy could be traded in a deregulated market. To a great extent, the company was successful, and twenty-four states adopted some form of energy deregulation from 1997 to 2000.

Before Enron became a major player in the energy market, the price of natural gas was highly regulated and the gas flowing through pipelines was not a commodity for speculation that could be bought and sold on the fly. But after oil prices plunged in the mid-1980s and major users began switching to cheaper fuel oil, Mr. Lay managed to convince officials in Washington to change the rules so that these users could shop for the best energy deals from gas producers and utilities. As a deregulated market emerged and natural gas prices began fluctuating wildly, Enron developed hedging contracts for gas like those used in markets for pork bellies, corn, and winter wheat. This resulted in the creation of a "gas bank" that allowed utilities to bid for and lock up long-term prices. In return for this privilege, Enron coordinated the flow of gas from the producers, arranged for delivery, and took a small cut on every deal.

The scheme was so successful that Enron became by 1995 the biggest participant in the natural gas industry, controlling 25 percent of the North American market. The company also used its vast network of researchers, lobbyists, pundits, and influence peddlers to promote the deregulation of the wholesale electricity markets. This industry had previously charged rates approved by state officials that allowed power plants to recover costs and still make a reasonable profit. But in the deregulated market that emerged in the 1990s, states changed their rules to allow new independent power generating and marketing companies to build plants, sell power, and trade power among utilities. Enron moved aggressively to capture the biggest share of trading in these new markets by lining up contracts to purchase electrical power and gas and by cutting deals to sell the energy to customers, often over the long term. The most lucrative aspect of this business was the trading of financial contracts, or derivatives, based on the exchange value of gas and electricity at "hubs" around the country.

From an environmental perspective, it is important to realize that Enron's commodities-trading business was intended to make large profits on a resource, energy, that is critical to the economic stability of the nation and that receives billions of dollars in subsidies from the U.S. government. The only value added to this resource offered by Enron was a trading scheme that allowed buyers to purchase energy in a more open market or to contract for a future purchase at a fixed price. This new approach to trading energy was premised on the assumption in neoclassical economics that the lawful or lawlike machinations of market systems will resolve the supply problem and deliver the scare resource at the "right" or optimal price for both buyers and sellers if those mechanisms are not compromised or disabled by government regulation or other exogenous forces.

Lay and his colleagues were able to convince representatives of government to create the largely unregulated market that would make their new trading scheme possible by appealing to this assumption. The Enron executives were particularly adept in arguing that this was in the national interest because it would promote the overall growth of the U.S. economy by vastly increasing energy supplies. The scheme had nothing to do with energy conservation, adverse environmental impacts, alternate energy sources, or the long-term energy future of the American economy or other economies, but this was not apparent in the promotional material of the company or in the rhetoric used by its spokespersons and lobbyists. The consistent message here was that the only viable solution to these perceived problems was a deregulated energy market that would become increasingly global in scope.

One irony here is that Enron's enormous gains in energy-trading profits were due largely to price volatility and to overall higher gas prices, which also drove up the price of electricity because gas is widely used in electrical power plants. It is also worth noting that the beginning of the end for Enron came in the summer of 2001 when prices for electricity and gas collapsed and the company's chief financial officer, Andrew Fastow, chose to disguise losses in limited partnerships that could, in theory at least, be treated as separate entities. Because Enron was regarded as an energy trading company, it was also able to record as revenue the total amount of its transactions as opposed to profits made on each sale, as is typical of brokerage firms. In a practice known as "mark to market," Enron listed as earnings costs and revenues on deals that could stretch over long periods, and this often created the illusion of profitability when there was little cash actually coming in.[13]

If Enron had been regulated as a financial institution, it would have been obliged to certify its business practices, to report its activities, to back its leveraged trades with more collateral, and to use separate financing to set up its derivative business. The simply reason why Enron was not regulated in this fashion was that it was viewed as an energy trading company different in kind from a purely financial institution. But a better explanation for the regulatory black hole that surrounded the financial dealings of Enron is that the company was widely perceived as being in the process of creating a global market for energy in which the lawful or lawlike machinations of market systems would be increasingly freed from the exogenous constraints of government. Given that belief in the actual or real existence of these mechanisms was inconsistent with an emphasis on systematic regulation and oversight by government, Enron was able to exaggerate its gains and hide its losses with highly questionable accounting procedures and practices.

The reliance on these procedures and practices increased exponentially after Jeffery Skilling became president and chief operating office of Enron in 1997. Skilling attempted to move the company away from a business model based on hard assets and toward a model where capital as a substitutable resource for the exchange of a wide range of commodities and services in deregulated markets was the sole source of revenues and profits. Under his leadership, Enron's finance and trading empire was extended to include wood pulp, steel, advertising time on television, and insurance against credit defaults. What this business model assumes, of course, is that there is no difference in kind between business transactions in a market that trades scarce public resources and those in any other markets. After Enron shifted the bulk of its business transactions to the Internet, it was soon recognized as the biggest e-commerce business in the world.

As Enron moved into one new trading market after another, some executives resisted Skilling's desire to rid the company of all hard assets, and plans were made to build power plants around the world and to become the major player in the global water business via a subsidiary called Azurix. This company was launched in 1998 with the intent of transforming the $400 billion global water business in the same way that Enron had transformed the natural gas and electricity industries. The plan was to buy water infrastructures and to sell water in the new deregulated markets. The company quickly purchased large numbers of water and sewer utilities from California to Georgia and from Britain to Brazil, set up an online trading market called Water2Water.com to facilitate these transactions, and proceeded to sell shares in June 1999. The CEO of Azurix, a Lay protégé named Rebecca P. Mark, predicted a 20 percent profit in the short term, and its IPO, or initial public offering, opened at $19 a share.[14]

Perhaps the best way to illustrate the pitfalls of a wholesale reliance on assumptions in the neoclassical economic paradigm to resolve environmental problems in economic terms is to consider Azurix's proposed solution to help the state of Florida pay for its $3.9 billion share of the costs of reviving the Everglades. The proposal was straightforward—Azurix would help Florida pay these costs if the company could sell the water captured in this project. Because Enron had contributed generously to Governor Jeb Bush's political campaign and the governor and his aides had previously endorsed the concept of privatizing water, the executives at Azurix were, initially at least, quite confident that their proposal would be accepted by the Florida legislature.

As it turned out, the chairman of the legislature's Everglades Committee angrily denounced the plan as "the most sinister business proposition the state has ever had,"[15] and swift opposition developed from members of both parties in the legislature. The fundamental source of this opposition was the conviction that water is, or should be, a public resource, as opposed a commodity that be bought and sold in the private sector. Many members of the Florida legislature also felt that the preservation of a natural resource, such the Everglades, is a public responsibility that should not be entrusted to a for-profit corporation.

Meanwhile, Azurix discovered that it had paid far too much for inefficient utilities around the globe and that public resistance to privatizing water was making the process of deregulation excruciatingly slow. Water2Water.com was a complete business failure, and Azurix stock fell 75 percent in one year as the company went through more than $1 billion in capital. After Enron's bonds were downgraded to junk in the fall of 2001, the more than $900 million in Azurix debts was one of the major reasons for the decision to file for bankruptcy protection.

Most in the business community appear to view Enron as a corporate rogue and are fearful that the widespread concern and media frenzy following its collapse will generate excessive government regulation. As a spokesman for the Business Roundtable put it, these new regulations could inhibit the ability of U.S. corporations "to compete, create jobs and generate economic growth." On the other end of the spectrum, those who view Enron as emblematic of pervasive and systematic problems with American-style capitalism have called for fundamental changes in how executives are compensated, the rules and procedures for reporting financial results, the manner in which financial analysts rate stocks, the ways in which boards of directors are chosen, the definition of accounting standards, and the rules that govern the legal and accounting professions.[16]

To my knowledge, however, there has been no discussion thus far in print or the electronic media of the fact that the core business of Enron was to make enormous short-term profits by deregulating global markets for the exchange of scarce natural resources without any concern whatsoever for the long-term availability of those resources or the adverse environmental impacts associated with their wholesale exploitation and use. Another large something that seems to be conspicuously missing in the current soul-searching public debate is that the vast majority of resources traded by Enron were massively subsidized by taxpayers. The primary reason why there appears to have been no discussion of these matters is relatively simple and straightforward. Those who are seeking to understand the causes of this colossal business failure endorse, wittingly or unwittingly, the same assumptions about the character of economic reality in the neoclassical economic paradigm that simultaneously explain why Enron was able to quickly become the seventh largest corporation in the U.S. and why it collapsed with such dizzying speed.

NEOCLASSICAL ECONOMICS AND PUBLIC POLICY

Assumptions from mainstream economics have also greatly impaired efforts by governments and international organizations to respond effectively to problems in the global environment. When more than one hundred heads of state arrived at the UN Conference on Environment and Development at Rio de Janeiro in 1992, environmentalists had high hopes that the outcomes would be positive. But shortly after the so-called Earth Summit began, members of the American delegation demanded that all references to production processes and levels of consumption in developed industrial economies be deleted from proposals. The delegates also indicated that the United States would not sign the global warming convention on greenhouse gas emissions unless it was purely voluntary and that it would not sign the biodiversity convention in any event because it would compromise the intellectual property rights of American biotechnology companies.

A major dilemma at the Earth Summit was that the industrialized nations of the north were unwilling to accept proposals that reduced levels of consumption while the nations of the south, where widespread poverty exists, were unwilling to limit economic growth. The buzz phrase designed to appeal to nations in both north and south was "sustainable development," an idea that first came to international attention when the UN Bruntland Commission published *Our Common Future* in 1987. In this volume, sustainable development was defined as economic behavior that "meets the needs of the present without compromising the ability of the future generations to meet their own needs."[17] Although what sustainable development actually means, for present or future generations, was not a topic for discussion, the construct was vague enough to allow all parties to accept it in principle.

When the Earth Summit was over, it had approved two treaties, the Framework Convention on Climate Change and the Framework Convention on Biodiversity Preservation; three nonbinding statements of principle (the Rio Declaration, Agenda 21, and a set of Forest Principles); and a budget that was woefully inadequate to translate any of these intentions into reality. This paucity of funds made little difference, however, because the treaties were badly flawed and the statements of principle were nonbinding.

During a conference held five years later to evaluate what had occurred since the Earth Summit, it was determined that although some progress had been made in dealing with the population problem, other environmental problems were larger and less tractable than ever before. Meanwhile, mainstream economists plugged information from sources such as the national accounts into their equations and reported that the global economy was growing. They did so at about the same time that scientists at the IPCC announced that a 50 percent to 70 percent reduction in greenhouse gases was required if global earth temperatures were to remain at something like the current levels.

Before the Kyoto Conference on Climate Change in 1997, President Clinton agreed that global warming is a serious problem and proposed that the Annex 1 countries, which comprise the industrialized nations of Europe, North America, and the former Soviet bloc along with Japan, reduce greenhouse gas emissions to 1990 levels by 2012. Although Clinton indicated that the proposal would be binding, it would still delay emissions reductions for an extra twelve years. After the fossil fuel lobby concluded that even these modest reductions would result in loss of revenue, it embarked on a $13 million print and broadcast advertising campaign that essentially claimed that the Kyoto Conference could target the United States for special punishment and ruin its economy.

At the Kyoto Conference, the U.S. delegation appealed once again to assumptions about economic reality in mainstream economics to argue that dramatic reductions in greenhouse gases would slow the growth of the global economy. Fearing this prospect, industrialized nations pledged to reduce greenhouse gas emissions by a mere 5.2 percent below 1990 levels by 2012. But even this very small and wholly inadequate decrease in emissions was not acceptable to delegations from the Third World, and the proposal was tabled until a follow-up meeting in Buenos Aires in 1998. Another proposal passed at the Conference allowed the industrialized nations to maintain current levels of emissions of greenhouse gases by buying emissions rights from countries such as Russia and the Ukraine. The idea was that these countries had rights to sell because previous levels of industrial output and carbon emissions had been greatly reduced when their economies collapsed following the breakup of the former Soviet Union.

In this scheme, emissions are treated as commodities, and the sale of the excess commodities to other industrialized nations by Russia and the Ukraine was intended to generate revenue that would allow these countries to grow their economies much above previous levels of production and consumption. This proposal was particularly attractive to the Annex 1 countries because it would effectively eliminate the obligation to reduce greenhouse emissions to the level called for in the Clinton proposal. If the sale of emissions rights worked as planned, the 5.2 percent target by 2012 would be reduced to less than 1 percent. What was obviously privileged here is the assumption that growth in the global market is natural and that any measure that enhances this growth is by definition good, regardless of the state of the global environment.

In November 2000, delegates from 175 countries gathered in The Hague to consider environmental and economic policies that would oblige thirty-eight industrial nations to reduce greenhouse emissions to the levels agreed on in 1997 at Kyoto. At the beginning of this meeting, IPCC scientists declared, for the first time in the twelve-year period that this group has been in existence, that the results of their research had "proven" that the crisis in the global environment was directly attributable to human economic activities. In the face of what should have been a stark reminder that the industrial nations must make good on the commitments made in Kyoto, the American delegation made a proposal that would effectively eliminate the economic burden of those commitments on the U.S. economy. The proposal contained another scheme for trading in emissions credits and a scheme for granting credit for planting forests and crops. After representatives of the European Union rejected this proposal on the grounds that it would provide the United States with an unfair economic advantage, negotiations broke down and nothing of substance was accomplished.

When President Bush announced in March 2001 that the United States was unwilling to meet the modest reductions in greenhouse gas emissions provided in the Kyoto Treaty, representatives of the European Union (EU) were outraged. During an emergency visit to Washington a few days later, the EU representatives made their case to Christine Todd Whitman, the administrator of the Environmental Protection Agency. Whitman said that she told the representatives she was as "optimistic as the President that, working constructively with our friends and allies through international processes, we can develop technologies, market-based incentives and other innovative approaches to global climate change."[18]

The U.S. decision to withdraw from the Kyoto Treaty was also a central point of contention in a meeting between President Bush and the chancellor of Germany, Gerhard Schroeder, held a day earlier. When asked to comment on the meeting, Bush said, "We will not do anything that harms our economy, because first things first are the people who live in America."[19] This comment provoked an interesting response from the president of the EU Commission, former Italian Prime Minister Romano Prodi: "If one wants to be a world leader, one must know how to look after the entire earth and not only American industry."[20]

President Bush's apparent belief that the natural laws of economics will, if left alone, resolve environmental problems was also apparent during a meeting in Quebec in April 2001 where representatives of thirty-four nations discussed ways in which to implement a vast Free Trade Area of the Americas. This agreement, which could be implemented by 2005 or earlier, would create a single market from the Arctic to the tip of South American that includes roughly 800 million people, and the World Bank and the Inter-American Development Bank have committed more than $20 billion to the effort.[21] Although the environmental impacts of this new phase of globalization will be enormous, the details in this agreement were worked out behind closed doors over a seven-year period and became public for the first time only during the closed summit meeting in Quebec.

The vast majority of the estimated twenty thousand protestors who marched in the streets outside this meeting were peaceful, and most were members of environmental groups and human rights organizations. The core argument of spokespersons for these protestors was that although the accord will promote free commerce and protect foreign investors, it will do little to improve the lives of poor people and almost nothing to protect the environment.[22] In his brief address at the conference, President Bush appeared to reflect these concerns when he said that the United States would proceed with negotiations over a Free Trade Area of the Americas only if it was accompanied by "a strong commitment to protecting our environment and improving labor standards."[23] There were, however, few concrete provisions in the draft agreement that reflected these concerns, and business groups, along with several powerful members of the Republican Party, responded to Bush's remark by claiming that labor and environmental standards have no place in free trade agreements and only inhibit commerce.

Meanwhile, in a much less publicized meeting in New York, ministers of the UN Commission on Sustainable Development were discussing ways in which to continue to implement the agenda of the 1992 Earth Summit. The main item of business was to set the stage for the resumption of negotiations over the Kyoto Protocol in July 2001 in Bonn, Germany, in the hope that other industrialized nations would ratify the treaty. Bishnu Tulsie, planning minister of the Caribbean island of St. Lucia, indicated that his country would sign the Kyoto agreement no matter what industrialized nations might do because the issue before the small island state "is not economics—it is survival." A number of African ministers complained that global warming was contributing to an increase in floods and droughts on the African continent and made an open appeal to the Bush administration to reconsider its position on the Kyoto Protocol. Nigerian Environment Minister Alhiji Muhammad Kabir Said was more direct. He noted that the "withdrawal" of the United States from this agreement "condemns us in the developing world."[24] At the meeting in Bonn in July 2001, representatives from 178 countries endorsed the rules of the Kyoto Protocol. The United States, a country where carbon dioxide emissions have increased 15 percent above the 1992 levels, was not a party to this agreement.

In November 2001, in Marrakech, Morocco, negotiators from more than 160 countries, including Great Britain, Japan, and Russia, finally agreed on the terms of the Kyoto Treaty after four years of incessant haggling. The terms require forty industrialized countries to reduce worldwide emissions of carbon dioxide and other heat-trapping gases by an average of 5.2 percent below 1990 levels by 2012. They also spell out rules for compliance and set binding penalties for countries that fail to meet the agreed-on targets. But because the United States was not a party to this agreement, virtually all of the negotiators conceded that it will have, at best, only modest impacts and does not even begin to speak to the problem of global warming.

The effectiveness of the agreement was also greatly diminished by the willingness of the negotiators to satisfy the last-minute demands of delegates from Japan, Russia, Australia, and Canada. These delegates insisted on more flexibility in the rules and more privileged treatment in the use of market-based mechanisms for purchasing carbon credits from countries with smaller greenhouse gas emissions and for reducing quotas by expanding forests and farmlands that absorb carbon dioxide. For example, Russia extracted a concession that doubles the amount of credits it can claim for its carbon-absorbing forests and agricultural land from 17.6 million tons of carbon dioxide to 33 million tons. The principal objections to the last-minute compromises were raised by members of the European Union who have long argued that these market-based mechanisms simply make it easier for the major polluters to meet their goals at less cost.[25]

When President Bush announced that the United States would not be a party to the Kyoto Treaty, he indicated that there would be a cabinet-level review of alternative solutions to global warming. But this initiative was put on hold following the September 11, 2001, terrorist attack, and the U.S. delegation at the Marrakech conference merely observed the proceedings and offered no alternatives. This inaction prompted Jan Ponk, the Dutch environmental minister, to comment, "After the events of September 11, if there is any reason for the United States to call for international, global approaches, it should also join a global approach to the existing global problem of climate change."[26] There was, however, no sign of inaction on the part of the American delegation to the meeting of the World Trade Organization in the Persian Gulf emirate of Qatar in December 2001. The head of this delegation, Robert B. Zoellick, effectively argued for increased cross-border sales of American farm goods and services, ranging from mutual funds to genetic engineering, and was instrumental in forging an agreement that commits the 142 nations in the WTO to lowering tariffs and eliminating agricultural export subsidies.

In stark contrast with the WTO meeting in Seattle two years earlier, the four thousand-odd official delegates, representatives, and journalists in Qatar did not have to contend with angry protestors. Because of limited hotel space, the WTO allowed only one representative each from nongovernmental agencies such as environmental groups, labor unions, and other organizations critical of globalization. In a session with U.S. officials, these nongovernmental representatives were told to observe scrupulously the laws of Qatar, particularly those that forbid insulting the emir and "shaming the state," and reminded that violators could be sentenced to more than three years in prison. In this climate, the most contentious source of disagreement was not adverse environmental impacts of global economic activity; it was complaints by poor countries that the current rules of global trade favor the rich.[27] At the end of this meeting, however, delegates from the European Union did manage to pass a declaration that requires the WTO to examine the relationship between international trade agreements and environmental pacts.[28]

When President Bush unveiled his long-awaited plan to resolve the crisis in the global environment on February 14, 2002, he said, "This new approach is based on the common-sense idea that sustainable economic growth is the key to environmental progress because it is growth that provides the resources for investment in clean technologies."[29] The "common-sense idea" in the Bush proposal is predicated on the metaphysically based assumption in the neoclassical economic paradigm that the mechanisms of closed market systems will simultaneously promote economic growth and resolve environmental problems if there is minimal interference from government or other exogenous forces.

The proposal calls for a set of voluntary measures and tax incentives that will allegedly reduce "greenhouse gas intensity" by 18 percent over the next decade without harming the growth of the American economy. Under this plan, fixed targets for power plant emissions of carbon dioxide would be replaced by voluntary "emission intensity" targets that expand by a fraction of the accompanying economic growth. For example, if the U.S. gross domestic product increased at an annual rate of 3 percent, utilities and manufacturers would be asked to hold voluntarily the rate of growth of their carbon emissions by 1 percent.

Assuming, as most economists predict, that the gross domestic product (GDP) increases over the next decade by 30 percent or more, the overall amount of carbon dioxide emissions would expand accordingly, and the proposed 18 percent reduction merely serves to disguise the fact that total emissions would be significantly larger. The only mechanism in the plan for monitoring these emissions is a program created in 1992 under President George H. W. Bush's administration that asks all utilities and manufacturers to report voluntarily their carbon dioxide emissions to the Department of Energy. The plan also provides "base line protection and credit" for companies that participate in the program that essentially guarantee that they will not be penalized for participating or miss out on future credits if the policies of the government change.

The current President Bush also intends to put forward a plan developed by the Environmental Protection Agency that would oblige utilities and manufacturers to limit future emissions of sulfur dioxide, nitrogen oxide, and mercury based on a "cap and trade" approach. In this scheme, the government would set mandatory limits on emissions of these pollutants while establishing a new market in which major polluters can purchase "credits" toward meeting their pollution targets from nonpolluting companies.[30] But even if we assume that the market for purchasing credits actually reduces the overall level of pollutants, the deadline for complying with the new emissions targets is the year 2018, much longer than existing deadlines and long after Bush has left office.

The obvious problem with the Bush plan is not only that it appeals to metaphysically based assumptions in the neoclassical economic paradigm to create the illusion of environmentalism in impressive sounding policies that are virtually content-free. It also implicitly endorses the validity of those assumptions by allowing the U.S. economy to increase emissions of carbon dioxide and other pollutants at roughly the same rate as it has over the last decade. The only aspect of this plan that could make a marginal contribution to solving environmental problems would provide $4.6 billion in tax incentives over the next five years to encourage energy conservation, the use of renewable fuels, and the implementation of technologies that reduce emissions of greenhouse gases and other pollutants. For example, utilities could get tax credits for building power-generating windmills and consumers tax credits for installing solar panels or buying energy efficient cars. When we consider, however, the scope of the crisis in the global environment and the enormous extent to which economic activities in the United States contribute to this crisis, it becomes clear that the proposed $4.6 billion in tax incentives cannot even begin to speak to these problems. Because this amount over a five-year period is less than a penny a day for each American, there is simply no prospect that this scheme could promote any major changes in the ways that energy is produced and consumed in the United States.[31]

NO FREE LUNCH: ENERGY AND
THE GLOBAL ECONOMIC RRDER

The UN Bruntland Commission report (1987) defines minimal annual growth in any healthy national economy as 3 percent, which means that an economy that sustains this rate of growth must double production every twenty-three years. This definition of minimal growth rate is the baseline measure for healthy economies and one of the major concerns of those who make decisions about monetary policy at the World Bank and the International Monetary Fund. But it is not in accord with any realistic assessment of our situation in the real economy of the global environment.

For example, Peter Vitousek at Stanford University demonstrated in 1986 that the human population already consumes about 40 percent of the total biomass production of the land-based biosphere. Assuming that our numbers double in forty years, the percentage of terrestrial biomass required to feed this population would be 80 percent, and 100 percent shortly thereafter. This means that limits to the growth of market economies are starkly real, that sustainable development as normally defined is not possible, and that the global economy cannot grow its way out of poverty and environmental degradation based on existing technologies and energy resources. As Hermann Daly puts it, "In its physical dimensions, the economy is an open subsystem of the earth's ecosystem, which is finite, nongrowing and materially closed. As the economic subsystem grows, it incorporates an ever greater proportion of the total ecosystem into itself and must reach a limit at 100 percent, if not before. Therefore its growth is not sustainable. The term *sustainable growth* when applied to the economy is a bad oxymoron—self-contradictory as prose and unevocative as poetry."[32]

To grow, says Daly, means "to increase naturally in size by the addition of material by assimilation or accretion," and to develop means "to expand or realize the potentials of; to bring gradually to a fuller, greater or better state." More simply put, something that grows gets larger, whereas something that develops becomes different. Because the global ecosystem develops or evolves but does not grow, the global economy may develop but must eventually stop growing at the point at which foodstuffs are not sufficient to feed the global human population. The term *sustainable development*, says Daly, makes sense in economic terms only if it is defined as "development without growth," or as "qualitative improvement of a physical economic base . . . within the assimilative and regenerative capacities of the ecosystem."[33]

Some of the more ardent promoters of globalization make the extraordinary claim that market forces will eventually allow all people in the world to enjoy the same level of income and consumption as in the United States. For this to occur, however, the global economy must grow by a factor of seven, and this growth must also keep pace with increases in the global human population. But because the present scale of global economic activities cannot be sustained without occasioning massive disruptions in the global ecosystem, and because humans already consume about 40 percent of the net product of global photosynthesis, even growth by a factor of two seems quite unrealistic. When we also factor into this picture adverse environmental impacts resulting from a seven-fold increase in the level of consumption, the prediction that all human beings on this fragile planet will eventually live like those in the United States seems even more absurd.

There is, however, no conceptual basis in neoclassical economics for entertaining the prospect that there are insuperable biophysical limits to economic growth, and many neoclassical economists appear to be unaware that such limits exist. When they are obliged to confront this prospect, the usual response is that that there is no conceivable limit on economic growth because scientific and technological advances will dramatically increase productivity in agricultural and in other economic sectors without adverse environmental impacts. Even if we ignore the fact that there is no such thing as an immaterial good and that all large-scale economic activities have adverse environmental impacts, this argument is specious for other reasons as well.

Suppose that people in advanced industrialized nations are content with their current standard of living, about $25,000 per capita, and that the standard in these countries does not increase beyond this figure. Also assume that advances in science and technology allowed people in poor and middle-income nations to achieve this standard and that the population in these nations does not increase. The question now becomes, how much more efficient must technologies become in this scenario to raise the average global standard of living to $25,000 per capita? The answer is that because average per-capita income in rich nations is about twenty-three times that in poorer nations, the advances must improve the efficiency of what economists term "want-satisfaction per unit of resource consumption" by a factor of 23. If, however, the global population increases, as the World Resources Institute predicts, to 9.4 billion by 2050, the advances during this period must improve efficiency by a factor of 37.[34] It is conceivable, of course, that our scientific understanding of the processes of nature is fundamentally flawed and that an improved understanding could allow us to build technologies that could increase technological efficiencies by such incredible orders of magnitude. However, the likelihood that this will happen is slim to none.

Assumptions from neoclassical economics also explain why the adverse environmental impacts of globalization are conspicuously missing from the system of national accounts that serves as one of the prime indexes of the "health" of economies. These accounts summarize the flows of services, materials, and products within national markets in units of monetary transactions. The assumption that national markets are closed explains why the gross national product (GNP) accounts only for production and services and why external natural resources are not included. It also explains why the gross domestic product (GDP) accounts only for the goods and services consumed in a national economy and makes no mention of the depletion of natural resources. The GDP also treats costs associated with the extraction of natural resources as income and makes no distinction between renewable and nonrenewable resources.

When neoclassical economists attempt to factor into their equations costs associated with the use of the external resources of nature, they typically use a device called shadow pricing. A shadow price is an imputed valuation of a commodity that lies outside the closed market system and has, therefore, no market price. Used in cost-benefit analysis, shadow prices represent the planned opportunity cost, or the cost of an action represented as the value of a forgone alternative action, associated with a commodity that is not generally traded. As the name implies, shadow prices are not viewed as "real" or "natural" market prices; they represent imputed prices for alternative actions designed to maximize returns on the market. Because what is privileged in this scheme is the assumption that markets must expand and consume more scarce resources, shadow prices typically serve to keep actual costs to the environment in the shadows or, more often, completely in the dark.

Some economists have argued that shadow prices should be constructed for environmental functions that are directly comparable to market prices with the use of supply and demand curves. The supply curve would estimate the costs of measures needed to prevent a loss of an environmental function, and the demand curve would represent the individual preferences of consumers for environmental functions in units of money.[35] The presumption here is that the sovereign arbiter of economic value in neoclassical economics, the atomized economic actor, would defy the laws of economics and privilege the long-term welfare of the whole (global ecosystem or biosphere) over short-term economic advantage. But even if sufficiently large numbers of people were willing to do so, they would need to possess a truly prodigious amount of knowledge about environmental problems and solutions to arrive at a price for an environmental function comparable to a market price.

LIMITS TO GROWTH AND CHEAP OIL

The real limits to economic growth since 1960 have been disguised in no small part by an accounting system that does not recognize the real or actual costs associated with vast increases in the use of an oozy black substance formed from ancient vegetation in the earth's crust called oil. The wholesale exploitation of this natural resource provided enormous economic benefits to roughly one billion people in advanced industrial societies and generated much of the capital required to create the new global economy.[36] It also resulted, however, in the creation of a global energy regime and a very extensive network of related technologies and technological processes that constitute the greatest contributing factor to the environmental crisis.

Global demand for this combustible substance increased so significantly that at any time after 1970 about five gallons of oil were in transit on large seagoing tankers for every man, woman, and child on the face of the earth. This prodigious flow of cheap oil spurred the phenomenal growth of industrialization worldwide and the exponential expansion of the petrochemical industry, which was producing by 1999 more than a thousand million tons of organic chemicals annually.[37] This industry replaced degradable materials, such as wood and paper, with new nondegradable materials, most notably plastics. As a result, landfills, rivers, streams, and ocean beds have become increasingly saturated with the remains of these unwanted but very durable products. The industry also manufactured the prodigious amounts of chemical fertilizers, herbicides, and pesticides that contributed, along with the heavy use of farm equipment powered by gasoline and diesel fuels, to the widespread mechanization and industrialization of agriculture in countries where arable land was plentiful and labor costs were high.

By the 1990s, the new economic realities associated with the green revolution had utterly transformed agricultural processes and practices in Europe, North America, Japan, Australia, and New Zealand. Farmers in these countries now specialize in single crops that plant geneticists have bred for responsiveness to chemical fertilizers, resistance to chemical pesticides and compatibility with mechanized harvesting. The dependence of this new agricultural system on cheap oil was greatly amplified after patchwork quilt farms were displaced with vast fields dedicated to monoculture. Because monoculture crops are more vulnerable to insects and other pests, this required a vast increase in the use of chemical pesticides. And because these crops also depleted specific nutrients in the soil much faster, this forced farmers to vastly increase their use of chemical fertilizers as well.

The foodstuffs produced in this global market and the packaged goods and other products made from these materials are transported over great distances by another system that owes its existence to prodigious supplies of cheap oil—a vast network of barges, ships, cargo vessels, railroads, and trucks. It is estimated, for example, that items purchased in American grocery stores travel on average more than two thousand miles before appearing on the shelves. It is also not unusual for those who grow crops transported thousands of miles on a transportation system fueled by cheap oil to consume products made from those crops that travel back over this system to local wholesalers and retailers.

The green revolution provided some marginal economic benefits to Latin America and helped Taiwan, South Korea, and Indonesia to industrialize their economies. Yet only a few nations, such as India, became a net exporter of food and/or achieved food independence. The real winners in economic terms are transnational corporations in agribusiness and related industries. These corporations may have become, to borrow as phrase from a recent advertising campaign of one of them, "supermarkets to the world." On the other hand, the natural resource that made this market possible is "cheap" only because we have failed to evaluate its actual or real costs in environmental terms.

Cheap oil also fuels another transportation system of roughly a billion cars, buses, small trucks, and motorbikes that travel along a network of roads that covers roughly 10 percent of the landmass in North America, Europe, and Japan and about 2 percent of the landmass worldwide.[38] The average American car, assuming that it actually gets the federally mandated 27.5 miles per gallon, travels approximately 100,000 miles in its lifetime and emits around thirty-five tons of carbon dioxide or monoxide. The more than 500 million cars in use worldwide generate about 25 percent of global greenhouse gas emissions, and the UN Population Fund projects that by 2025 cars in developing countries will be emitting four times as much carbon as in the industrialized countries today.[39] Also consider that the process of manufacturing a car generates on average about as much air pollution as driving a car for ten years and produces approximately twenty-nine tons of waste.[40]

In the absence of these transportation systems and other systems dependent on abundant supplies of cheap oil, such as electrical power plants, the massive increase worldwide in the numbers and sizes of cities would not have occurred. By 1990, more than eight hundred cities on the planet had populations in excess of half a million, nearly three hundred had more than a million, and fourteen had in excess of ten million. If present trends continue, over half the population of countries throughout the world will soon be living in oil-hungry cities that will not, in most cases, have adequate sewage disposal systems and wastewater treatment facilities.[41]

The energy regime of oil was also the economic engine that provided much of the capital required for globalization. During the 1970s, members of the Organization of Petroleum Exporting Countries (OPEC) deposited large amounts of their windfall profits in world banks. After states ceased to regulate capital flows during the Reagan-Thatcher era, it became much easier to make money from finance than from trade or manufacture, and after 1980 international financial flows dwarfed trade flows. Most of this capital was channeled into the global banking system, and much of it passed through development banks.

The World Bank, the Inter-American Development Bank, the Asian Development Bank, and a few smaller institutions used their own funds and those borrowed from flush financial markets in New York, London and Tokyo to invest heavily in economic development in poorer countries. Based on economic guidelines and predictions developed by neoclassical economists, the development banks invested the vast majority of their funds in infrastructure and energy projects. After 1960, the World Bank became the single largest financier of new roads, power plants, dams, coal mines, and oil wells. Because the economic forecasts that argued in favor of investing in such projects were predicated on the assumption that markets are closed systems, virtually no attention was paid to the adverse environmental impacts of the lending programs. Also consider that the states borrowing these billions, notably Brazil, India, China, and Indonesia, were too concerned about improving economic conditions to worry about environmental concerns. Consequently, the leaders of these countries, along with most representatives of the development banks, have resisted all efforts to require assessments of potential environmental impacts of any development projects regardless of scale.

Meanwhile, tens of billions of dollars have been disbursed by the development banks annually to finance projects, such as irrigation schemes and roads through rainforests, that may make financial sense based on assumptions about economic reality embedded in the mathematical formalism of neoclassical economics. However, a large number of these projects have proven to be quite disastrous in ecological terms and make no sense at all in the real economy of the global environment. For example, the World Bank in the five years following the Earth Summit funded fossil fuel development projects in China, Russia, and elsewhere that will generate more carbon dioxide omissions in their lifetimes than the entire world produced in 1997.[42]

Global politics since 1960 has also been driven in no small part by efforts on the part of major powers to protect existing sources of oil and to gain access to additional sources. The decision by OPEC in 1973 to restrict oil production, the nationalization of the large oil concessions in Saudi Arabia, Kuwait, and Venezuela in 1975 and 1976, and the 1979 revolution in Iran contributed to higher prices and spurred a new era of oil exploration and extraction. New oil operations soon appeared in Alaska, Alberta, the Gulf of Mexico, the North Sea, Angola, Ecuador, and Siberia, and most of these projects were subsidized by the tax breaks from governments and loans from development banks. And last but certainly not least, the constant preoccupation of the major powers with events in the emotionally charged and unpredictable political landscape of the Middle East has much to do with the vast reserves of oil in the region.

MAINSTREAM ECONOMICS AND THE TELOS OF GLOBALIZATION

In a discussion of the globalization of the market economy, some consideration should be given to two large claims that are central to the arguments of its most ardent proselytizers and promoters—a global free market system is an historical inevitability, and the progressive emergence of this system is inextricably connected, as Milton Friedman and others have claimed, with the spread of political liberty and the appearance of new democratic governments. The notion that a global free market system is the telos of economic reality is an extension of the assumption in the neoclassical economic paradigm that the natural laws of economics are universal and act on atomized economic actors and firms in the same ways regardless of cultural contexts. In the mathematical formalism of neoclassical economics, this assumption manifests in the presumption that market forces are the primary determinants of economic behavior, and there is no place or function in this formalism for culturally specific variables. This explains why most mainstream economists tend to view cultural differences as incidental and unimportant, or as merely temporary sources of resistance to the market mechanisms that act in accordance with the natural laws of economics.

This understanding of the lawful character of market mechanisms also manifests in the mathematical formalism of neoclassical economics in the assumption that a specific set of initial conditions is required for the efficient operation of a market system regardless of cultural contexts. It also explains why mainstream economists presume that any fully functioning market systems that eventually emerge in any cultural contexts will be quite similar. The large problem here is that the conditions under which market systems develop, the role that government plays in their control and management, and the extent to which their implementation enhances political liberty and the growth of democratic institutions are massively conditioned by cultural contexts. Perhaps the easiest way to illustrate this point is briefly to discuss the manner in which successful market systems developed in Asia during the post–World War II period and some recent experiments with market systems in China and Russia.

The "Asian tigers," South Korea, Taiwan, Hong Kong, and Singapore, and the "new Asian tigers," Malaysia, Indonesia, Thailand, and the Philippines, built their industrial economies on the economic model that had proved successful in Japan. In all of these countries, economic activities have been centrally controlled by dictators or by authoritarian leaders in de facto one-party systems, and the principal means of control has consistently been government regulation and coercion. From the perspective of mainstream economists, the "market friendly" outcomes in "Countries, Inc." are "paradoxical" because they did not result from the unimpeded operation of the mechanisms of closed market systems. They resulted from massive government intervention in the economic process in countries where living memories of colonization, conquest, secession, civil conflict, and war engendered a strong sense of collective purpose and a willingness to privilege the economic interests of the nation-state over that of the individual.

If the economic success of "Countries, Inc." seems paradoxical in the view of mainstream economists, the phenomenal economic growth of the market system in China's Guangdong Province should make no sense at all. This "Asian miracle" resulted from an experiment with the market economy instigated by the Chinese government in 1987 in the hope of earning more hard currency from international trade and absorbing surplus labor. In this experiment, three Special Economic Zones were established and their directors given unprecedented authority to make trade and investment decisions. The two zones in which economic growth was most dramatic are strategically located in Shenzhen, across from Hong Kong, and in Fujian, across from Taiwan. By 2000, the external trade of Guangdong Province, meaning both exports and imports combined, totaled $175.5 billion, or about 40 percent of the total for all of China.[43]

What makes the results of this experiment virtually impossible to explain from the perspective of neoclassical economics is that none of the initial conditions that must presumably be in place before a viable market system can develop existed in Guangdong Province. This market system emerged in the absence of a system of private ownership, commercial banks, capital markets, commercial laws, a legal system, and a judicial system. But this did not frustrate in any discernible ways its rapid economic growth and development, and the only way in which one can begin to understand why this occurred is to consider the influence of something that has no place or function in the formalism of mainstream economic theory—culturally specific variables.

For example, most mainstream economists were convinced that the experiment was doomed to failure because foreign investors would not invest large amounts of capital in the absence of contractual legal frameworks and a means of enforcing the terms of contractual agreements. What these economists apparently failed to appreciate is that roughly 80 percent of overseas ethnic Chinese trace their origins to Guangdong Province and still have friends and relatives there, and it was "foreigners" in this group that were willing to invest billions of dollars in the new state-controlled enterprises based on little more than mutual trust and the expectation of a quick return. The informal connections that made this possible, which the Chinese refer to as *guanxi*, operate on all levels, from principal decision makers appointed by the government down to people in local neighborhoods. The second major source of investment was ethnic Chinese businessmen in Hong Kong who were seeking to reduce labor costs by moving production and assembly operations to the industrial center located in nearby Shenzhen.[44]

From an environmental perspective, the large-scale movement toward a more market-oriented economy in China, which is largely based on older technologies and technological processes, is very troubling. It has already resulted in severe damage to the global environment, and that damage will grow exponentially if the present plans to expand this economy are implemented. For the moment, however, let us consider what this development allows us to reasonably conclude about the directions in which the global economy is moving and the extent to which this movement will contribute to the emergence of new democratic governments.

It seems clear that the decision by the fourteenth Congress of the Chinese Communist Party in 1992 to shift from a "socialist planned commodity economy" to a "socialist market economy" signaled a recognition that the market system is more efficient and productive than the command and control economy.[45] And one can also make a good case that the greater autonomy of economic actors in this new market system has tended to promote a larger awareness of the benefits of individual freedom and the value of democratic institutions. But there is absolutely nothing in this history that allows us to conclude that movement toward a global free market system is in any sense a preordained lawful process that is necessarily accompanied by enhanced political freedoms and the emergence of democratic governments.

This point can be illustrated in a slightly different way by briefly examining some recent developments in a country that has attempted to transform its command and control economy into a free market economy with all deliberated speed—the Russian Federation. After the president of the Soviet Union, Mikhail Gorbachev, failed to convince the leaders of the fifteen restive republics to create a voluntary union with himself as president in late 1991, hard-line Communists responded by staging a coup. The coup fizzled after it met with determined resistance, and Gorbachev, who had been put under house arrest in Crimea, returned to power for the four-month period in which the republics established themselves as new nation-states and the former Soviet Union ceased to exist. Gorbachev then turned over the reins of power to the president of the Russian Federation, Boris Yeltsin, at a time when the economy was plunging into a deep depression. Orders for military equipment had dried up, inflation was soaring, coal supplies were disrupted, and there was good prospect that St. Petersburg would have no heat in the coming winter.[46]

As social unrest mounted, Yeltsin was angered by the reluctance of Parliament to approve some of his more radical economic reforms and he attempted to dissolve this body in September 1993. When a majority of the members resisted this order and refused to leave the Parliament building, Yeltsin forced their surrender by setting the building on fire. He then proceeded to implement his economic reform program without the approval of Parliament. The first major item on the list of proposed reforms was the privatization of state-owned businesses. This formidable task was entrusted to a group of young economists on the State Committee on the Management of State Property, headed by economist Anatoly Chubais. Under his leadership, the committee decided to create a large property-owning population by distributing vouchers, worth about ten thousand rubles, or roughly thirty U.S. dollars each, to all Russian citizens, including children.

In this program, which ran from October 1992 to July 1994, people could use the vouchers to acquire shares in specific companies or in the company where they worked, exchange them for shares in mutual funds, or sell them to other individuals. But because the auctions where vouchers could be used to buy shares were rarely publicized and often hard to reach, this created a situation in which hungry Russians strapped for cash typically sold them to the highest bidder. Consequently, the voucher system did not place the ownership of formerly state-owned companies in the hands of ordinary Russian citizens. It resulted in the acquisition of these companies by a small group of nouveau riche who were either party officials and former directors of state enterprises or members of a new business class known as the oligarchs.[47] By all accounts, this was also the biggest garage sale in history. By 1996, eighteen thousand industrial enterprises had been privatized, the proportion of industrial workers employed in this new private sector had grown to 80 percent, and 70 percent of GNP was generated in this sector.

There was widespread public anger and resentment over the results of the economic reforms, and this become quite apparent when the Communists made a strong showing in the 1995 elections to the sixth Duma. Yeltsin's approval rate at this time was at 5 percent, and Gennady Zyuganow, the leader of the Communist Party, was favored to win the 1996 presidential election by a landslide. Fearing this prospect, some of the oligarchs offered to lend Yeltsin money for his reelection campaign in exchange for shares in strategic state-owned enterprises that would be held "in trust." Under this agreement, the loans would mature in a few months and the government would then have the option of repaying them or ceding control of the shares to the trustees. Because no one involved had any expectation that the government could repay the loans, the agreement essentially sold to a few Russian businessmen billions of dollars in state property at a fraction of its actual value. For example, Vladimir Potanin, a former trade official turned banker, acquired a company with annual revenues of $1.5 billion, Norilsk Nickel, for $180 million, and instantly became the owner of one of the world's richest reserves of nickel, copper, platinum, palladium, and silver.[48] For Yeltsin, however, the loans for shares scheme paid off. He used the monies provided by the oligarchs to finance the slick media campaign that resulted in his come-from-behind victory in the 1996 election.

But what is most important here for our purposes is that the Russian economy during this period was an experiment in pure capitalism in which market forces were not constrained by commercial laws, legal frameworks, regulatory agencies, central banks, or by any government regulation and control whatsoever. The unfortunate result was that a small group of unexceptional Russians were transformed into billionaires who own the seven largest commercial banks, dominate the media, and control large sectors of the industrial economy. It also seems clear that the emergence of this market economy did not enhance political freedoms and promote democratic governance. But it did massively contribute to the creation of a political system that Russian analyst Lilia Shevtsova describes as a "hybrid regime" built on the "incompatible principles of democracy, authoritarianism, populism, oligarchy, nepotism, and even anarchy."[49]

Following the 1996 election, Yeltsin, who was recovering from double pneumonia following open-heart surgery, was not active in the political process. When Yeltsin reemerged in his familiar role as "Boris the czar" in 1997, he told the Russian Parliament that government must play a much more active role in managing the movement toward a functional market system: "From the policy of nonintervention, we are resolutely going over to policy of preemptive regulation of economic processes. . . . In itself, the market is not a cure-all. In any civilized state, the market mechanism and state regulation work in harmony."[50] During this period, new banking and securities regulations were instituted, and by 1997 the recently created Russian stock market was yielding very high returns for investors. But after two major shocks to the economy in 1998, the collapse of oil and other commodity prices, and the flight of international investors following the Asian economic crisis, the Russian stock market crashed, the government defaulted on its debt, and the ruble was devalued.

In August 1999, Yeltsin chose as prime minister Vladimir Putin, a career KGB officer who had served in East Germany and who tried his hand at business and politics following the collapse of the Berlin Wall. The first step of the new prime minister was to renew the war in Chechnya, a move that most observers viewed as politically disastrous. But because the Russian public had been unnerved by a series of bombings attributed to Chechen terrorists and apparently felt the need for some renewed sense of national purpose and unity, the war enhanced Putin's reputation as a strong leader. His popularity also increased after the government managed to pay pensioners, teachers, and doctors, most of whom had survived for months without any income, the monies owed them by the state.

Sensing an opportunity to enhance his political fortunes, Putin created a new political party called Unity that took the leading position in the Duma elections in December 1999. A month later he emerged as the leader of this party and the president of the Russian Federation. By 2001, Putin had revamped the tax code, lowered the flat rate, and the resulting 36 percent increase in the tax collection rate vastly increased state revenues. He also managed to privatize large amounts of state-owned land and to institute some long awaited and sorely needed judicial reforms.

The willingness of Putin to cooperate with the Bush administration in the war on terrorism has obviated much of the hostility between the Russia and the United States that was a constant feature of the Cold War. But there are no indications that the Russian Federation is on the verge of instituting a truly democratic system of government, and its fledging experiment with the market system has not as yet provided any appreciable benefits for ordinary citizens. In fact, some statistics indicate that living conditions for the vast majority of these people have become much harsher. The infant mortality rate in Russia is now three times that of the EU countries, life expectancy for males has fallen to fifty-seven years, and environmental problems are far more massive and much less tractable than in other industrialized countries.

Once again, the intent here is not to denigrate the free market system or to suggest that it is in any sense inferior to any other economic system. It is to make the case that blatantly unscientific assumptions about economic reality in the neoclassical economic paradigm have not only served to obviate the prospect of realistically accounting for the costs of doing business in the global environment. They have also been used in an effort to legitimate the absurd claim that the future of the global economy has been predetermined by the natural laws of economics or the lawful dynamics of market mechanisms.

Part of what makes this claim invidious is the presumption that a global market system will come into existence without any willful or conscious intent on the part of human beings outside of the "inherent" impulse to maximize personal utility in the service of selfish interests. But what is most invidious is the assumption that the lawful dynamics are such that the resulting "closed" global market system must perpetually expand and consume increasingly larger amounts of exogenous natural resources. And this leads to the totally irrational conclusion that the preordained emergence of a global market system obliges us to view the resources of nature as either unlimited or replaceable by other resources and/or technological processes.

The belief that natural resources are unlimited was, until fairly recently, reinforced by the perceived existence of what Kenneth Boulding terms an "inexhaustible frontier somewhere beyond the known world, an illimitable plane in which respite could be found once one's immediate surroundings deteriorated socially or environmentally." It was, he says, only after World War II that we began to realize that the "illimitable plane" was fast becoming a "closed sphere" where the "cowboy economy of the past" would be displaced by a "spaceman economy in which the earth has become a spaceship."[51]

Given that the energy resources of spaceship earth are finite, the costs of doing business in the global environment must obviously take into account the depletion of energy resources. Such an account must also reflect the actual relationship between parts (economic systems and processes) and whole (ecosystem) in terms of the damage done to the whole by the activities of the parts. And this will require the development of a new economic theory premised on the assumption that parts exist in embedded relationship to the whole and manifest as new wholes with different emergent properties on ascending levels of scale and complexity.

If assumptions about part–whole relationships in the neoclassical economic paradigm were commensurate with the actual or real dynamics of part–whole relationships in the global environment, there would be no need to develop and implement an environmentally responsible economic theory. But because the assumptions are utterly different from and wholly incompatible with these dynamics, there is simply no basis in this paradigm for coordinating global economic activities in ways that could lead to a sustainable environment.

In an effort to demonstrate why this is "in principle" the case, we will now examine the manner in which two diverse groups of economists have attempted to posit economic solutions to environmental problems. Most, but not all, members of the first group, the so-called environmental economists, have sought to develop "market solutions" within the framework of neoclassical economic theory and are viewed as mainstream economists. Those in the second group, the "ecological economists," are not considered mainstream economists for an interesting reason—they have attempted to posit economic solutions to environmental solutions by enlarging the framework of neoclassical economics in ways that tend to require revisions in assumptions about part–whole relationships that are foundational to the theory in both conceptual and mathematical terms.

As we will see, the market solutions proposed by the vast majority of the environmental economists are driven by assumptions about part–whole relationships in the neoclassical economic paradigm that effectively undermine the prospect of realistically accounting for the costs of doing business in the global environment. The ecological economists, in contrast, have articulated a number of viable and potentially very effective economic solutions to environmental problems. But these solutions have not been taken seriously because they clearly imply that neoclassical economic theory is premised on erroneous assumptions. For our purposes, this discussion is important because it serves to dispel the now very dangerous myth that viable economic solutions to environmental problems can be implemented within the framework of neoclassical economics or by enlarging that framework.

CHAPTER 5

A GREEN THUMB ON THE INVISIBLE HAND
Environmental Economics

> Nature! We are surrounded and embraced by her: powerless to separate ourselves from her, and powerless to penetrate beyond her.
>
> —Johann Wolfgang von Goethe

Research in environmental science clearly indicates that global economic activities are massively disrupting the web of interactions between parts (organisms) and compromising the ability to the whole (ecosystem or biosphere) to sustain the growing number of our species. The causes of this problem may be staggeringly complex, but the most effective way to deal with it seems obvious. We must use scientifically valid measures of the damage done to the global environment by our economic activities as a basis for assessing the costs of this damage in economic terms and develop means and methods for including these costs in the economic system.

If this could be accomplished within the framework of neoclassical economics, we could quickly begin to posit viable economic solutions to environmental problems based on assumptions about the character of economic reality that are well known and almost universally accepted. The business of managing natural resources and developing more environmentally friendly technologies and processes would be "business as usual," and global economic planners and environmental scientists could work together in harmony to fashion a global economic order that is both prosperous and secure. Unfortunately, this cannot and will not happen because assumptions about part–whole relationships in the neoclassical economic paradigm are categorically different from and wholly incompatible with the actual or real dynamics of part–whole relationships in the global environment.

The effort to demonstrate why this is "in principle" the case begins with an examination of the manner in which mainstream economists have attempted to graft a green thumb on the invisible hand in a subfield called environmental economics. This orthodox approach to positing economic solutions to environmental problems is taught in universities and practiced in government agencies and development banks, and the solutions are usually embedded in the mathematical formalism of general equilibrium theory. In this formalism, the point of convergence that allegedly points to the existence of the natural laws of economics is U, the symbol for the utility function, and the concrete effects of the operation of these laws allegedly manifest in decisions made by economic actors.

Because market economies must in accordance with this theory grow or expand, environmental economists generally presume that the health of these economies is sensitively dependent on the consumption of increasingly larger amounts of environmental resources. And because the theory stipulates that a market system exists in a domain separate and distinct from the global environment, environmental resources outside this domain are viewed as "goods, services, and amenities" that are not subject to the pricing mechanisms that operate within the system. The theory also assumes that because the pricing mechanisms are the indexes of the lawful or lawlike decisions made by economic actors, the "real" value of environmental resources can be determined only by these mechanisms.

Although mainstream economists rarely talk openly about the natural laws of economics that are foundational to the formalism of general equilibrium theory, they often make references to assumptions about economic actors implicit in the formalism. These actors are typically described as suprarational decision makers who invariably make choices that maximize their utility, or their economic satisfaction or well-being. But when we examine the manner in which these actors are actually depicted in the mathematical formalism appropriated from mid-nineteenth century physics, these assumptions become more than a little problematic. In this formalism, the actors are described as point particles that move about and interact in an immaterial field of utility and economic decisions are largely predetermined by mechanisms associated with the natural laws of economics. The following passage from one of the leading textbooks on environmental economics illustrates the logical confusion that results:

> An individual is assumed to have a set of preferences over goods and services that can be ordered in a logical and consistent manner. . . . The utility function is an ordinal representation of preferences that allows us to express the most preferred consumption bundles by the highest level of utility. Utility is an unobservable continuous index of preferences. If we impose a policy that changes the consumption bundle so that utility increases, then economists measure this change as consumer surplus—the money metric of the unobservable utility function. Consumer surplus can be either a willingness to pay or a willingness to accept compensation measure. . . . Consider an individual choosing between alternative consumption bundles defined by n levels of environmental quality, $Q_1, Q_2, \ldots, Q_n.$[1]

The statement that "an individual is assumed to have a set of preferences over goods and services that can be ordered in a logical and consistent manner" infers that the preferences are freely chosen. But the statement that the "utility function is an ordinal representation of preferences that allows us to express the most preferred consumption bundle at the highest level of utility" suggests that the choices are predetermined by the function. We are then told that the utility represented by the function is "an unobservable continuous index of preferences" and the inference is that the function discloses the preferences of economic actors even though the preferences are unobservable.

In an evaluation of the potential impact of an environmental policy, this unobservable function becomes a money metric that represents a surplus value in consumer preferences. The index of this surplus value is defined as the willingness of consumers to pay or to accept compensation for a change in the utility of something consumed, or something potentially consumable, that results from the implementation of an environmental policy. Hence the unobservable becomes observable in units of money that reflect changes in a utility function revealed by consumer preferences that are necessarily consistent with this function.

The hidden assumption here is that the utility function actually decodes or reveals the action of forces associated with the natural laws of economics on the preferences of consumers. This explains why the unobservable utility function can allegedly disclose these preferences as surplus value in assessing the economic impacts of environmental policies on self-regulating market systems. What we have, then, is a view of a market as a self-referential system of equations in which the value of "environmental goods and resources" is a function of consumer preferences that are consistent with calculations based on this self-referential mathematical system.

Another related problem occasioned by the substitution of utility for energy in the equations of mid-nineteenth century physics is that neoclassical economists must assume that production and consumption does not alter the material substances out of which goods and commodities are made. Recall why the creators of neoclassical economics made this assumption. They were obliged to do so in order to make the case that that there is a symmetry between production and consumption in an immaterial field of utility in which lawful or lawlike mechanisms govern and control decisions made by economic actors and determine the value of goods and commodities. This explains why there is no basis in neoclassical economics for representing economic activities as physical processes embedded in and interactive with natural processes in the global environment. The environment in this formalism has value only as environmental goods, services, and amenities that can be bought, sold, traded, saved, or invested, like any other commodity, in a closed market system that must, if it is functioning properly, grow or expand.

GETTING THE PRICES RIGHT

When environmental economists calculate environmental costs, they assume that the relative price of each bundle of an environmental good, service, or amenity reveals the "real marginal values" of the consumer. As noted earlier, the creators of neoclassical economics conceived of the construct of marginal values after substituting utility for energy in the equations borrowed from mid-nineteenth century physics. In the resulting formalism, a marginal value essentially represents how much a consumer is willing to pay a little bit more of something to acquire a little bit more of something else. Note what the writers of our standard textbook on environmental economics have to say about the dynamics of this process:

> The power of a perfectly functioning market rests in its decentralized process of decision making and exchange; no omnipotent planner is needed to allocate resources. Rather, prices ration resources to those

that value them the most and, in doing so, individuals are swept along by Adam Smith's invisible hand to achieve what is best for society as a collective. Optimal private decisions based on mutually advantageous exchange lead to optimal social outcomes.[2]

In environmental economics, the presumption that optimal private decisions "based on mutually advantageous exchange" lead to optimal social outcomes for the state of the environment is a primary article of faith. According to these economists, however, this will not occur unless the following conditions apply. The market system in which economic actors make optimal private decisions must operate more or less perfectly, and the prices, or values, of environmental goods and services must be represented as a function of those decisions. But if these conditions are met, environmental economists generally assume that the lawful or lawlike operation of the market system will resolve environmental problems when the "prices are right."

Because the "right price" in neoclassical economic theory is a function of the dynamics allegedly revealed in the mathematical formalism of this theory, the results of computations determine if a putative price is actually right. This explains why much of the work of the environmental economists attempts to represent environmental costs of economic activities in terms of prices that economic actors have paid, or are willing to pay, in order to realize some marginal benefits of environmental goods and services. This view of right prices also explains why the term *environmental externalities* has a rather peculiar meaning in the literature of mainstream economists.

Externalities are situations in which the production or consumption of one economic actor affects another who did not pay for the good produced or consumed, and externalities can be either negative or positive. For example, environmental economists often cite pollution as an example of the former and preservation of biological diversity as an example of the latter. When these economists use the phrase "environmental externalities," they are referring to environmental goods and services that are "external" to market systems in the sense that they lie outside of the alleged lawful operations of these systems.

From the perspective of environmental economists, markets fail if prices do not accurately communicate the desires and constraints of a society and an environmental problem is a negative externality that represents such a failure. A market system is alleged to operate properly when a set of competitive markets generates a sufficient allocation of resources at a level of efficiency known as "Pareto optimality"—a state or condition where it is impossible to reallocate resources to enhance the utility of one economic actor without reducing that of another. The assumption here is that if the natural laws of economics are allowed to maximize the private net benefits of consumers and producers with minimal restraint, a set of markets will emerge in which each economic actor will have access to a socially optimal allocation of resources.

The most traditional approach to internalizing a negative environmental externality is to impose a tax defined by Pigou in *The Economics of Welfare* (1932), which is presumably equal to the value of the marginal social damage associated with the externality. The aim of this tax, says Pigou, "is to ascertain how the free play of self-interest, acting under the existing legal system, tends to distribute the country's resources in the way most favorable to the production of a large national dividend, and how it is feasible for State action to improve upon 'natural' tendencies."[3] There are, suggests Pigou, natural tendencies at work in market systems associated with the operation of the natural laws of economics, and any tax imposed by the state should enhance these tendencies. He also claims that the value of production will be maximized in the vast majority of economic situations if government refrains from interfering with these natural tendencies. He also argues, however, that "human institutions" can interfere with the lawful dynamics of market systems, and government must therefore take some limited action "to control the play of economic forces in such ways as to promote the economic welfare, and through that, the total welfare, of their citizens as a whole."[4]

When environmental economists are asked to assess the potential impacts on market economies of environmental tax reforms, they typically factor a Pigouvian tax into the mathematical formalism of neoclassical economic theory. One problem with the optimal social outcomes that the predictions are intended to disclose is that they are almost invariably premised on the assumption that the gross national product of healthy market economies must grow at an annual rate of 3 percent or more. Consequently, the calculated impacts of proposed environmental tax reforms tend to emphasize economic losses associated with decreases in the consumption of environmental goods and services and to minimize the environmental costs associated with this consumption.

In dealing with pollution problems, environmental economists generally favor emissions charges or fees, and they often appeal to Pigou to make the case that this instrument is more efficient and effective than command and control regulations. The charges or fees are designed to reduce the quantity or improve the quality of pollution by making polluters assume a portion of the costs for every unit of harmful pollution they release into the environment. The scheme is Pigouvian in the sense that the anticipated result is that the charges or fees will be equal to the marginal social damage associated with the externality. The expectation is that firms will be induced to lower their emissions to the point where the incremental cost of pollution control equals the emissions charges they might otherwise pay. It is also presumed that if individual polluters use pollution-control strategies that represent least cost solutions, market forces will cause the aggregate costs of pollution control to be minimized.

Another traditional approach in environmental economics to getting the prices right by internalizing negative environmental externalities was originally proposed by economist Ronald Coase in a paper published in 1960.[5] Coase objected to the use of any environmental tax or subsidy that would have an adverse distributional impact or that would impose economic burdens not directly related to or a function of specific economic activities. He also argued that the value judgments implied in the use of taxes or subsidies were inconsistent with neoclassical assumptions about the character of economic reality and the lawful dynamics of market processes.

Coase claimed that the essence of environmental problems is that no one owns the environment, and this disallows the prospect that the lawful mechanisms of market processes can resolve these problems. He concluded, therefore, that the most effective way to internalize negative environmental externalities was to revise the legal system to allow for the assignment of ownership rights to environmental resources. If these resources were owned, argued Coase, the mechanisms of the market would eliminate undesirable uses, and adverse environmental impacts would disappear without the need for government intervention. In this situation, he said, there would be an equivalence between paying someone for a good and charging someone for a bad in a state of general equilibrium where optimal social outcomes are necessarily realized.

Environmental economists often appeal to Coase to make the case that tradable pollution permits, like those mentioned in the discussion of the Kyoto accords, are a more effective market-based solution than Pigouvian taxes. In these schemes, a predetermined level of emissions is established within a specific region, and permits equal to the permissible total emissions are distributed among producers in the region. Polluters who keep their levels of emissions below that allowed in their permits can sell or lease their surplus permits to other producers or use them to offset emissions in other parts of their production system. Because the permits are limited and therefore have scarcity value, the environmental economists claim that this should provide sufficient incentives to create a market in which they are actively traded.

Beginning in the 1970s, the Environmental Protection Agency allowed states to use tradable permits to implement the provisions of the Clean Air Act, and they were used in the 1980s in the petroleum industry to accomplish the phasing down of leaded gasoline.[6] This scheme was also employed to facilitate the worldwide reduction of emissions of ozone-depleting chlorofluorocarbons, to lower ambient ozone levels in the northeastern United States, and to implement stricter air pollution controls in the Los Angeles area.[7] Experience has shown, however, that tradable permits are difficult to administer and costly to implement, and that the infrastructure required for actively trading them rarely emerges. A number of studies have also indicated that these schemes have not achieved more reductions in emissions than standard regulatory systems and that they failed to stimulate more innovation in pollution control technology than command-and-control restrictions.[8]

There is, however, a more primary reason why both emissions charges and tradable permits cannot even begin to effectively resolve the crisis in the global environment. The assumption in neoclassical economics that the economic activities of parts (production or distribution systems) must be viewed as distinct and separable functions in wholes (closed market systems) effectively undermines the prospect that the market-based solutions of the environmental economists can effectively deal with pollution problems in economic terms. This assumption obliges these economists to represent the costs of pollution as a function of the economic activities of parts that has value only in the mental space of economic actors operating within closed and isolated wholes (regional economies or national economies). But for reasons that will become more apparent in the chapters on part–whole relationships in both biology and physics, parts in physical reality are invariably embedded in and interactive with wholes, and there is no such thing in nature as an isolated system.

The fact that national economies are not closed or isolated systems in physical terms should be obvious to anyone who has watched the weather channel. The precursors of acid rain produced in Great Britain (sulfur dioxide and nitrogen dioxide) travel on a prevailing western wind and are deposited in Scandinavia, and industrial facilities in northern Britain cause more pollution in Scandinavia than in southern England. Huge amounts of greenhouse gases and other pollutants produced in the United States cause environmental problems in Canada, and CFCs emitted from any region on the globe damage the ozone layer. But because the atmospheric physics is such that the thinning of the ozone layer is nonuniform, some countries, such as Australia and New Zealand, suffer more damage from higher concentrations of UV radiation than countries that are located further from the poles.

It is, of course, theoretically possible for environmental economists to enlarge the zones, regions, or "bubbles" within which emissions schemes and tradable permits apply. And they did so in the failed U.S. proposal that would have allowed highly industrialized nations to meet the reductions in carbon dioxide emissions required in the Kyoto accords at less cost. This does not, however, obviate the fact, as that proposal nicely demonstrated, that the intent in such schemes is to expand market economies at the great expense of a sustainable global environment. The market-based solutions of the environmental economists may appear to result in "win-win" outcomes in the equations of neoclassical economics. But this is only because assumptions about part–whole relationships in economic reality implicit in the formalism preclude the prospect that actual or real costs associated with damage done to the environment by economic activities can be included in the calculations.

The fundamental disjunction between constructions of part–whole relationships in neoclassical economic theory and the actual dynamics of part–whole relationships in physical reality is also apparent in attempts by environmental ecologists to assess long-term economic impacts of changes in the global environment. For example, a well-known environmental economist notes in a study on the potential impact of global warming on the global economy that "climate change is likely to have different impacts on different sectors in different countries." He then writes, "In reality, most of the U.S. economy has little interaction with climate. For example, cardiovascular surgery and parallel computing are undertaken in carefully controlled environments and are unlikely to be directly affected by climate change. More generally, underground mining, most services, communications, and manufacturing are sectors likely to be largely unaffected by climate change—sectors that comprise about 85 percent of GNP."[9]

The assumption that various sectors of an economy can be isolated from the impacts of global warming because they have little or no "interaction" with climate makes no sense at all from the perspective of environmental science. In the climate models that these scientists use to study the potential long-term impacts of global warming, it is quite clear that parts (organisms) are sensitively dependent on changes in the whole, such as increases in average global temperature. Virtually all of these models show that increases in global temperature in the range of three to six degrees centigrade will massively alter the interaction between these parts globally and that all natural environments, including those within the national boundaries of the United States, will be transformed dramatically. Imagine that 80 percent of the corn crop in the United States failed, that the waters flowing down Colorado River dropped in volume by 70 percent, and that fisheries in most coastal waters collapsed, and one begins to get a sense of the scope of these potential transformations.

Other market-based instruments that environmental economists use to posit economic solutions to environmental problems, such as subsidies, incentive structures, performance bonds, and deposit refund schemes, are also premised on assumptions about part–whole relationships in economic reality that are foundational to neoclassical economic theory. For those interested in a more detailed discussion of the entire range of market-based solutions developed by the environmental economists, a good place to begin is *Economics of the Environment*, edited by Robert Stavins.[10] This book contains a number of useful overview articles and a wealth of bibliographical material.

ENVIRONMENTAL POLICY AND COST-BENEFIT ANALYSIS

Another way to illustrate why the neoclassical economic paradigm is incapable of realistically assessing the costs of doing business in the global environment is to examine the methods used by environmental economists to value environmental externalities in cost-benefit analyses. Developing methods to conduct these analyses became a growth industry after Ronald Reagan issued Executive Order 12291 in 1981. The order required that cost-benefit analyses be performed for all environmental regulations in the United States with annual costs in excess of $100 million and stipulated that regulations could be implemented only if the benefits to society exceed the costs.

In theory, this concept seems straightforward and very appealing. Why should we spend money dealing with an environmental problem if the costs exceed the benefits? But when translated into the methods for evaluation used by environmental economists, "benefits to society" means the optimal social outcomes that result from the alleged operation of the natural laws of economics within closed market systems. And the "costs" against which those benefits are measured refers to other alleged manifestations of these nonexistent laws—the amounts that economic actors are willing to pay to protect or preserve environmental goods, services, and amenities, or the amounts they are willing to accept for the exploitation or consumption of them.

One dilemma faced by environmental economists in conducting cost-benefit analyses is that the only "real marginal value" they can confer on the environment is allegedly determined by the operation of the natural laws of economics within closed market systems. Because the vast majority of the damage occasioned by economic activities cannot be valued in these terms, these economists have developed two methods for valuing "nonmarket" resources—indirect methods designed to estimate the "use-value" of these resources (hedonic pricing and the travel cost method), and direct methods designed to estimate both "use-value" and "non-use value" of the resources (contingent valuation methods). From the perspective of environmental economists, the question of whether the results produced by these measures can be viewed as "empirically valid" is no trivial matter. If the results are invalid in these terms, they cannot be used to implement Pigouvian taxes or Coase liability rules, and there is no basis for believing that cost-benefit analyses based on general equilibrium theory are anything more than artifacts of a self-referential mathematical paradigm.[11]

In the hedonic pricing method, environmental economists seek to explain the value of a commodity as a bundle of valuable characteristics, one or more of which may be environmental. For example, the value of a house may depend on number of rooms, the size of the lawn, proximity to shopping, air quality levels, and distance from toxic-waste sites. A hedonic price for this house would be arrived at by estimating a hedonic price function, calculating prices for the environmental variables, and creating a demand curve that allows the variables to be given an approximate monetary value. The presumption is that the "real" marginal value of preserving air quality or eliminating toxic wastes can be reasonably inferred from the results of hedonic price methods and compared with other results based on these methods.[12]

The travel cost method is predicated on the assumption that the value a nonmarket resource, such as national parks and public forests, can be estimated based on the amount of money an economic actor would be willing to sacrifice to appreciate natural beauty. In this method, a statistical relationship between observed visits to nonmarket resources of natural beauty and the costs of visiting those resources is derived and used as a surrogate demand curve from which the consumer's surplus per visit-day can be measured. Although this may seem rather esoteric and strange, travel cost methods have been widely used in cost-benefit analyses of proposals in the United States and Britain to create or preserve publicly owned recreational areas.[13]

Contingent valuation methods have been increasingly used to assess the economic value of recreation, scenic beauty, air quality, water quality, species preservation, bequests to future generations and other nonmarket environmental resources. The methods are intended to assess the willingness to pay of economic actors to preserve natural environments (preservation or existence values), to maintain the option of using natural resources (option values), and to bequeath natural resources to future generations (bequest values).[14] Most contingent valuation surveys ask individuals for either their maximal willingness-to-pay for an increase in the quality of an environmental resource or their minimal willingness to accept some compensation to forgo such an increase.

The word *contingent* is used to highlight the fact that the values disclosed by the respondents are contingent upon the constructed or simulated market described in the survey. A description of this simulated market might include an estimate of the reduction in annual mortality risk that could accompany an improvement in air quality or the rate at which an endangered species could recover if afforded additional protection.[15] The questions take many forms, ranging from open-ended ("What is the maximum you would be willing to pay for —") to specific yes-no responses ("The government is considering a proposal X. Your per annum tax bill if this proposal passes would be Y. How would you vote?"). The surveys also usually solicit information about the socioeconomic characteristics of the respondents, their environmental attitudes and/or recreational behavior, and other variables that pertain to a willingness-to-pay function.

There is, however, no standard approach to the design of contingent valuation surveys, and the level of environmental quality is typically predetermined by a third party, such as a government that is seeking to achieve a particular level of air quality. The resulting methodological problems and uncertainties have raised large questions about the efficacy of the results, and there is a lively debate among mainstream economists about whether the measures should be used at all. In spite of these problems, however, contingent evaluations are now routinely used by government agencies and the World Bank, and the most recent bibliography of this research (1994) lists 1,600 studies and papers published in more than forty countries on a wide range of environmental goods and services.[16]

However, the primary reason why mainstream economists have questioned the validity of contingent valuation studies has nothing to do with flaws in designs, problems with statistically based probability sampling, or lack of controls.[17] According to most of these economists, the fundamental problem is that these studies are based on principles that are inconsistent with assumptions about the character of economic realty in neoclassical economics.[18] Objections that appeal to principles are often presumed to be self-evident, but uncovering what these economists are really saying requires some explanation.

As we have seen, an economic actor in general equilibrium theory is represented as an atomized entity moving like a point particle in a field of utility in accordance with the natural laws of economics. These laws allegedly manifest as economic decisions quantifiable in units of money, and the decisions are viewed as the interface with forces associated with the natural laws. But the subjective reality of the actors remains atomized, the laws allegedly act on this subjectivity from the outside, and the decisions are presumably unaffected by ideas, impulses, emotions, and desires that would make the outcomes indeterminate.

When, however, as the game theorists have discovered, the black box of human subjectivity is opened and economic decisions are examined based on individual criteria of rational decision making, there is an infinite regress into the complexities of language and culture. Because this clearly suggests that the natural laws of economics do not exist, what is the most effective way in which a mainstream economist might seek to obviate this conclusion? Simply put, he or she can claim that the laws manifest only in actual decisions made in closed market systems and therefore that the only data that can be used in the equations of general equilibrium theory are those that reflect these decisions. Mainstream economists do not, of course, frame their objections to the use of contingent valuation methods in these terms. On careful examination, however, this is essentially what they are saying.

Interestingly, a number of studies done by mainstream economists on the manner in which people make decisions in various economic contents have shown that there are often no discernible regularities in the process.

For example, one study suggested that "for many purchases a decision process never exists, not even for first purchase,"[19] and another on economic behavior in grocery stores found that shoppers construct a "choice heuristic on the spot about 25% of the time."[20] What these and other studies have revealed is something that most of us intuitively know—people often make complex consumer choices based on irrational impulses that they rationalize after the fact by making up reasons why a purchase was needed or necessary.

For the sake of argument, however, let us assume that the natural laws of economics actually exist and that contingent valuation studies are capable of fully revealing maximal social outcomes of environmental policy decisions. Are we then to believe, as one such study showed, that reductions in chemical contaminants in drinking water was not important in economic terms because the value of a statistical life associated with a reduction in risk of death in thirty years was only $181,000?[21] Is $26 a measure of the real marginal costs of pollution because this is the average price that a household is willing to pay annually for a 10 percent improvement of visibility in eastern U.S. cities?[22] Is the value of whooping cranes the $22 per year average that one set of households was willing to pay to preserve this species[23] and that of the bald eagle the $11 per year average that another set of households would spend to preserve this apparently less valuable species?[24] The point here is obvious, and I will not belabor it. These values are predicated on assumptions about part–whole relationships in economic reality that completely misrepresent and distort what should and must be the ultimate value of achieving the goal of a sustainable global environment.

DEVELOPMENTAL ECONOMICS

Many environmental economists work in the field of development economics, formally defined as "the study of economic transformations of developing countries."[25] The origins of development economics can be traced to the Marshall Plan, which financed the reconstruction of infrastructures and production capacities destroyed during World War II and demonstrated that large capital investment could lead to rapid economic development. The notion that deficiency in capital is the fundamental cause of underdevelopment was the basic principle underlying the creation of the Bretton Woods institutions, the World Bank and the International Monetary Fund, and bilateral foreign aid programs. Until roughly 1970, international financial institutions sponsored large development projects in transport and energy, and decisions about whether to fund such projects were almost invariably based on studies predicated on general equilibrium theory. Consequently, those who administered these programs typically admonished developing countries to "get the prices right" by allowing the invisible hand to operate with minimal constraints and making policy decisions that would remove existing constraints.[26]

The presumption that the natural laws of economics are universal and apply equally well to all emerging market systems resulted in a situation where institutional differences in developing economies, as well as unique cultural and historical factors, were largely ignored. The economic planners assumed that the market mechanisms that govern the interaction between resources, preferences, and technology would lead to Pareto-efficient outcomes and tended to view any other considerations as largely irrelevant. When market failures occurred, as they did with some frequency, the economists typically cited "outside" intervention by government as the cause of the failures. All that was required to prevent such failures, said most mainstream economists, was to provide information about the consequences of different policies and Coasian rationality would ensure that the parties would arrive at an efficient solution.

From the beginning of the Reagan-Thatcher era to the present, the prescription for economic development in poorer countries has been consistently based on predictions and analyses derived from neoclassical economic theory. The prescription says, in essence, that trade liberalization will induce development, yield economies of scale, and make industries more internally competitive if governments do not disrupt the lawful dynamics of market processes.[27] Gross national product and gross domestic product have been generally viewed as the best proxies for all aspects of developing economies, and much of the work of the development economists has focused on evaluating projects based on cost-benefit analysis. Over the last decade, these economists have also articulated new models for economic growth based on income distribution and development, coordination failures, and incomplete information.

During the economic recession of the 1980s, previously optimistic forecasts about the state of the global economy were suddenly in need of revision. Average growth rates in developing economies either fell or became stagnant, and the average developing country was obliged to use resources greater than its entire gross domestic product to service foreign debts.

After two thirds of these countries failed to achieve a balance surplus capable of servicing their debts, the crisis came to a head when Mexico, Brazil, and Turkey defaulted on their debt-service obligations. Because commercial banks in developing countries were unwilling to extend additional loans to developing countries, they became utterly dependent on the IMF and World Bank for economic survival. These institutions used this as an opportunity to impose conditions for additional loans that were consistent with assumptions about the character of economic reality in the neoclassical economic paradigm.

During the 1990s, development economists at the IMF and World Bank placed a great deal of emphasis on government failures and on "getting the prices right" via stabilization, liberalization, deregulation, and privatization.[28] The result was that much of the developing world reduced trade and investment barriers, dismantled domestic price controls in agriculture and industry, and reduced fiscal deficits. The success stories during this period were the newly developing economies in East Asia. The proportion of the population living in absolute poverty in this region fell from 60 percent in 1975 to 20 percent in 1995, life expectancy increased by nine years, education levels rose 60 percent or more, and infant mortality fell from seventy-three to thirty-five per thousand births.[29] But the environmental costs associated with these successes were considerable. The growth of the global economy during the 1990s resulted in large-scale damage to the environment that was unprecedented, and efforts to curb this destruction were in most cases frustrated or undermined by assumptions about economic reality in mainstream economics.

In East Asia, the environmental damage occasioned by economic growth during the 1990s, measured in terms of pollution, congestion, deforestation, and loss of biodiversity, was greater than in any other part of the world. Approximately 20 percent of the arable land was dramatically degraded by waterlogging, erosion, and overgrazing, and biodiversity in 50 percent to 75 percent of coastlines and protected marine areas was greatly reduced. Vast increases in pollution and the use of new fishing techniques destroyed coral reefs throughout this region, and levels of carbon dioxide in countries that embarked on rapid economic growth a decade earlier (China, Malaysia, and Thailand) tripled.[30] But the problem here and elsewhere in the developing world was not rapid economic growth per se. It was a program for developing the global economy predicated on assumptions about conditions for economic growth in the neoclassical economic paradigm.

There are, however, a small but growing number of development economists who have openly challenged these assumptions based on careful studies of market failures throughout the developing world. Some of these scholars have shown that market failures in developing countries often occur in the absence of government failures,[31] that government plays a critical role in the effective management of developing economies,[32] and that only capable and efficient governments can manage successful reforms.[33] Others have convincingly argued that the sources of poverty must be understood in terms of a multiplicity of factors in cultural and historical terms[34] and that GNP and GDP are very poor measures of general welfare in developing economies.[35] Some of these individuals have also claimed that trickle-down economics must be supplemented by policies that lessen sharp disparities in income and assets, enhance employment opportunities, and provide safety nets for the most vulnerable members of society.[36] Many, if not most, of these economists have also openly rejected general equilibrium theory and argue that predictions based on this theory are nothing more than probability distributions derived from an analysis of stochastic processes that affect the relevant variables.[37]

The development economists who embrace these unorthodox views, most of whom also identify themselves as environmental economists, are very much aware of the adverse environmental impacts of global economic activities. They have not, however, been able to develop standard measures for evaluating the sustainability of a country's environmental policies that would allow for more systematic consideration of the potential environmental damage that might be caused by large-scale development projects. It remains to be seen whether these scholars will have any discernible influence on policy decisions that shape global economic development. At the moment, however, most of the literature in development economics continues to be based on the neoclassical growth model on which decision makers in government and international financial institutions rely almost exclusively.[38]

It would be absurd to argue that the environmental economists are not committed to the resolution of the environmental crisis or that they fail to understand the enormity of this crisis. In fact, much of their research has contributed to an improved understanding of the potential economic impacts of proposed solutions to environmental problems and the manner in which these solutions can be implemented in cost-effective ways. It would also be absurd to claim that there is anything wrong with attempts to assess economic impacts of environmental policies or to develop economic solutions to environmental problems that have minimal impacts on market economies.

On the other hand, metaphysically based assumptions about the character of economic reality in the neoclassical economic paradigm are such that there is no basis for realistically accounting for the costs of doing business in the global environment. If environmental resources were unlimited, environmental sinks inexhaustible, and environmental impacts of global economic activities generally benign, the "usefulness" of neoclassical economic theory as a heuristic in managing market economies could be regarded as sufficient justification for the widespread application of this theory. But because none of these conditions apply, the theory can no longer be regarded as useful even in utterly pragmatic, utilitarian terms because it fails to meet what must now be considered the fundamental criterion for the usefulness of any economic theory—the extent to which the theory allows us to coordinate experience with economic reality in ways that can achieve the goal of a sustainable global environment.

MENDING THE CLOTHES OF THE EMPEROR

As we saw earlier, a number of Nobel laureates in economics are very much aware that assumptions about the character of economic reality in the neoclassical economic paradigm are fundamentally flawed. It is also significant that those who have made the most convincing case that these assumptions cannot be viewed as scientific have consistently been trained economists. For example, Alfred Eichner in *Why Economics Is Not Yet a Science* first provides a devastating critique of the many ways in which mainstream economists fail to adhere to the methods and procedures of science and then offers the following commentary on the discipline of economics as a social system:

> The refusal to abandon the myth of the market as a self-regulating system is not the result of a conspiracy on the part of the "establishment" in economics. It is not even a choice that any individual economist is necessarily aware of making. Rather it is the way economics operates as a social system—including the way new members of the establishment are selected—retaining its place within the larger society by perpetuating a set of ideas which have been found useful by that society, however dysfunctional the same set of ideas may be from a scientific under-

standing of how the economic system works. In other words, economics is unwilling to adhere to the epistemological principles which distinguish scientific from other types of intellectual activity because this might jeopardize the position of economists within the larger society as the defender of the dominant faith. This situation in which economists find themselves is therefore not unlike that of many natural scientists who, when faced with mounting evidence in support of first, the Copernican theory of the universe and then, later, the Darwinian theory of evolution, had to decide whether undermining the revelatory basis of Judeo-Christian ethics was not too great a price to pay for being able to reveal the truth.[39]

Disclosing the "revelatory basis" of neoclassical economic theory is not, as we have seen, terribly difficult. The French moral philosophers who first posited the existence of the natural laws of economics presumed that these laws, like the laws of nature, were created by the Judeo-Christian God. The creators of classical economists (Smith, Ricardo, and Malthus) appealed to this conception of natural law to legitimate the real or actual existence of the invisible hand. But they did so within the context of a mechanistic Newtonian worldview that did not require the presence of the willful and mindful agency of God. They concluded, therefore, that both the laws of physics and the natural laws of economics originated in the disembodied mind of a Deistic God who withdrew from the universe following the first moment of creation.

The presence of this deity was further disguised after the creators of neoclassical economics successfully promulgated the fiction that they had transformed economics into a rigorously scientific discipline with the use of higher mathematics. The presumption that mainstream economics is a purely secular enterprise was also grandly reinforced by subsequent generations of economists who refined and extended general equilibrium theory with the use of increasingly more sophisticated mathematical devices and techniques. This has resulted, as Nobel Prize-winning economist Robert Solow describes it, in a very strange situation:

> My impression is that the best and the brightest in the profession proceed as if economics is the physics of society. There is a single universal model of the world. It only needs to be applied. You could drop a modern economist from a time machine . . . at any time in any place, along with his or her personal computer; he or she could set up business with-

out even bothering to ask what time and which place. In a little while, the up-to-date economist will have maximized a familiar looking present-value integral, make a few familiar log-linear approximations, and run the obligatory regression. The familiar coefficients will be poorly determined, but about one-twentieth of them will be significant at the 5 per cent level, and the other nineteen did not have to be published. With a little judicious selection here and there, it will turn out that the data are just barely consistent with your thesis advisor's hypothesis that money is neutral (or non-neutral, take your choice) everywhere and always, module an information asymmetry, any old asymmetry, don't worry, you'll think of one.[40]

In the next chapter, we will briefly consider some efforts by a group of diverse scholars, known as ecological economists, to enlarge the framework of neoclassical economic theory to include means and methods of accounting for the damage done to the environment by economic activities. As noted earlier, the work of the ecological economists is considered unorthodox from the perspective of most mainstream economists because it is not consistent with assumptions about economic reality in neoclassical economics. The views and opinions of a few ecological ecologists, such as Nicholas Georgescu-Roegen and Herman Daly, are routinely mentioned and rather summarily dismissed in the scholarship of the environmental economists. And some environmental economists are sufficiently unorthodox in orientation to be included on occasion in the roster of ecological economists. There is, however, very little dialogue between the two groups, and the influence of the environmental economists on economic planners and decision makers in both government and business dwarfs that of the ecological ecologists.

If the framework of neoclassical economic theory could be enlarged in ways that would allow us to posit effective economic solutions to the environmental crisis, the prospects of resolving this crisis in a timely fashion would be greatly improved. After all, there have been numerous occasions in the history of thought when proposed revisions of theoretical paradigms that were initially perceived as unorthodox became orthodox because they enhanced our ability to coordinate a greater range of experience with some aspect of reality. Unfortunately, for reasons we will now more carefully examine, that will not be the case here.

CHAPTER 6

SCHISMS, HERESIES, AND KEEPING THE FAITH

Ecological Economics

> In the end, our society will be defined not only by what we create, but by what we refuse to destroy.
>
> —John C. Sawhill

The ecological economists have made numerous attempts to incorporate scientifically valid measures of the damage done to the ecosystem by economic activities into the framework of neoclassical economics. Scholarship in this discipline is also replete with carefully developed and documented reasons why neoclassical economic theory fails to account for the costs of doing business in the global environment. The mistake, if one can call it that, made by the ecological economists is the presumption that assumptions about part–whole relationships implicit in the mathematical framework of neoclassical economic theory can be revised.

Given the enormous extent to which assumptions about economic reality in this theory contribute to the crisis in the global environment and frustrate its resolution, there is obviously nothing unreasonable about this presumption. But the fact that there has been virtually no dialogue between ecological economists and mainstream economists clearly indicates that the former is saying something that the latter simply does wish to entertain. Part of what mainstream economists clearly do not wish to entertain is the prospect, implicit in the work of the ecological ecologists, that the emperor is not clothed in the raiment of scientific knowledge. There is, however, a much more fundamental reason why neoclassical economists have been unwilling to engage in this dialogue.

Because ecological economists are typically acquainted with research in environmental science, they know that assumptions about part– whole relationships in neoclassical economics are anything but sacrosanct. However, the presumption that mainstream economists would be willing to revise these assumptions was unrealistic because they are foundational to the mathematical theories used by these economists and the theories make no sense in their absence. As I hope to demonstrate, any proposed economic solutions to environmental problems that require even a slight modification of these assumptions threatens to undermine the efficacy of neoclassical economic theory because the validity of this theory is entirely dependent on the absolute validity of the assumptions.

Even a slight change in the assumptions would force mainstream economists to redefine initial conditions in the equations of neoclassical economics in ways that would require the introduction of new sets of complex variables. This would not only play havoc with the neat symmetry in these equations between consumption and production and produce results that describe very different outcomes, but it would also effectively undermine the presumption that the economic process exists in a separate and distinct domain of reality in which decisions of economic actors are a function of lawful or lawlike mechanisms that operate only within this domain.

In order to enlarge the framework of neoclassical economic theory in ways advocated by the ecological economists, mainstream economists would not only be obliged to admit that assumptions about parts and wholes in that theory are arbitrarily conceived constructs that do not describe the real of actual character of the economic process, but they would also be forced to concede that these assumptions preclude the prospect that their mathematical theories can realistically account for the costs of doing business in the global environment. Because this would amount to an open admission that neoclassical economic theory is merely a heuristic that describes tendencies-to-occur in market systems with well-developed institutional practices and frameworks, mainstream economists have been understandably reluctant to seriously consider the proposals of the ecological economists.

A BRIEF HISTORY OF ECOLOGICAL ECONOMICS

Many ecological economists base their understanding of the biophysical limits of economic growth on the first and second law of thermodynamics. The first law states that energy is conserved and cannot be created or destroyed, and the second that low-entropy matter-energy in a closed system is always transformed into high-entropy matter-energy. Entropy in physics is essentially a measure of disorder in a system—the higher the entropy, the greater the disorder. From the perspective of thermodynamics, an economic system converts matter-energy from a state of low entropy to a state of high entropy and matter-energy exists in two forms—available or free and unavailable or bound.

For example, the chemical energy in a piece of coal, which is low in entropy, is viewed as free, and the heat energy in waters of the oceans, which is high in entropy, is viewed as bound. Because the amount of bound matter-energy in a closed system must continually increase, the only way to lower entropy in such a system is to introduce matter-energy from outside. After this matter-energy is introduced into the system, however, the price paid for consuming what might initially appear to be a free lunch is an overall increase in the level of entropy.

Virtually every object with economic value has a highly ordered structure, and the matter-energy required to manufacture these objects inevitably increases the overall level of entropy in the global ecosystem. For example, an automobile is vastly more ordered than a lump of iron ore, and the matter-energy required to transform raw materials into an automobile is enormous. Manufacturing processes also produce waste, pollution, and greenhouse gases, and these by-products massively contribute to the overall level of disorder in the ecosystem. Even recycled products require energy inputs that increase entropy levels and convert free energy to bound energy. As Erwin Schrödinger put it, the life of all organisms, including our own, is necessarily an entropic process: "The device by which an organism maintains itself stationary at a fairly high level of orderliness (= a fairly low level of entropy) really exists in continually sucking orderliness from its environment."[1]

When the environmental movement emerged as a potent political force during the petroleum shortage in the 1970s, ecologist Howard Odum developed a systematic model based on energy flows to better understand the impact of human activity on the natural environment. He pointed out that wherever a flow of capital exists, there must be an energy flow in the opposite direction. Odum also noted that while a market system in neoclassical economics is represented as a closed loop with no inputs or outputs, low-entropy energy inputs always enter real or actual economic systems and are translated into high-entropy energy outputs. He also convincingly argued that other essential energy flows, such as solar, water, and wind, are misused because they are not represented in the flow of capital.

The work of economists Nicholas Georgescu-Roegen and Herman Daly was also seminally important in the development of ecological economics. In *The Entropy Law and the Economic Process* (1971), Georgescu-Roegen demonstrated that the mathematical analysis of production in neoclassical economics is badly flawed because it fails to incorporate the laws of thermodynamics. In his view, an economy must be viewed in thermodynamic terms as a unidirectional flow in which inputs of low-entropy matter and energy are used to produce two kinds of outputs—goods and services and high entropy waste and degraded matter. Because neoclassical economic theory assigns value only to the first output and completely ignores the costs associated with the second in environmental terms, Georgescu-Roegen attempted to refashion this theory to include these costs.

"Man's natural dowry," wrote Georgescu-Roegen, "consists of two essentially distinct elements: 1) the stock of low-entropy on or within the globe; and 2) the flow of solar energy." And we have not, in his view, used these resources well:

> If we abstract from other causes that may knell the death bell of the human species, it is clear that natural resources represent the limitative factor as concerns the life span of that species. Man's existence is now irrevocably tied to the use of exosomatic instruments and hence to the use of natural resources just as it is tied to the use of his lungs and of air in breathing, for example. We need no elaborated argument to see that the maximum of life quantity requires the minimal rate of natural resource depletion. By using these resources too quickly, man throws away that part of the solar energy that will still be reaching the earth after he has departed. And everything he has done during the last two hundred years or so puts him in the position of a fantastic spendthrift. There can be no doubt about it: any use of the natural resources for the satisfaction of nonvital human needs means a smaller quantity of life in the future.[2]

The writings of Georgescu-Roegen are well known and appreciated by ecological economists, but there are, to my knowledge, no discussions of his work in standard textbooks on mainstream economics. The obvious reason for this omission is that Georgescu-Roegen challenged three fundamental assumptions upon which the mathematical formalism of neoclassical economic theory is predicated: (1) market systems are closed; (2) nonmarket environmental resources must be viewed as existing outside of the market systems and treated as externalities; and (3) there are no limits on the growth and expansion of market economies.

Numerous writers in other fields, such as science and engineering, have wondered why the work of Georgescu-Roegen is not mentioned in the scholarship of mainstream economists and why none of these economists have even bothered to write a refutation of his positions. The best explanation for the studied unwillingness of neoclassical to entertain and systematically refute these positions in a reasoned and informed argument is that this exercise would require a defense of the assumptions upon which neoclassical economics is based from a scientific point of view. Consequently, neoclassical economists have chosen to either completely ignore the work of Georgescu-Roegen or to dismiss it with the lame comment that it is "not really economics."

In *Steady State Economics* (1977) Herman Daly, who was once a student of Georgescu-Roegen's at Vanderbilt University, criticized the failure of mainstream economics to account for the throughput of low-entropy natural resources. He also argued that the preoccupation with money flows, or with movement of quantities of money over periods of time, serves to perpetuate the fiction that perpetual economic growth is possible and morally desirable. One solution to this problem, says Daly, is to use constraints associated with the second law of thermodynamics to formulate policies for long-term sustainability, such as taxes on energy and virgin resources. He claims that such policies would increase social awareness of ecological limits and promote the realization that "physical flows of production and consumption must be minimized subject to some desirable population and standard of living."[3]

In Daly's view, the three basic goals of an economic system should be efficient allocation, equitable distribution, and sustainable scale. The first two goals are included in mainstream economics, and specific public policies have been formulated to realize them. But scale is not included and, consequently, there are no policy instruments in mainstream economics that deal with scale. Daly defines scale as the total physical volume of low-entropy raw materials that move through the open subsystem of an economy and back into the finite and nongrowing global environment as high-entropy wastes.[4]

Because the scale of the global economy has grown dangerously large relative to the fixed size of the ecosystem, this economy is sustainable, says

Daly, only if it does not erode the carrying capacity of the ecosystem. Consequently, he is critical of his fellow economists for assuming that environmental resources and sinks are infinite relative to the scale of the economy and that decisions about allocation merely move natural resources between alternative uses. The unfortunate result, says Daly, is that scale is not viewed as a constraint and economic policies encourage growth that cannot be sustained by the ecosystem.

Daly also notes that when neoclassical economists subsume scale under allocation, they assume that efficient allocation of resources will be achieved when prices are right. If production facilities increase in scale, the neoclassical economists claim that this merely reflects the judgment of the market that the marginal benefits of scale exceed the marginal costs to the environment. Even when these judgments are influenced by considerations of costs to the external environment, neoclassical economists contend that the right prices will internalize these costs. The result, says Daly, is that the ecosystem is excluded from the world of commodities where value is measured by market prices.

The fundamental problem is that there is no basis in neoclassical market price mechanisms, which are tied to the preferences of individual consumers, to account for scale. "Distribution and scale," writes Daly, "involve relationships with the poor, the future, and other species that are fundamentally social in nature rather than individual." Pretending that these social choices exist on the same plane as the choice between chewing gum and a candy bar seems, he continues, "to be dominant in economies today and is part of the retrograde reduction of all ethical choice to the level of personal tastes weighted by income."[5] Given that Daly privileges market mechanisms, one might suppose that his views would be welcomed by mainstream economics. This is not, however, the case because his scientifically valid claim that economic systems are open to and interactive with the global environment challenges the assumption that markets are closed.

The attempt by ecological economist Robert Costanza in 1980 to posit a biophysical basis for value illustrates some of the difficulties of wedding quantifiable physical processes to price mechanisms in neoclassical economics. Based on the assumption that input-output techniques allow economic inputs to be reduced to primary factors and that energy is the ultimate input,[6] Costanza begins his analysis with the conventional categories of capital, labor, natural resources, and government. He then extends the analysis to convert labor and government services to energy equivalents based on units of solar energy, and claims that a statistical analysis of his model reveals that inputs of energy values are closely related to outputs of monetary values.

One problem with Costanza's energy theory of value, or any other scheme that attempts to posit market prices for biophysical variables in neoclassical economics, is that the relative strength of closed market systems is measured in terms of "differences" in primary factors contributing to costs of production. When Costanza reduces all of these factors to inputs of energy, his claim that there is a constant relationship between units of energy and output value becomes a mere tautology. In eliminating differences in primary factors contributing to costs of production, such as fossil fuels, nuclear energy, materials, labor, and so on, he erases one of the bases upon which neoclassical economists assess the relative strengths of competing economies. If, however, other primary factors are included in a biophysical model of production, there is another problem. The market value of any resulting products in neoclassical economic theory is a function of consumer choice, and there are very few consumers who are capable of assessing environmental costs of goods and commodities based on the biophysical bases of their production.

ECOLOGICAL ECONOMICS AND GLOBALIZATION

In the current era of globalization, ecological economists have become increasingly concerned with the "tragedy of the commons," a dilemma first described by American biologist Garrett Hardin.[7] A commons, says Hardin, is any area where property-rights regimes do not apply and users have open access to its exploitation. He uses the example of a common grazing land where each cattle owner continues to enlarge his or her herd as long as doing so increases his income. Because each owner derives all the economic benefits from the sale of his cattle, and because the loss of grazing resources consumed by his or her cattle is borne by all the other owners, the tragedy is that all owners will increase the numbers in their herds to the point at which the grazing capacity of the land is utterly depleted or destroyed.

Economist H. S. Gordon came to very similar conclusion in an earlier study of fisheries. As long as fisherman can earn a profit, they continue to catch fish to the point at which overfishing occurs. If a particular species of fish is valuable, which often correlates with scarcity, fisherman tend to develop more technologically efficient means of catching these fish and this often threatens this species with extinction.[8] The problem here is that exploiters of common resources have little incentive to conserve them and a great deal of incentive to recklessly exploit them before others can do so, and this applies to the global commons of oceans, frozen poles, forests, and the entire genetic reserve. As mathematician and ecological modeler Colin Clark notes, "The tragedy of the commons constitutes perhaps the most powerful bias against sustainable development. As population and technology expand, the implications of our inability to solve the problem spread from local to global scales."[9]

Another related problem that mainstream economics fails to address, as a number of ecological economists have pointed out, is "intergenerational fairness." The usual way that neoclassical economists address this problem is by discounting benefits to future generations. Discounting is premised on the belief that because life is uncertain and the future is unpredictable, a benefit or loss in the present is more important than in the future. One problem with discounting is that it reflects the value that the present generation places on the natural environment without consulting future generations. Another is that the near future is assumed to have more worth than the distant future and at some point in the future that worth becomes negligible.

Neoclassical economists normally discount the future value of environmental assets by the present rate of interest, a practice that tends to favor wholesale exploitation of natural resources. For example, if the discount rate is 5 percent, sixty-one cents at compound interest would be worth a dollar in ten years, and sixty-one cents becomes the present value factor for the ten-year period. If the discount rate is higher and the time horizon is longer, the present value factor typically becomes lower. Higher discount rates may discourage development projects with large capital requirements, such as dams, and preserve large areas in their existing state. The usual result, however, is that the economic desires of those in the present are satisfied at the great expense of future generations.

Ecological economists Richard Norgaard and Richard Howard have made a convincing case that the use of traditional discount rates to balance present and future values is fundamentally flawed because discounting based on current commercial interest rates massively compromises the interests of future generations. If, for example, the commercial interest rate is 6 percent, costs and benefits will be discounted by a factor of four in twenty-five years and by a factor of eighteen in fifty years. Because the use of current interest rates assigns virtually all rights over resources to the current generation, Norgaard and Howard argue that discounting schemes should be based on the assumption that future generations have equal rights over resource allocation. But valuing these resources from the perspective of future generations would require a much improved understanding of long-term resource allocation and associated environmental impacts.[10]

ECOLOGICAL ECONOMICS AND NATIONAL ACCOUNTS

Another way in which ecological economists have attempted to revise assumptions in mainstream economics is to make substantive changes in the system of national accounts. Because the accounts do not reflect the costs of pollution and general environmental degradation, and because they also ignore deterioration of the environmental resource base, they paint a very distorted picture of the prospect of sustainable economic growth. The first comprehensive case for developing new accounting techniques was in the World Bank report *Environmental Accounting for Sustainable Development* (1989). The authors of the original articles in this report argued that a measure of sustainable income, which is not included in standard GDP measures, is badly needed. They noted that GDP not only fails to distinguish between income derived from production and income derived from depleting natural assets, such as forests, soils, and mineral reserves, but it also does not account for defensive expenditures, such as the costs of cleaning up oil spills or dealing with radioactive wastes.

The contributors to the report endorsed a systematic approach to these problems and offered methods of subtracting the value of natural resource depreciation and defensive expenditures from standard measures of GDP. However, they did not resolve the question of how to identify and assign value to these factors or what techniques should be used to adjust GNP figures. In the debate that followed, some ecological economists argued that GDP is inherently flawed and that a more ecologically based measure should be used, whereas others championed a pluralistic approach in which no single measure would dominate.

Richard Norgaard, one of the leading exponents of pluralism in national accounts, traces many environmental and resource problems to inconsistencies in the logic of GDP accounting and in mainstream economic theory.[11] In his view, there is no theoretical justification for creating a modified GDP that would compete with standard GNP for the attention of policymakers. The more viable approach, says Norgaard, is to abandon any single standardized system of accounts and seek to measure multiple and different dimensions of economic and ecological reality.

Norgaard also notes that market prices reflect subjective judgments by resource allocators about the existence of scarcity as opposed to real or actual resource scarcity.[12] But because the allocators presume that these prices accurately reflect resource scarcity, they regard any modification in these prices as the wrongful imposition of a value judgment based on their own value judgment that consumption today should take precedence over sustainability. The large irony here, says Norgaard, is that this "nonmarket variable" then becomes embodied in both market structures and discount rates.

Herman Daly and John Cobb have developed an alternative to GNP, the "Index of Sustainable Economic Welfare," for the United States that essentially divides national income accounts into sectors and imposes standards of sustainability, as well as equity, on these sectors.[13] When Daly and Cobb used their index to adjust GNP in the United States during the period 1945–1980, the surprising result was that net income has been virtually flat over this twenty-five year period. In another study of the U.S. economy based on the index from 1951 to 1990, a period during which per-capita GNP more than doubled, the ISEW grew less than 20 percent and even declined slightly between 1980 and 1990. If these results are reasonably accurate, the conclusion is rather devastating—all apparent economic growth in the U.S. economy from 1951 to 1990 is a delusion that resulted from a failure to account for losses in natural capital.

Similarly, Robert Repetto and his associates at the World Resources Institute have done a number of natural resource accounting studies on developing nations such as Indonesia, the Philippines, and Costa Rica.[14] These studies show that growth trends in GNP massively distort the health of economies in these developing nations because they do not account for such factors as petroleum depletion, forest loss, and soil erosion. When net investment was adjusted to account for these factors, the results showed that it was negative during a period when gross investment by standard GDP measures was very high and rising. And when ecological economist Kirk Hamilton factored in resource depletion and environmental damage to calculate net savings in national economies, he arrived at the disturbing conclusion that these savings in most of the developing world have been negative since the mid-1970s.[15]

Mark Sagoff, a scholar in public policy, makes a convincing case that neoclassical market valuation is simply not capable of effectively assessing environmental impacts. As we have seen, market value in mainstream economics is based on a vague something that is not subject to direct observation or measurement—individual utility or individual happiness and well-being. Sagoff argues that even if individuals could be enticed into placing a marginal money valuation on an environmental "amenity," they might be happier if they paid this amount in exchange for the opportunity to destroy the amenity. He also cites the results of a study in Wyoming in which participants refused to place a dollar evaluation on the environment.[16]

Ecological economists Silvio Funtowicz and Jerome Ravetz argue that market valuation in mainstream economics is not an appropriate tool for dealing with problems in complex ecosystems or with the ethical concerns that are at the center of environmental policy issues.[17] In their view, the essential problem with these evaluations is the assumption that environmental considerations can be "scientifically" measured as money equivalents. If this is not the case, as they reasonably argue, then any numerically precise measure of GNP or GDP can never reflect the costs of doing business in the global environment.

Ecological economist Bruce Hannon has taken a different approach. Rather than revise standard GNP measures, he proposes that we develop a contrasting measure of the health of the ecosystem—the gross ecosystem product, or GEP.[18] He argues that the GEP would recognize limits to growth and would compete with the GNP by showing that increased economic output tends, almost invariably, to lower the GEP. If the proposed GEP existed, and if economic planners were committed to making GEP and GNP more compatible, this could, says Hannon, result in more efficient production techniques and promote the recognition that there are upper limits to economic growth.

Rather predictably, however, mainstream economists have not welcomed this ecological approach. The problem is not merely that there is no viable basis in the neoclassical economic paradigm to establish market prices for environmental resources that are commensurate with their actual value in the real economy of the global environment. It is also that any successful attempt to value the resources in these terms would require the introduction of a new set of variables that would falsify the assumption that markets tend toward a state of equilibrium.

The ecological economists have been successful in convincing some leaders in other nations that GNP is not necessarily the best indicator of human satisfaction and that accounting for the depreciation of national capital is a necessary part of the economic process. Norway has developed a system for calculating balances for mineral and living resources, France is using a system of accounts that attempts to track the status of all resources influenced by human activity, and the Netherlands has a system that includes environmental damage and the costs for repairing this damage. The governments of these nations use this information to assess environmental impacts of economic activities and to make policy decisions. However, these studies are often ignored by their own economists and almost completely ignored by economists who assess the relative "health" of their national economies.

In recent years, the discipline of ecological economists has been increasingly more fragmented in a variety of different, often contradictory, approaches and there is no single economic paradigm that encompasses these approaches.[19] On one side there are those who take the more traditional approach and argue that ecological criteria for sustainability should serve as the basis for making policy recommendations. On the other side there are those who are attempting to redefine the discipline as a science of social change that is committed to developing institutional frameworks that feature sustainable production and consumption patterns.[20] This inability to evolve a set of assumptions that could serve as the basis for a commonly shared economic paradigm also explains why many ecological ecologists have migrated toward solutions derived from more humanistic disciplines in the social sciences, such as public policy, psychology, and sociology.

TOWARD A NEW THEORY OF ECONOMICS

What this brief overview of ecological economics illustrates is that any attempt to incorporate costs associated with real or actual damage to the ecosystem within the framework of neoclassical economics, however well intentioned, is doomed to failure. Once again, this approach to solving the environmental crisis simply will not work because the relationship between parts (economic actors and firms) and wholes (market systems) in mainstream economics is categorically different from and wholly incompatible with the actual dynamics of the relationship between parts (organisms) and whole (ecosystem) in physical reality.

Entropy is a lawful dynamic of the relationship between parts and wholes in the ecosystem, but it does not exist in the relationship between parts and wholes in the virtual reality of mainstream economics. Consequently, there is no quantitative basis for linking the amount of individual utility, or pleasure, enjoyed by parts (economic actors) to the amount of low entropy they consume and to the impacts of this consumption on the whole (global increases in entropy). Similarly, there is no unique relationship between discount rates and environmental degradation because there is no real or actual linkage between the maximal utility or pleasure of parts (economic actors) and the state of the whole (ecosystem). This leads to a conclusion that carries large implications for our future efforts to resolve the ecological crisis in economic terms—*markets and price mechanisms in neoclassical economics are such that they cannot create appropriate incentive structures to achieve the goal of a sustainable global environment.*

The disjunction between part–whole relationships in mainstream economics and the actual dynamics of part–whole relationships from the perspective of environmental science also results in major differences in the manner in which ecological resources are valued. The concept of value in the relationship between parts (economic actors) and whole (market systems) is immeasurable, subjective, and allegedly revealed in its money equivalent by pricing mechanisms associated with the operation of the immeasurable utility function in the equations of neoclassical economic theory. But the concept of value in the relationship between parts (organisms) and whole (global ecosystem or biosphere) in environmental science is measurable, objective, and associated with the relative stability of complex interactive ecosystems that have no monetary value.

These disparate conceptions of part–whole relationships also result in utterly different views of the state or condition that is most conducive to an optimal relationship between parts and wholes. The optimal state or condition of the whole (market system) in mainstream economics results from maximization of utility, or economic satisfaction or well-being, by the parts (economic actors). But from the perspective of environmental science, the optimal state or condition in the whole (global environment or biosphere) is sustainability, and the well-being of all parts, including human beings, is ultimately dependent on whether this state or conditions exists. Although mainstream economists assume that the whole (market system) can perpetually expand because there are no limits on resources in the external environment, environmental scientists rightly argue that market systems are open to the whole (ecosystem) and cannot perpetually expand because environmental resources are limited.

When global economic planners are asked to confer a monetary value

145

on natural resources for purposes of discounting for future generations, they are normally quick to point out that scientific predictions about the future state of the environment are plagued with uncertainties. They typically view these uncertainties as grounds for dismissing the predictions or as potential liabilities that members of future generations will have the technical expertise to overcome. One irony here is that the future of economic systems is plagued with uncertainties that are not reflected in the theories used by the neoclassical economists. Another is that whereas the scientists are obliged by the scientific method to develop theories that allow for predictions that are potentially falsifiable, the economists use theories that do not and cannot meet these standards.

Let us also keep in mind that when scientists talk about degrees of uncertainty in predicting the future of the global environment, they are dealing in statistical probabilities that describe a range of possibilities that are rather uniformly disastrous for the future of our species. The point in time where the predicted impacts will begin to massively threaten this future is not several generations removed—it is roughly when children who are now at the age of five reach adulthood. If we are to deal properly with these uncertainties in environmental planning, we must practice what Charles Perrins terms "the precautionary principle":

> The class of problems for which the precautionary principle is advocated as an alternative to conventional decision-making models is that for which the level of uncertainty and the potential costs of current activities are both high. Global warming is one example. . . . The optimal policy is then the one that minimizes the maximum environmental costs over variation in the unobserved part of the history of the system.[21]

One great advantage of observing the precautionary principle in global economic planning is that it would allow more time for scientists to assess present environmental impacts and to predict future impacts. The discipline of environmental science is fairly new, and advances in knowledge in this discipline over the last two decades have been staggering. Over the next decade it is not unrealistic to assume that better observational techniques, enhanced understanding of the physics of nonlinear systems, and improved computer models will result in more accurate assessments of the present and future state of the global environment. Minimizing negative environmental impacts of global economic activities over this ten-year period is not a great price to pay in exchange for the opportunity to acquire knowledge that could allow our children and grandchildren to live out their lives on a hospitable planet. But economic planners will not be able to adhere to the precautionary principle if they continue to base their decisions on assumptions about economic reality in mainstream economics.

Clearly, the time has come when we must proceed with deliberate speed to develop and implement an environmentally responsible economic theory. This theory must obviously be premised on the assumption, as the ecological economists have consistently argued, that markets are open systems that exist in embedded and interactive relationship with the global environment. It must also mirror or reflect in economic terms the dynamic relationship between the activities of the parts (production and distribution systems) and the state of the whole (global ecosystem) in empirical terms. Our current understanding of part–whole relationships in biology and physics is quite complex, but it is not necessary, for our purposes, to explore the full range of this complexity. If, however, we are to consider how this new understanding could be wed to an environmentally responsible economic theory that retains most of the substantive benefits of free markets, some familiarity with the dynamics of these relationships is required.

CHAPTER 7

THE REAL ECONOMY IN BIOLOGY
Emergence and a New View of Order

> Overpopulation, the destruction of the environment, and the malaise of the inner cities cannot be solved by technological advances, nor by literature or history, but ultimately only by measures that are based on an understanding of the biological roots of the problem.
>
> —Ernst Mayr

Charles Darwin (1809–1882) was a great admirer of the work of Isaac Newton, and his theory of evolution is predicated on a relationship between atomized parts (organisms) and wholes (species) that mirrors the relationship between parts (atoms) and wholes (physical systems) in New-tonian physics. Darwin was also greatly influenced by two classical economists who premised their theories on the part–whole relationship in the classical paradigm—Adam Smith and Thomas Malthus. Darwin's note-books reveal that he read a number of Smith's works, including *The Theory of Moral Sentiments*, during the summer of 1838 and 1839. Although there is no record indicating that Darwin read *The Wealth of Nations* in its entirety, he was familiar with a detailed summary of this book written by Dugald Stewart.[1]

Darwin was impressed by Smith's thesis that order in human existence is maintained by immaterial eternal natural laws that obviate the need to appeal to human agency or to willful interventions by God. He was also taken with Smith's claim that these laws ensure that order will sponta-neously emerge in the competition between atomized economic actors for scarce resources and sustain the market system in equilibrium. There were, however, several aspects of Smith's theory that for obvious reasons were not useful to Darwin. For example, Smith claimed that the stability of market systems is maintained by natural laws in spite of individual changes in preferences or propensities and that differences in skills are a consequence, as opposed to a cause, of the division of labor. As a result, Smith's theory did not allow for two dynamics that became critically important in Darwin's theory– the development, or evolution, of individual goals and purposes, and the development, or evolution, of cumulative processes that result in different populations of individuals.

The crucial intellectual stimulation that led Darwin to refine fundamental aspects of his theory, as his notebooks attest, came from reading Malthus's *Essay on Population* in 1838.[2] Although some elements of Darwin's gestating theory had already been formed, Malthusian population theory provided him with a vision of human survival grounded in "crowding and struggle," and these dynamics became defining characteristics of his agent of evolution—natural selection in the quest for survival.[3] Malthus's essay also exposed Darwin to a mechanistic description of the struggle for survival that dealt in whole populations, as opposed to individuals, in a situation where population growth is exponential. He was also influenced by Malthus's suggestion that diversity and variety are essential aspects of the natural order and that birth and death are inextricably intertwined in the struggle for existence.

Darwin made his theory public for the first time in a paper delivered to the Linnean Society in 1858. The paper begins, "All nature is at war, one organism with another, or with external nature."[4] In *Origins of the Species,* Darwin is more specific about the character of this war: "There must be in every case a struggle for existence, either one individual with another of the same species, or with the individuals of distinct species, or with the physical conditions of life."[5] All of these assumptions are apparent in Darwin's definition of natural selection:

If under changing conditions of life organic beings present individual differences in almost every part of their structure, and this cannot be disputed; if there be, owing to their geometrical rate of increase, a severe struggle for life at some age, season, or year, and this certainly cannot be disputed; then, considering the infinite complexity of the relations of all organic beings to each other and to their conditions of life, causing an infinite diversity in structure, constitution, habits, to be advantageous to them, it would be a most extraordinary fact if no variations had ever occurred useful to each being's own welfare, in the same manner as so many variations have occurred useful to man. But if the variations useful to any organic being ever do occur, assuredly individuals thus characterized will have the best chance of being preserved in the struggle for life; and from the strong principle of inheritance, they will tend to produce offspring similarly characterized. This principle of preservation, or the survival of the fittest, I have called Natural Selection.[6]

Based on the assumption that the study of variation in domestic animals and plants "afforded the best and safest clue" to understanding evolution, Darwin concluded that nature could by crossbreeding and selection of traits produce new species. His explanation of the mechanism in nature that results in new species took the form of the following argument: (1) the principle of geometric increase indicates that more individuals in each species will be produced than can survive; (2) the struggle for existence occurs due to shortage of resources; (3) in this struggle for existence, slight variations, if they prove advantageous, will accumulate in interbreeding groups and produce new species. In analogy with the animal breeder's artificial selection of traits, Darwin termed the elimination of the disadvantaged and the promotion of the advantaged "natural selection."

In Darwin's view, the "struggle for existence" occurs *between* an atomized individual organism and other atomized individual organisms in the "same species," *between* an atomized individual organism of one species and that of a "different species," or *between* an atomized individual organism and the "physical conditions of life." The whole as Darwin conceived it is the collection of all atomized individual organisms, or parts, and the struggle for survival occurs *between* or *outside* the parts. Because Darwin viewed this struggle as the only limiting condition in the rate of increase of organisms, he assumed that the rate will be "geometrical" when the force of struggle between parts is weak and that the rate will decline as the force becomes stronger.

Natural selection occurs, says Darwin, when variations "useful to each being's own welfare," or useful to the welfare of an atomized individual organism, provide a survival advantage and the organism produces "offspring similarly characterized." Because the force that makes this selection operates outside the atomized parts, Darwin describes the whole in terms of "relations" between the totality of parts. For example, the "infinite complexity of relations of all organic beings to each other and to their conditions of life" refers to relations between parts, and the "infinite diversity in structure, constitution, habits" refers to "advantageous" traits

151

within the atomized parts. It also seems clear that the atomized individual organisms in Darwin's biological machine resemble classical atoms and that the force that drives the interactions of the atomized parts, the "struggle for life," resembles Newton's force of universal gravity. Although Darwin parted company with classical determinism in the claim that changes, or mutations, within organisms occurred randomly, his view of the relationship between parts and wholes was essentially Newtonian.

Darwinian theory was not of any great importance in the development of mainstream economics until the 1930s and 1940s. By this time, however, general equilibrium theory was the reigning economic paradigm, its origins in mid-nineteenth physics had been almost completely forgotten, and the presumption that this theory was a science comparable to the physical sciences made it largely immune from challenges from the distant field of evolutionary biology. The only mainstream economist who attempted to apply evolutionary ideas in the socioeconomic sphere was Friedrich Hayek, but his use of these ideas was less than systematic and contained many of the same misrepresentations and distortions of Darwinian theory found in the work of Herbert Spencer.[7]

However, Darwinian evolution did lend scientific credence to some of the fundamental assumptions about part–whole relationships in the neoclassical economic paradigm. Darwin's presumption that individual organisms are atomized entities that struggle for survival in terms of lawful or lawlike mechanisms that operate on these entities from the outside massively reinforced the view of economic actors in neoclassical economic theory, for obvious reasons. The actors in this theory are also viewed as atomized entities that compete with one another for survival in accordance with the lawful or lawlike mechanisms that operate on these entities from the outside, and the future state of this system is the sum of the resulting interactions. The notion that individuals and firms that survive in market systems have a competitive advantage that proves their fitness also derives from and has consistently been reinforced by Darwinian theory.

PARTS AND WHOLES IN MICROBIAL LIFE

During the last three decades, a revolution in the life sciences has enlarged the framework for understanding the dynamics of evolution. This new understanding has revealed that the relationship between parts, or individual organisms, is often characterized by continual cooperation, strong interaction, and mutual dependence. It also suggests that the view of evolution as a linear progression from "lower" atomized organisms to more complex atomized organisms is no longer appropriate. The more appropriate view is that all organisms (parts) are emergent aspects of the self-organizing process of life (whole), and, therefore, that the proper way to understand the parts is to examine their embedded relations to the whole. According to Lynn Margulis and Dorian Sagan, this is particular obvious in the study of microbial life:

> It now appears that microbes—also called microorganisms. germs, bugs, protozoans, and bacteria, depending on the context, are not only the building blocks of life, but occupy and are indispensable to every known living structure on the Earth today. From the paramecium to the human race, all life forms are meticulously organized, sophisticated aggregates of evolving microbial life. Far from leaving microorganisms behind on an evolutionary "ladder," we are surrounded by them and composed of them.[8]

During the first two billion years of evolution, bacteria were the sole inhabitants of the earth, and the emergence of more complex life forms is associated with networking and symbiosis. During these two billion years, prokaryotes, or organisms composed of cells with no nucleus, transformed the earth's surface and atmosphere. It was the interaction of these "simple" organisms that resulted in the complex processes of fermentation, photosynthesis, oxygen breathing, and the removal of nitrogen gas from the air. In the life of bacteria, bits of genetic material within organisms are routinely and rapidly transferred to other organisms. At any given time, an individual bacterium has the use of accessory genes, often from very different strains, that can perform functions not performed by its own DNA. Some of this genetic material can be incorporated into the DNA of a bacterium, and some may be passed on to other bacteria. What this picture indicates, as Margulis and Sagan put it, is that "all the world's bacteria have access to a single gene pool and hence to the adaptive mechanisms of the entire bacterial kingdom."[9]

Because the whole of this gene pool operates in some sense within the parts, the speed of recombination is much greater than that allowed by mutation alone, or by random changes inside parts that alter interaction between parts. The existence of the whole within parts explains why bacteria can accommodate change on a worldwide scale in a few years. If the

153

only mechanism at work were mutations inside organisms, much longer periods of time would be required for bacteria to adapt to a global change in the conditions for survival. "By constantly and rapidly adapting to environmental conditions," write Margulis and Sagan, "the organisms of the microcosm support the entire biota, their global exchange network ultimately affecting every living plant and animal."[10]

The discovery of symbiotic alliances between organisms that become permanent is another aspect of the modern understanding of evolution that challenges Darwin's view of universal struggle between atomized individual organisms. For example, the mitochondria found outside the nucleus of modern cells allow the cell to utilize oxygen and to exist in an oxygen-rich environment. But because mitochondria also have their own genes composed of DNA, reproduce by simple division, and do so at times different from the rest of the cell, it is "as if" mitochondria are discrete organisms performing integral and essential functions in the life of the cell.

The most reasonable explanation for this extraordinary alliance between mitochondria and the rest of the cell is that oxygen-requiring bacteria in primeval seas combined with other organisms. These ancestors of modern mitochondria entered other organisms and provided waste disposal and oxygen-derived energy in exchange for food and shelter, and the previously separate organisms evolved together into single more complex forms of oxygen-requiring life. Because the whole of these organisms was larger than the sum of their symbiotic parts, this allowed for life functions that could not be performed by the mere collection of parts. The existence of the whole within the parts coordinates metabolic functions and overall organization.[11]

PARTS—WHOLES IN COMPLEX LIVING SYSTEMS

The more complex organisms that evolved from this symbiotic union are sometimes referred to in biology texts as factories or machines. But a machine, as Darwin's model for the relationship between part and whole suggests, is a unity of order and not of substance, and the order that exists in a machine is external to the parts. The whole within the part that sets the boundary conditions of cells is DNA, and a complete strand of the master molecule of life exists in the nucleus of each cell. DNA evolved in an unbroken sequence from the earliest life forms and the evolution of even the most complex life forms cannot be separated from the coevolution of microbial ancestors. DNA in the average cell codes for the production of about two thousand different enzymes, and each of these enzymes catalyzes one particular chemical reaction. The boundary conditions within each cell resonate with the boundary conditions of all other cells and maintain the integrity and uniqueness of whole organisms.

The machine metaphor, which is still widely used in biology textbooks, assumes that genes are a set of instructions on how to make a body and that organisms are computable from initial inputs coded in DNA. However, the genetic information in DNA that codes for an initial protein is a necessary but not sufficient cause in the process of creating an organism because this protein typically changes its form and function via interactions with other proteins. For example, most of roughly thirty thousand genes in human DNA code for the production of a single protein that is subsequently broken up into smaller sequences and recombined to form some ten other proteins that perform specialized functions. Similarly, a large repertoire of regulatory mechanisms change the function of human proteins to perform specialized functions on a moment-to-moment basis and these mechanisms also respond to a wide range of environmental stimuli. Hence the whole (human organism) cannot be reduced to or explained in terms of the sum of initial computable parts (proteins) and displays unique and complex emergent behavior that results from a complex web of interactions within and between these parts.

Recent studies have also revealed that human DNA evolved in an unbroken sequence from the first self-replicating molecule of life in a process in which parts (sequences of DNA in other species) recombined to form new wholes (genes in ancestral human species) that display unique behavior. For example, human DNA contains sequences of DNA from ancient bacteria that recombined to perform more than two hundred metabolic functions in human cells, and human DNA also contains sequences of DNA from flies and worms that code for the development of the complex human immune system. From the perspective of the new biology, it is now clear that the mechanistic assumption that the human genome is "merely" a sequence of nucleotides that codes for discrete parts that fit together into a functioning whole is false.

Artifacts, or machines, are constructed from without, and the whole is simply the assemblage of all parts. Parts of machines can also be separated and reassembled and the machine will run normally. But if we separate a living organism into its "component" parts, this results in the inevitable death of this whole. "Living processes and living organisms," writes biologist J. Shaxel, "simply do not exist save as parts of single whole organisms."[12] Hence we must conclude, as the eminent biologist Ludwig von Bertalanffy does, that "mechanistic modes of explanation are in principle unsuitable for dealing with certain features of the organic; and it is just these features which make up the essential peculiarities of organisms."[13]

Modern biology has also disclosed that life appears to be a property of the whole that exists within the parts, and the whole is, therefore, greater than the sum of parts. As Ernst Mayr puts it, living systems "almost always have the peculiarity that the characteristics of the whole cannot (not even in theory) be deduced from the most complete knowledge of components, taken separately or in other partial combinations. This appearance of new characteristics in wholes has been designated emergence."[14]

The concept of emergence essentially recognizes that an assemblage of parts in successive levels of organization in nature can result in wholes that display properties that cannot be explained in terms of the collection of parts. As P. B. and J. S. Medawar put it, "Each higher-level subject contains ideas and conceptions peculiar to itself. These are the 'emergent' properties."[15] Because reductionism requires that we explain properties of a whole organism in terms of the behavior of parts at a lower level, it obliges us to view emergent properties as irrational and without cause. If, however, we assume that the whole exists within the parts, emergent properties at a higher level can be viewed as properties of a new whole that exists in more complex relation to biological life. From this perspective, organisms are not mixtures or compounds of inorganic parts but new wholes with emergent properties that are embedded in or intimately related to more complex wholes with their own emergent properties.

Some evidence also suggests that the whole (biosphere) displays unique behavior that is an emergent property of the interactions of parts (organisms). The fossil record indicates that the temperature of the earth's surface and the composition of the air appear to have been continuously regulated by the whole of life or the entire biota. Although the complex network of feedback loops that maintains conditions suitable for the continuance of life is not well understood, much evidence suggests that the entire biota are responsible. For example, the stabilization of atmospheric oxygen at about 21 percent was achieved by the whole biota millions of years ago and has been maintained ever since. If the oxygen concentration had risen a few percent above 21 percent, the volatile gas would have caused living organisms to combust spontaneously.

If we fail to factor in the self-regulating emergent properties of the whole of the biota, the mixture and relative abundance of gases in the atmosphere makes no sense at all on the basis of inorganic chemistry. Oxygen gas forms about 21 percent of the atmosphere, and the relative disequilibria of other gases, such as methane, ammonia, methyl chlorine, and methyl iodine, are enormous. If the whole of the biota did not display emergent properties that regulated these parts, chemical analysis suggests that all of these gases, which readily react to oxygen, should be so minute in quantity as to be undetectable. Yet nitrogen is ten billion times more abundant, carbon dioxide ten times more abundant, and nitrous oxide ten trillion times more abundant that they should be if these parts had interacted without mediation from the whole.[16]

Physics also indicates that the total luminosity of the sun, or the total quantity of energy released as sunlight per year, has increased during the last four billion years by as much as 50 percent. According to the fossil record, however, the temperature of the earth during this period has remained fairly stable, about 22 degrees centigrade, in spite of the fact that temperatures resulting from the less luminous early sun should have been at the freezing level. One of the emergent properties of the whole that maintained earth's temperature was the regulation of this atmospheric gas by the carbon dioxide cycle. This cycle involves a vast network of feedback loops between volcanic eruptions, rock weathering, soil bacteria, oceanic algae, and the production of limestone sediments.

COMPETITION VERSUS COOPERATION WITHIN SPECIES

Because Darwin assumed that individual organisms, like classical atoms, are atomized, and that the dynamics of evolution acted between or outside organisms, he concluded that competition for survival between organisms was the rule of nature and that this competition would be more pronounced between members of the same species. As Darwin put it, "The struggle will almost invariably be most severe between the individuals of the same species, for they frequent the same districts, require the same food, and are exposed to the same dangers."[17]

In the absence of a struggle for existence between species, Darwin assumed that the rate of increase of numbers of single species would be exponential. "Every single organic being," wrote Darwin, "may be said to be striving to the utmost increase in numbers."[18] If this "utmost increase" is not checked with competition for survival from other species, the consequences, in Darwin's view, are easily imagined: "There is no exception to the rule that every organic being naturally increases at so high a rate, that, if not destroyed, the earth would soon be covered by the progeny of a single pair."[19]

Using the example of elephants, Darwin attempted to estimate the minimal rate of increase in the absence of competition with other species. He assumes that a pair of elephants begins breeding at thirty years old and continues breeding for ninety years, and that six young elephants are born during this period. If each offspring survives for one hundred years and continues to breed at the same rate, Darwin calculated that nineteen million elephants descended from the first pair would be alive after a period of 740 to 750 years.[20] He then concludes that this natural tendency for species to increase in number without limit is checked by four "external" causes: predation, starvation, severities of climate, and disease.[21]

Large numbers of field studies by ecologists suggest, however, that one of the primary mechanisms that regulates the number of members of a particular species operates within the parts, or within individual members of that species. Take the example of Darwin's elephants. In a study of more than three thousand elephants in Kenya and Tanzania from 1966 to 1968, biologist Richard Laws found that "the age of sexual maturity in elephants was very plastic and was deferred in unfavorable situations." Depending on those situations, individual elephants reached "sexual maturity at from 8 to 30 years."[22] Laws also found that females do not continue bearing until ninety, as Darwin supposed, but cease to become pregnant around fifty-five years of age. The primary mechanisms that regulate the population of elephants is the "internal" adjustment of the onset of maturity in females which lowers the birth rate when overcrowding occurs, and not the "external" mechanisms of predation and starvation.

Numerous other studies have shown that internal adjustments in the onset of maturity in females regulate population growth in a large number of species. Linkage between age of first production of offspring and population density has been found in the white-tailed deer, elk, bison, moose, bighorn sheep, ibex, wildebeest, Himalayan tahr, hippopotamus, lion, grizzly bear, harp seal, southern elephant seal, spotted porpoise, stripped dolphin, blue whale, and sperm whale.[23] A large number of animal species also internally regulate populations by varying their litter and clutch size in response to the amount of food available. According to the biologist Charles Elton, "The short-eared owl (*Asio flammeus*) may have twice as many young in a brood and twice as many broods as usual, during a vole plague, when its food is extremely plentiful."[24] Similarly, nutcrackers, which normally lay only three eggs, increase the clutch to four when there are plentiful hazelnuts, the arctic fox produces large litters when lemmings are abundant, and lion bear fewer or more cubs according to the available food supply.[25]

COMPETITION VERSUS COOPERATION BETWEEN SPECIES

Some evidence also suggests that competition for survival between species (parts) is regulated by a whole (an ecology or ecosystem) that is resident within the parts in terms of the evolved behavior of organisms in an ecology or ecosystem. Even very similar organisms in the same habitat can display internal adaptive behaviors that serve to sustain the whole when food and other resources are in short supply. One such adaptive behavior involves the division of the habitat into ecological niches where the presence of one species does not harm the existence of another similar species. For example, the zebra, wildebeest, and gazelle are common prey to five carnivores: the lion, leopard, cheetah, hyena, and wild dog. These predators coexist, however, because they developed five different ways of living off the three prey species that do not directly compete with one another. As the ethologist James Gould explains, "Carnivores avoid competing by hunting primarily in different places at different times, and by using different techniques to capture different segments of the prey population. Cheetahs are unique in their high-speed chase strategy, but as a consequence must specialize on small gazelle. Only the leopard uses an ambush strategy, which seems to play no favorites in the prey it chooses. Hyenas and wild dogs are similar, but hunt at different times. And the lion exploits the brute-force niche, depending alternately on short, powerful rushes and strong-arm robbery."[26] Herbivores also display evolved behavior that minimizes competition for scare resources in the interests of sustaining other life forms in the environment. Paul Colinvaux has studied such behavior on the African savanna:

> Zebras take the long dry stems of grasses for which their horsy incisor teeth are nicely suited. Wildebeest take the side-shoot grasses, gathering with their tongues in the bovine way and tearing off the food against their single set of incisors. Thompson's gazelles graze where others have

been before, picking out ground-hugging plants and other tidbits that the feeding methods of the others have overlooked and left in view. Although these and other big game animals wander over the same patches of country, they clearly avoid competition by specializing in the kinds of food energy they take.[27]

Similarly, three species of yellow weaverbirds in Central Africa live on the same shore of a lake without struggle because one species eats only hard black seeds, another soft green seeds, and the third only insects.[28] In North America, twenty different insects feed on the same white pine—five eat only foliage, three live off birds, three on twigs, two on wood, two on roots, one on bark, and four on cambium.[29] A newly hatched garter snake pursues worm scent over cricket scent and a newly hatched green snake in the same environment displays the opposite preference. Yet both species of snake could eat the same prey.[30]

Although emergent cooperative behaviors within parts (organisms) that maintain conditions of survival in the whole (environment or ecosystem) appear to be everywhere present in nature, the conditions of observation are such that we distort results when we view any of these systems as isolated. All parts (organisms) exist finally in an embedded relation to the whole (biota) where the whole seems to operate in some sense within the parts. As Lynn Margulis explains:

> All organisms are dependent on others for the completion of their life cycles. Never, even in spaces as small as a cubic meter, is a living community of organisms restricted to members of a single species. Diversity, both morphological and metabolic, is the rule. Most organisms depend directly on others for nutrients and gases. Only photo and chemo-autotrophic bacteria produce all their organic requirements from inorganic constituents; even they require food, gases such as oxygen, carbon dioxide, and ammonia, which although organic, are end products of the metabolism of other organisms. Heterotrophic organisms require organic compounds as food; except in rare cases of cannibalism, this food comprises organisms of other species or their remains.[31]

When we consider that emergent properties of the whole (biota) appear to have consistently maintained conditions for life by regulating large-scale processes such as global temperature and relative abundance of gases, the idea that this whole exists within all parts (organisms) becomes rather imposing. Traditional metaphors for the cooperative aspects of life, such as "chain of being" and "web of existence," suggest that the self-regulating properties of the whole are external to or between parts. And the more recent metaphor of life in the Gaia hypothesis as a single organism or cell is a distortion in that it implies that there is no separate existence of parts. Perhaps the more appropriate view is that the relationship between parts (organisms) and whole (life) is complementary.

Obviously, our most advanced scientific understanding of nature in the biological sciences clearly indicates that the assumption in neoclassical economics that closed market systems exist in a domain that is separate and distinct from the environment is dangerously wrong. Not as obvious are the threats posed to the stability of the global environment by the assumption that the collection of atomized parts (economic actors and firms) constitutes wholes (markets) and that the equilibrium of these wholes is maintained by lawful or lawlike forces that act outside or between the parts. First, this assumption greatly frustrates our ability to appreciate the fact that parts (economic actors and activities) exist in embedded relation to the whole (global ecosystem). Second, it suggests that economic actors and firms are isolated atomized entities that cannot be fully responsible for the environmental impacts of their economic decisions because these decisions are largely determined by forces over which they have no control. Third, the presumption that national economies are controlled by these forces greatly diminishes the power of government to exercise its proper role and responsibility in resolving environmental problems. Fourth, this view of national economies in an era of globalization has created a situation in which we sanction and encourage open-ended competition between nation-states and transnational corporations for economic hegemony and scarce resources with little concern about impacts on the global environment.

The mechanistic relationship between parts and wholes in neoclassical economics also grandly conditions how we view the resources of nature and the manner in which they are exploited. In this paradigm, areas where natural resources are being exploited are viewed as parts that are isolated and distinct from other parts, and the collection of these parts constitutes the whole of the external resource currently used by the closed global market system. When resources in one of these parts are exhausted, it is assumed that this part can be replaced by another where natural resources exist, or by an artificial part, a new technology or process, that can substitute for the resource. The value of resources in these parts, after they become inputs into the market system, is determined by their market value and there is no effective means for valuing them in any other terms.

We now know, however, that the natural resources that exist in specific regions, or parts, evolved via a complex network of feedback loops in which self-regulating properties of wholes (ecological systems and global ecosystem) exist within the parts. These parts cannot be systematically and massively exploited for their natural resources without disrupting these feedback mechanisms and eventually disabling the self-regulating properties of the wholes. And because the parts (organisms and ecosystems) have evolved very specific properties that sustain via their complex interaction conditions for life in the whole (global ecosystem), this whole is clearly not a machine with substitutable or replaceable parts.

The next chapter will demonstrate that part–whole relationships in the new physics are remarkably similar to those in biology. The emergence of new wholes that display properties that cannot be explained in terms of the sum of their constituent parts is also a feature of inorganic systems. Attempts in physical theory to comprehend the dynamics of emergence in biological systems have disclosed an essential indeterminacy in these macro-level processes comparable to that on the micro-level in quantum physics. This improved understanding of the physics of living systems has also led to the sobering conclusion that small changes in ecological systems can result in large-scale changes in the global environment in relatively short time frames. This discovery could be critically important if we are to develop and implement an environmentally responsible economic theory before we arrive at the point where global economic activities occasion massive irreversible changes in the conditions for human survival.

CHAPTER 8

THE REAL ECONOMY IN PHYSICS
Cosmic Connections

> The paradox is only a conflict between reality and what you think reality ought to be.
> —Richard Feynman

In 1905, five years after Leon Walras published *Elements of Pure Economics*, an obscure patent office clerk in Geneva published three papers that signaled the beginning of the second scientific revolution. The "new physics" that Albert Einstein and others developed over the next thirty years undermined every assumption about the character of physical reality in the physics on which neoclassical economic theory is based.[1] More important for our purposes, it also disclosed a relationship between parts (quanta) and whole (cosmos) that is remarkably similar to the relationship between parts (organisms) and whole (ecosystem) in the new biology. Part of what makes this understanding vitally important in the effort to develop an environmentally responsible economic theory is that it will allow us to deal more effectively with the problem of uncertainties in predicting potential long-term impacts of economic activities on the global environment.

All that is required to understand the special character of part–whole relationships in this physics and their resemblance to those in biology is a willingness to exercise one's imagination and visualize a physical reality that lies outside the domain of everyday experience. But because this is not possible in the absence of some familiarity with the physical theories that disclosed these relationships, these theories will be described in terms that can be easily understood by those without prior training in higher mathematics and physics. This material will also serve as background for the argument at the close of this discussion that the philosophical implications of part–whole relationships in contemporary science could be critically important in coming to terms with the environmental crisis.

Einstein developed the special theory of relativity (1905) in an effort to eliminate some asymmetries in mathematical descriptions of the behavior of light, or electromagnetic radiation, in Newtonian mechanics and Maxwell's electromagnetic theory. The Newtonian construct of three-dimensional absolute space existing separately from absolute time implied that one could find a frame of reference absolutely at rest. Newtonian mechanics also implied that it was possible to achieve velocities that are equal to the speed of light and that an observer traveling at such velocities would perceive the speed of light as zero.

Einstein's first postulate was that it is impossible to determine absolute motion, or motion that proceeds in a fixed direction at a constant speed. The only way, he reasoned, that we can assume that absolute motion exists is to compare it with that of other objects. In the absence of such a comparison, said Einstein, one can make no assumptions about movement. He concluded, therefore, that the assumption that there is an absolute frame of reference in which the speed of light is reducible to zero must be false. Sensing that it was Newton's laws rather than Maxwell's equations that required adjustment, Einstein concluded that there is no absolute frame of reference or that the laws of physics hold equally well in all frames of reference. He then arrived at the second postulate of the absolute constancy of the speed of light for all moving observers. Based on these two postulates, the relativity of motion and the constancy of the speed of light, the entire logical structure of relativity theory followed.

Einstein mathematically deduced the laws that related space and time measurements made by one observer to the same measurements made by another observer moving uniformly relative to the first. One consequence was that the familiar law of simple addition of velocities does not hold for light or for speeds close to the speed of light. If, for example, one could chase a quantum of light, or photon, in a spaceship at increasingly greater larger velocities, it would still move away at its own constant speed. The reason why these relativistic effects are not obvious in our everyday perception of reality, said Einstein, is that light speed is very large compared with ordinary speeds, and this creates the illusion that we perceive events in the instant that they occur. There was nothing new here in the notion that frames of reference in conducting experiments are relative. Galileo arrived at that conclusion. What Einstein did, in essence, was extend the so-called Galilean relativity principle from mechanics, where it was known to work, to electromagnetic theory, or the rest of physics as it was then known. What was required to achieve this greater symmetry was to abandon the Newtonian idea of an absolute frame of reference.

This led to the conclusion, as Einstein put it, that the "electrodynamic fields are not states of the medium [the ether] and are not bound to any bearer, but they are independent realities which are not reducible to anything else."[2] In a vacuum, light traveled, he concluded, at a constant speed, c, equal to 300,000 km/sec, and all frames of reference are relative to this constant. There is, therefore, no frame of reference absolutely at rest, velocities in various frames of reference must be measured in relationship to the constant speed of light, and the laws of physics apply equally well to all frames of reference moving relative to each other.

Einstein also showed that the results of measuring instruments themselves must change from one frame of reference to another. For example, clocks in the two frames of reference would not register the same time and two simultaneous events in a moving frame would appear to occur at different times in the unmoving frame. In the space-time description used to account for the differences in observation between different frames, time is another coordinate in addition to the three space coordinates forming the four-dimensional space-time continuum. In relativistic physics, transformations between different frames of reference express each coordinate of one frame as a combination of the coordinates of the other frame. For example, a space coordinate in one frame usually appears as a combination, or mixture, of space and time coordinates in another frame.

The special theory of relativity dealt only with "constant," as opposed to "accelerated," motion of the frames of reference. In 1915-1916, Einstein extended relativity to account for the more general case of accelerated frames of reference in the general theory of relativity. The central idea in general relativity theory is that it is impossible to distinguish between the effects of gravity and of nonuniform motion. If we did not know, for example, that we were on an accelerating spaceship and dropped a cup of coffee, we could not determine whether the mess on the floor was due to the effects of gravity or the accelerated motion. This inability to distinguish between a nonuniform motion, such as an acceleration, and gravity is known as the principle of equivalence.

Einstein then posits the laws relating space and time measurements carried out by two observers moving uniformly, as in the example of one observer in an accelerating spaceship and another on earth. Force fields, like gravity, cause space-time, Einstein concluded, to become warped or curved and hence non-Euclidean in form. In the general theory the motion of material points, including light, is not along straight lines, as in Euclidean space, but along "geodesics" in curved space.

What is important here for our purposes is that relativity theory disclosed a startling new relationship between parts and wholes that would be massively reinforced by subsequent developments in both physics and biology. According to Einstein's general relativity theory, wrote Max Planck, "each individual particle of the system in a certain sense, at any one time, exists simultaneously in every part of the space occupied by the system."[3] And the system, as Planck makes clear, is the entire cosmos. As Einstein put it, "physical reality must be described in terms of continuous functions in space. The material point, therefore, can hardly be conceived any more as the basic concept of the theory."[4]

In general relativity, field is identified with space-time curvature, and fundamental constants, such as the speed of light, physical laws and primary entities, such as mass, are intimately linked with one another. Any measurement in relativity theory is dependent upon the relative velocity of the reference frame in which the measurement is made, and every frame is related to every other frame. The relationship between moving frames can be visualized as a rotation of axes in the four-dimensional space-time continuum, and the mutual relation of entities determines their nature and properties along with the curvature of space-time.

With the elimination of the construct of discreteness, Einstein concluded that the sense that the collection of matter that constitutes "self" is separate from the whole is merely another macro-level illusion:

A human being is a part of the whole, called by us the "Universe," a part limited in time and space. He experiences himself, his thoughts and feelings as something separate from the rest—a kind of optical illusion of his consciousness. This delusion is a kind of prison for us, restricting us to our personal desires and to affection for a few persons nearest to us. Our task must be to free ourselves from the prison by widening our circle of compassion to embrace all living creatures and the whole of nature in its beauty. Nobody is able to achieve this completely, but

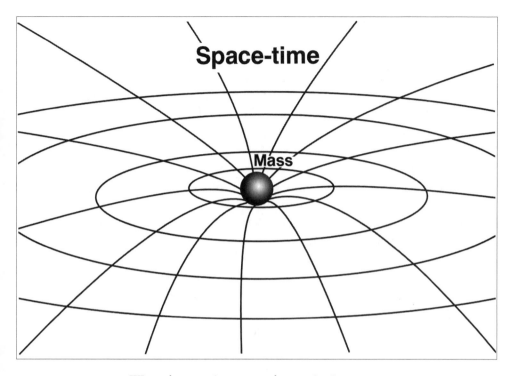

FIGURE 8.1. Warped space-time around a gravitating mass

the striving for such achievement is in itself a part of the liberation and a foundation for inner security.[5]

PARTS AND WHOLES IN QUANTUM PHYSICS

The suggestion that the part (self) is not separate and discrete but an integral manifestation of the whole (cosmos) was considerably amplified after the emergence of quantum physics in the 1920s. Those who developed this physics uncovered a part–whole relationship between quanta, or matterlike entities, and fields that displaced the earlier view of atoms as mass points and undermined the assumption of unrestricted determinism. In this understanding of the character of physical reality, parts (quanta) exist in embedded relation to the whole (cosmos), and no physical system can be viewed in theory or in fact as closed or isolated from other systems.

167

Appreciating why this is the case requires some understanding of a fundamental dualism in quantum physics between waves and particles. In classical physics, all properties of a system, including those of microscopic atoms and molecules, are assumed to be "real" in the sense that they are exactly definable and determinable. But in the quantum world, properties of a system cannot be said to have definite values and are described in terms of probabilities.

This inherent aspect of observation of quantum systems challenged the classical assumptions that the observer was separate and distinct from the observed system and that acts of observation did not alter the system. In quantum physics, a definite value of a physical quantity can be known "only" through acts of observation, which include us and our measuring instruments, and we cannot assume that the quantity would be the same in the absence of observation. Put differently, we cannot assume that a physical system exists in a well-defined state prior to measurement or that this state will be the same when a measurement is made. Even if our predictions are based on complete knowledge of initial conditions, the future state of this system cannot be entirely predicted.

Picture the particle as a pointlike entity, like the period at the end of this sentence, and the wave as a multidimensional entity spreading out in all directions at once like a water wave created when a stone is thrown into a pond. The wave aspect of quanta is responsible for the formation of interference patterns that are crudely analogous to the actions of water waves in the ocean. These patterns result when two waves produce peaks in places where they combine and troughs where they cancel each other out. In quantum physics, the wave function is completely deterministic and allows us to predict theoretically the future of a quantum system with certainty as long as the system is not observed or measured. But when an observation or measurement does occur, the wave function does not allow us to predict precisely where the particle will appear at a specific location in space. It allows us to predict only the "probability" of finding the particle within a range of probabilities associated with all possible states of the wave function.

In an effort to better visualize the relationship between parts (quanta) and whole (cosmos), imagine that the universe is a 3-D movie. What we can detect or measure in this movie are quanta, or particle-like entities. Quanta are associated with infinitely small vibrations in what can be pictured as a grid-lattice filling three-dimensional space. Potential vibra-

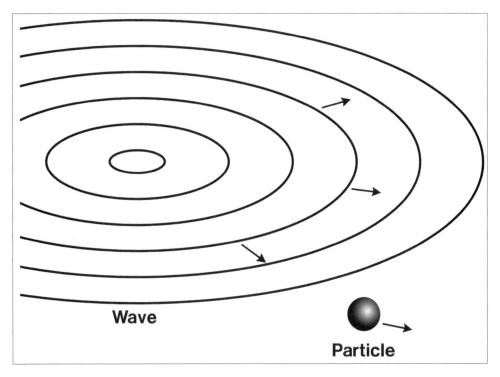

FIGURE 8.2. Wave and particle picture

tions at any point in a field are capable of producing quanta that can move about in space and interact, and it is the exchange of quanta within and between fields that allows the cosmic 3-D movie to emerge and evolve.

The projectors in this movie are the four known fields—strong, electromagnetic, weak and gravitational. The carriers of these fields, or messenger quanta, are the graviton for gravity, the photon for electromagnetism, the intermediate bosons for the weak force, and the colored gluons for the strong force. Material reality emerges from the transformations and organization of the fields and their associated quanta, and material substances emerge from six strongly interacting quarks and six weakly interacting bosons. In quantum field theory, particles are not discrete and separate entities that are acted upon, as classical physics supposed, by "forces." They are emergent phenomena that "interact" with each other through the exchange of other particles.

Making observations or measurements in quantum physics can be likened to putting on glasses to see a 3-D movie. The action that we might presume to be there on the micro level in the absence of measurement, or before putting on the glasses, is not the same as what we actually observe in physical experiments. In this cosmic movie, we are confronted with two logically antithetical aspects of one complete drama, wave and particle, and the price of admission is that we cannot perceive or measure both simultaneously.

One of the easiest ways to demonstrate that wave-particle dualism is a fundamental dynamic of the life of nature is to examine the results of the famous two-slit experiment. As physicist and Nobel laureate Richard Feynman put it, "any other situation in quantum mechanics, it turns out, can always be explained by saying, 'You remember the case with the experiment with two holes? It's the same thing.' "[6] In our idealized two-slit experiment we have a source of quanta, electrons, an electron gun, like that in TV sets, and a screen with two tiny openings. Our detector is a second screen like a TV screen, which flashes when an electron impacts on it and allows us to record where and when an electron hits the detector.

With both slits S_2 and S_3 open, each becomes a source of waves. The waves spread out spherically, come together, and produce interference patterns that appear as bands of light and dark on our detector. In terms of the wave picture, the dark stripes reveal where the waves have canceled each other out, and the light stripes where they have reinforced one another. If we close one of the openings, there is a bright spot on the detector in line with the other opening. The bright spot results from electrons impacting the screen in direct line with the electron gun and the opening like bullets. Because we see no interference patterns or no wave aspect, this result can be understood by viewing electrons as particles.

Physics has recently provided us the means of conducting this experiment with a single particle and its associated wave packet arriving one at a time. Viewing a single electron as a particle, or as a pointlike something, we expect it, with both slits open, to go through one slit or the other. How could a single, defined something go through both? But if we conduct our experiment many times with both slits open, we see a buildup of the interference patterns associated with waves. Because the single particle has behaved like a wave with both slits open, it does, in fact, reveal its wave aspect. And yet we have no way of knowing which slit the supposedly particle-like electron passed through.

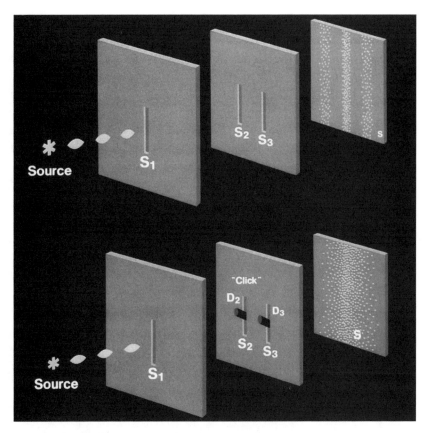

FIGURE 8.3. Double slit experiment

Suppose that we refine our experiment a bit more and attempt to determine which of the slits a particular electron passes through by putting a detector (D_2 and D_3) at each slit (S_2 and S_3). After we allow many electrons to pass through the slits, knowing from the detectors which slit each electron has passed through, we discover two bright spots in direct line with each opening that a detector indicated the electron passed through. Because no interference patterns associated with the wave aspect are observed, this is consistent with the particle aspect of the electron. Yet the choice to measure or observe what happens at the two slits reveals only the particle aspect of the total reality, and we cannot predict which detector at which slit will fire or click. All that we can know is that there a 50 percent

171

probability that the electron in its particle aspect will be recorded at one slit or the other.

The "essential reality" in quantum field theory, says physicist Steven Weinberg, "is a set of fields subject to the rules of special relativity and quantum mechanics; all else is derived as a consequence of the quantum dynamics of those fields."[7] Because events at the quantum level cannot be directly perceived by the human sensorium, we are not normally aware that every aspect of physical reality "emerges" through the interaction of fields and quanta. But from the perspective of our most advanced scientific knowledge, this is the actual or real ground for our existence and requires that we view the part that is our "self" in terms of dynamic patterns of interconnections embedded in a seamless web of activity that is the entire cosmos.

As Milic Capek puts it, "There can hardly be a sharper contrast than that between the everlasting atoms of classical physics and the vanishing 'particles' of modern physics."[8] We now know that the classical notion of substance as composed of indestructible building blocks is false and that particles cannot be viewed as separate and discrete. According to physicist Henry Stapp, "each atom turns out to be nothing but the potentialities in the behavior pattern of others. What we find, therefore, are not elementary space-time realities, but rather a web of relationships in which no part can stand alone; every part derives its meaning and existence only from its place within the whole."[9]

Similarly, the characteristics of these parts are not isolatable given particle-wave dualism and the incessant exchange of quanta within and between fields. Quanta cannot be dissected from the omnipresent sea of energy, nor can we in theory or in fact observe them from the "outside." At each step in the journey toward a grand unified theory incorporating all forces, the constituents of matter and the basic phenomena involved appear increasingly more interconnected, interrelated, and interdependent. As the physicist Werner Heisenberg put it, the cosmos "appears as a complicated tissue of events, in which connections of different kinds alternate or overlay or combine and thereby determine the texture of the whole."[10]

A NEW FACT OF NATURE

In the strange new world of quantum physics, we have consistently uncovered aspects of physical reality that are at odds with our everyday sense of reality. But no previous discovery has posed more challenges to our usual understanding of the "way things are" than an amazing new fact of nature known as nonlocality. Perhaps the best way to begin to appreciate why this is the case is to imagine that you are one of two observers in a scientific experiment involving two photons, or quanta of light.

These photons originate from a single source and travel in opposite directions an equal distance halfway across the known universe to points where each will be measured or observed. Now suppose that before the photons are released, one observer is magically transported to one point of observation halfway across the known universe and that the second observer is magically transported to the other. The task of the observers is to record or measure a certain property of each of the photons with detectors located at the two points in order that the data gathered at each can later be compared.

Even though the photons are traveling from the source at the speed of light, each observer would have to wait patiently for billions of years for one of the photons to arrive at his observation point. Suppose, however, that the observers are willing to endure this wait because they hope to test the predictions of a mathematical theorem. This theorem not only allows for the prospect that there could be a correlation between the observed properties of the two photons, but it also indicates that this correlation could occur instantly, or in no time, in spite of the fact that the distance between the observers and their measuring instruments is billions of light years. Now imagine that after the observations are made, the observers are magically transported back to the source of the experiment and that the observations recorded by each are compared. The result of our imaginary experiment is that the observed properties of the two photons did, in fact, correlate with one another over this vast distance instantly or in no time, and the researchers conclude that the two photons remained in communication with one another in spite of this distance.

This imaginary experiment distorts some of the more refined aspects of the actual experiments in which photons released from a single source are measured or correlated over what physicists term *spacelike separated regions*. But if we assume that the imaginary experiment were conducted many times, there is good reason to believe that the results would be the same of those in the actual experiments. Also like the imaginary experiment, the actual experiments were designed to test some predictions made in a mathematical theorem.

The theorem in question was published in 1964 by physicist John Bell and the predictions made in this theorem have been tested in a series of increasingly refined experiments. Like Einstein before him, John Bell was discomforted by the threat quantum physics posed to a fundamental assumption in classical physics—there must be a one-to-one correspondence between every element of a physical theory and the physical reality described by that theory. This view of the relationship between physical theory and physical reality assumes that all events in the cosmos can be fully described by physical laws and that the future of any physical system can, in theory at least, be predicted with utter precision and certainty. Bell's hope was that the results of the experiments testing his theorem would obviate challenges posed by quantum physics to this understanding of the relationship between physical theory and physical reality.

The results of these experiments would also serve to resolve other large questions. Is quantum physics a self-consistent theory whose predictions would hold in this new class of experiments? Or would the results reveal that quantum theory is incomplete and that its apparent challenges to the classical understanding of the correspondence between physical theory and physical reality were illusory? The answer to this question in the experiments made possible by Bell's theorem would not merely serve as commentary on the character of the knowledge we call physics. It would also determine which of two fundamentally different assumptions about the character of physical reality is correct. Is physical reality, as classical physics assumes, local? Or is physical reality, as quantum theory predicts, nonlocal? While the question may seem esoteric and the terms innocuous, the issues at stake and the implications involved were enormous.

Bell was personally convinced the totality of all of our previous knowledge of physical reality, not to mention the laws of physics, would favor the assumption of locality. The assumption states that a measurement at one point in space cannot influence what occurs at another point in space if the distance between the points is large enough so that no signal can travel between them at light speed in the time allowed for measurement. In the jargon of physics, the two points exist in "spacelike" separated regions, and a measurement in one region cannot influence what occurs in the other.

Quantum physics, however, allows for what Einstein disparagingly termed "spooky actions at a distance." When particles originate under certain conditions, quantum theory predicts that a measurement of one particle will correlate with the state of another particle even if the distance between the particles is millions of light years. And the theory also indicates that even though no signal can travel faster than light, the correlations will occur instantaneously, or in "no time." If this prediction held in experiments testing Bell's theorem, we would be forced to conclude that physical reality is nonlocal.

After Bell published his theorem in 1964, a series of increasingly refined tests by many physicists of the predictions made in the theorem culminated in experiments by Alain Aspect and his team at the University of Paris-South. When the results of the Aspect experiments were published in 1982, the answers to Bell's questions were quite clear—quantum physics is a self-consistent theory and the character of physical reality as disclosed by quantum physics is nonlocal.[11] In 1997, these same answers were provided by the results of twin-photon experiments carried out by Nicolas Gisin and his team at the University of Geneva.[12]

Whereas the distance between detectors in spacelike separated regions in the Aspect experiments was thirteen meters, the distance between detectors in the Gisin experiments was extended to eleven kilometers, or roughly seven miles. A distance of eleven kilometers is so vast compared with distances on the realm of quanta that the experiments were essentially seeking to determine whether the correlations would weaken or diminish over any distance, no matter how arbitrarily large. If the strength of the correlations held at eleven kilometers, physicists were convinced they would also hold in an experiment where the distances between the detectors was halfway to the edge of the entire universe. But if the strength of the correlations significantly weakened or diminished, physical reality would be local in the sense that nonlocality does not apply to the entire universe. This did not prove to be the case. The results of the Gisin experiments provided unequivocal evidence that the correlations between detectors located in these spacelike separated regions did not weaken as the distance increased.

One of the gross misinterpretations of the results of these experiments in the popular press was that they showed that information traveled between the detectors at speeds greater than light. This was not the case and relativity theory, along with the rule that the velocity of light is the absolute limit at which signals can travel, was not violated. The proper way to view these correlations is that they occurred instantly or in "no time" in spite of the vast distance between the detectors. The results also indicate that similar correlations would occur even if the distance between the detectors were billions of light-years.

A number of articles in the popular press also claimed that the results of the Gisin experiments showed that faster-than-light communication is possible. This misunderstanding resulted from a failure to appreciate the fact there is no way to carry useful information between paired particles in this situation. The effect that is studied in these experiments applies only to events that have a common origin in a unified quantum system, like the annihilation of a positron-electron pair, the return of an electron to its ground state, or the separation of a pair of photons from the singlet state. Because any information that originates from these sources is, in accordance with quantum theory, a result of quantum indeterminacy, the individual signals are random and random signals cannot carry coded information or data.

The polarizations, or spins, of each of the photons in the Gisin experiments carry no information, and any observer of the photons transmitted along a particular axis would see only a random pattern. This pattern makes nonrandom sense only if we are able to compare it with the pattern observed in the other paired photon. Any information contained in the paired photons derives from the fact that the properties of the two photons exist in complementary relation, and that information is uncovered only through a comparison of the difference between the two random patterns. Although the discovery that nonlocality is a fact of nature will not result in a technological revolution in the telecommunications industry, it does represent a rather startling new addition to our scientific worldview.

For our purposes, what is most important to realize is that the new fact of nature revealed in these experiments, as Bernard d'Espagnat has pointed out, is a "general" property of nature.[13] All particles in the history of the cosmos have interacted with other particles in the manner revealed by the Aspect experiments. Virtually everything in our immediate physical environment is made up of quanta that have been interacting with other quanta in this manner from the big bang to the present. Even the atoms in our bodies are made up of particles that were once in close proximity to the cosmic fireball, and other particles that interacted at that time in a single quantum state can be found in the most distant star. Also consider, as the physicist M. Mermin has shown, that quantum entanglement grows exponentially with the number of particles involved in the original quantum state and that there is no theoretical limit on the number of these entangled particles.[14]

This means that the universe on a very basic level is a vast web of particles that remain in contact with one another over any distance in no time in the absence of the transfer of energy or information. However strange or bizarre it might seem, physical reality now appears to be a "single" quantum system that responds together to further interactions. The quanta that make up our bodies could be as much a part of this unified system as the photons propagating in opposite directions in the Aspect and Gisin experiments. Thus nonlocality, or nonseparability, in these experiments could translate into the much grander notion of nonlocality, or nonseparability, as the factual condition in the entire universe.[15]

EMERGENCE IN CONTEMPORARY PHYSICS AND BIOLOGY

As we saw in the last chapter, our most advanced scientific understanding of biological reality has disclosed that life appears to be a property of the whole that exists within the parts, and that the whole is, therefore, greater than the sum of parts. From this new perspective, organisms are not mixtures or compounds of inorganic parts but new wholes with emergent properties that are embedded in or intimately related to more complex wholes with their own emergent properties. At the most basic level of organization, quanta interact with other quanta in and between fields, and fundamental particles interact with other fundamental particles to produce the roughly one hundred naturally occurring elements that display emergent properties that do not exist in the particles themselves. The parts represented by the elements combine to form new wholes in compounds and minerals that display emergent properties not present in the elements themselves. For example, the properties in salt, or sodium chloride, are novel and emergent, and do not exist in sodium or chloride per se.

The parts associated with compounds and minerals combined to form a new whole in the ancestor of DNA that displays emergent properties associated with life. During the first two billion years of evolution, it was the exchange of parts of DNA between prokaryotes as well as mutations within parts that resulted in new wholes that displayed new emergent properties. Combination through synergism of these parts resulted in new wholes in eukaryotes that display emergent properties not present in prokaryotes.

Meiotic sex, or the typical sex of cells with nuclei, resulted in an exchange of parts of DNA that eventually resulted in new wholes with emergent properties in speciation. And recombinations and extensions of the parts resident in all parts (DNA) resulted in emergent properties in whole organisms that do not exist within the parts or in the series of nucleotides in DNA. Through a complex network of feedback loops the interaction of all organisms as parts resulted in a whole, biological life, which exists within the parts and displays emergent regulatory properties not present in the parts.

Over the last three decades, new mathematical tools and techniques have been developed in an effort to better understand living systems as self-organizing networks. This new field of study is most widely referred to as dynamical systems theory, but it is also known as systems dynamics, complex dynamics, and nonlinear dynamics. The term dynamical systems theory is, however, a bit confusing because the word "theory" in the jargon of science normally applies to a mathematical description of the dynamics of specific physical systems. However, the object of study in dynamical systems theory is the "hidden" dynamics of nonlinear systems that result in the emergence of new structures or behavior that cannot be explained in terms of the sum of their parts.

The systems that display these emergent properties are embedded in a complex web of dynamic interconnections with their environment in a state or condition known as "far-from-equilibrium." A physical system is in equilibrium when its energy is distributed in the most statistically probable way, or when the forces, influences, reactions, and so on balance each other out and there is no change. In the 1960s, Nobel laureate Ilya Prigogine realized that systems that display spontaneous self-organization are in an inherently unstable condition far-from-equilibrium. And this led to the realization that dramatic large-scale changes occur in these systems as a result of feedback loops that are "nonlinear."

In linear systems, small changes produce small effects and large effects result from the accumulative impact of small changes. In nonlinear systems, in contrast, small changes can produce large effects because initial effects are amplified by self-reinforcing feedback loops. A feedback loop is essentially a series of causally connected elements in which an initial element "causes" effects on other elements that propagate around a loop and "feed back" into the original element. In other words, an original input affects the last output in repeated cycles and each input is modified or changed by the previous cycle. In the past few decades, we have learned that living systems are nonlinear and exist in far-from-equilibrium conditions where an increase in entropy, or in the level of disorder, results in instabilities and a corresponding increase in the number of feedback loops.

Nonlinear dynamics are an essential aspect of the self-organizing and self-perpetuating behavior of organic life. But scientists, until recently, have avoided the study of these systems due to their seemingly chaotic nature and the fact that nonlinear equations are usually too difficult to solve. Rather than deal with nature in its full complexity, scientists routinely described nonlinear processes with linear approximations that could be represented in formulas and solved analytically.

Efforts were made to solve nonlinear equations numerically by using various combinations for the variables until some approximation fit the nonlinear equations. For most nonlinear equations, however, this is a very cumbersome and time-consuming process that yields only very approximate solutions. This situation changed dramatically with the availability of powerful computers that can compute the large collection of values that satisfy the nonlinear equations and provide solutions represented graphically as a curve or set of curves.

Using these new computational tools, Prigogine found that a system far-from- equilibrium interacts with other systems via feedback loops and that the corresponding equations for the loops are nonlinear. He also found a correlation between the level of complexity in these systems and the degree of nonlinearity in the mathematical equations describing the feedback loops. Recognizing the critical connection between nonequilibrium and nonlinearity, Prigogine used the techniques of dynamical systems theory and the mathematics of complexity to develop a nonlinear thermodynamics for systems far-from-equilibrium.

In the nonlinear equations in this theory, there is usually more than one possible solution and the number of solutions increases in proportion to the degree of nonlinearity. When a nonlinear system arrives at a bifurcation point, or the point where new structures or behavior may suddenly emerge, there are typically a number of paths or branches that can be followed. Equally important, the path or branch that is realized is unique for each system and cannot be predicted with any degree of certainty. This means that there is an irreducible random element in these systems and that the behavior of a particular nonlinear system can be predicted for only a short period. For example, the essential indeterminacy in the nonlinear system of the atmosphere is such that we can never hope to make accurate predictions about weather conditions on both regional and global levels beyond a limited time. The current estimate is ten days or less.

Obviously, this understanding of the character of physical reality is utterly different from that of classical physics. In classical physics, it is assumed that physical laws act on or between discrete and separable atoms in a completely causal and deterministic manner, that a particular physical system can be completely isolated from other systems, and that the future of any physical system, if initial conditions are known, is entirely predictable. In the linear equations of classical physics, all processes are reversible, the past is interchangeable with the future, and there is no room for novelty or creativity. This view was challenged in the nineteenth century when the second law of thermodynamics, the entropy law, revealed that isolated physical systems as well as the universe as a whole move inevitably in the direction of disorder.

But while irreversibility in classical thermodynamics is associated with energy losses and disorder, irreversibility in dynamical systems theory can play a constructive role and lead to higher levels of order. For example, it has been shown that the catalytic feedback loops that are essential to living organisms result in instabilities and self-amplifying feedback loops that allow new structures of increasingly complexity to emerge at successive bifurcation points. As Prigogine puts it, "Irreversibility is the mechanism that brings order out of chaos."[16]

Dynamical systems theory, which includes chaos theory and the theory of fractals, has evolved into a rich and varied field in which the hidden dynamics of an enormous variety of self-organizing systems are investigated. This new branch of science is in the process of disclosing that the whole universe is more than the sum of its parts and that new wholes that display novel structures and behavior are emergent at all levels of physical reality. Given that this science is only in its initial stage of development, the process by which parts are organized into new wholes will undoubtedly be much better understood over time. What is now clear, however, is that indeterminacy is an essential ingredient in this process and there will always be a severe limit on our ability to predict the future of nonlinear systems.

INDETERMINACY AND GLOBAL ECONOMIC PLANNING

Most of us have been taught to believe that science can predict the future of physical systems with a high degree of accuracy and that any ambiguities or uncertainties that frustrate such predictions will, for all practical purposes, be eliminated over time. However, this is certainly not the case with nonlinear systems. If the ecosystem were a linear system in which atomized organisms interact with one another in accordance with completely deterministic laws, we could reasonably expect that its future could be predicted with great certainty. But this expectation is not reasonable or even rational because the ecosystem is a nonlinear system in which organisms are "open" nonlinear systems that maintain and reconstitute themselves via a vast web of highly indeterminate interactive feedback loops. Predictions based on improved computer-based models will, of course, provide a more accurate view of what is likely to occur within an increasingly narrow range of statistical probabilities. On the other hand, there is clearly no prospect that these predictions will ever be accurate to a degree demanded by those who believe that we live in a Newtonian universe.

In public debates about environmental problems, this is a large and menacing problem. For example, when scientists testify before committees in the U.S. Congress about future conditions in the global environment in terms of a range of statistical probabilities, this testimony is almost invariably dismissed by one or more committee members on the grounds that the less than precise predictions indicate that the scientists do not really understand the problems. Those who make this claim then typically argue that we should not implement large-scale economic solutions to environmental problems in the absence of a "proper" scientific understanding of those problems. Clearly, this response is utterly irresponsible for a now-obvious reason—the future of the nonlinear system of the global environment cannot, in principle, be predicted with a high degree of accuracy and the levels of uncertainty increase in direct proportion to the amount of time involved.

Another reason why this will always be the case has to do with the relationship between parts and wholes in the nonlinear system of life. In most of the media commentary on population patterns, species diversity, global warming, ozone depletion, and global weather patterns, there is the implication that these phenomena can be viewed as separate and distinct parts. This is simply not the case. Nonlinear systems are embedded in interactive relationships to one another and to a whole that is larger than the sum of the parts. The number of dynamic interconnections between the parts (nonlinear systems) and the whole (biosphere) is incalculably large, and there is an inherent indeterminacy at the bifurcation points in the nonlinear feedback loops between the parts when large-scale changes occur.

The dynamics of nonlinear living systems are such that small changes may produce small effects for an extended period. When, however, the system as a whole reaches a state that is farther from equilibrium, small changes can trigger very large effects and these effects can cause other nonlinear systems to become less stable and to move further away from equilibrium. For example, the loss of habitats in a particular ecological niche can proceed for several generations with only a gradual increase in the rate of species extinction and the loss of biological diversity. But if this process continues, the entire system eventually reaches a point where even very marginal losses in habitat result in sudden and massive changes, and this is reflected in a dramatic increase in extinction rates and a huge loss of biological diversity.

Because the feedback loops in this nonlinear system interact strongly with those in other nonlinear systems in the region, these systems also tend to move toward a far-from-equilibrium state where similar large-scale changes can occur. When we consider that the feedback loops between these nonlinear systems are embedded in a seamless web of interaction with those of all other nonlinear systems in the ecosystem, including the climate system, this leads to another imposing conclusion. None of these parts (nonlinear systems) can be isolated from the whole (biosphere or ecosystem), and the movement of progressively larger numbers of parts to a state that is further from an equilibrium state can result in very large-scale changes in the whole.

The ability of this whole to perpetuate conditions of life even in situations where massive changes in those conditions occur is due in large part to the fact that novel structures and behavior can emerge in far-from-equilibrium states. When, for example, a ten-kilometer wide meteor impacted earth some sixty-five million years ago near the Yucatan, the resulting explosion probably generated an enormous cloud of dust and ash that blocked out sunlight for a prolonged period and drastically changed global weather patterns. Under these conditions, it is now widely believed that the dominant species, dinosaurs, became extinct along with roughly 98 percent of other existing species. But the mutual interaction of nonlinear parts (organisms) sustained conditions that perpetuated the whole (life), and surviving organisms evolved into myriad new species that adapted to changing conditions in their environments in an incredible variety of ways.

From the perspective of science, the economic activities of more than six billion people are clearly embedded in a web of dynamic, interrelated, and interdependent activities that constitutes the massive nonlinear system of life. We can, of course, continue to ignore the costs of doing business in the real economy of the global environment based on the assumption these activities are, as neoclassical economics requires, separate from nature. And we can also continue to expand the global economy based on the assumption that the resources of nature are free and inexhaustible and the lawful mechanisms of market systems will resolve environmental problems. But if we do so for any extended period, the prospect that our species, like the dinosaurs, could become extinct must be taken very seriously. The irony, of course, is that while the dinosaurs became extinct as a result of the chance collision of earth with a meteorite, our species could become extinct as a result of its own willful and conscious behavior.

If we wish to avoid this prospect, we must begin to develop an economic theory that is capable of realistically accounting for the costs of doing business in the global environment. This cannot be accomplished by presuming, like the creators of neoclassical economic theory, that the scientific map in physical theories is identical to the vast complexities of human thought and behavior for an obvious reason—human behavior cannot be ultimately reduced to or entirely explained in terms of the interactions of quanta, atoms, molecules, or even the biophysical and neuronal processes in our bodies and brains.

The range of biologically predetermined behavior in our species is very small in comparison to other species because the evolved human capacity to acquire and use complex language systems made us free in a very radical sense. Meanings in our symbolic universes may be a function of themes and narratives invented by those who came before us. And the unfortunate tendency of groups of human beings to assume that the truths of their own cultural narratives are universal and that all other human beings must embrace these truths as well has been a major source of discord and conflict. Yet it is also demonstrable true that the ability to coordinate an increasing range of experience in social and political reality based on new narratives that enlarge the sense of shared meaning and purpose between all human beings has been critical to our survival.

The narrative called science bestowed the power upon us to control fundamental aspects of nature and to create complex technological systems that have allowed our numbers to increase the point where our economic activities are threatening the capacity of the system of life to sustain these numbers. This narrative has also provided us, however, with an understanding of the relationship between the parts (production and distribution systems) and whole (ecosystem or biosphere) that can serve as the basis for constructing a new narrative for organizing our experience in economic reality. For reasons that will become clear in the next chapter, however, the task developing an environmentally responsible economic theory will be formidable.

Even if this effort is successful, many powerful economic interests will oppose the implementation of this theory with something like the same zeal that the fossil-fuel industry has opposed regulations on emissions of greenhouse gases. It might be possible to frustrate the implementation of an environmentally responsible economic theory in the short term, but this will not be case in the longer term for a simple reason. Much of the recent research on nonlinear systems indicates that massive large-scale changes in the global environment could occur very quickly and that the resulting conditions could constitute a major threat to human life.

For example, scientists at the University of Wales in Bangor have recently shown that increases in droughts caused by global warming could activate dormant enzymes in peaty northern soils and trigger the decomposition of their organic matter. What makes this situation very dangerous is that these soils are estimated to hold about 60 percent of the amount of carbon that now exists in the atmosphere as carbon dioxide, and the carbon in the soils would be released as carbon dioxide in the decay process. The release of huge amounts of this greenhouse gas into the atmosphere would dramatically speed up the process of global warming. Even more disturbing, this could result in feedback loops between additional droughts, higher levels of decomposition in the soils, greater increases in the release of carbon dioxide, and more rapid global warming.[17]

As the dynamics of nonlinear systems are better understood and larger amounts of reliable data become available, predictions based on improved climate models will become increasingly more accurate. However, these predictions, for now obvious reasons, will never be entirely free of uncertainties. But in spite of this limitation, it is very likely that we will soon arrive at the point where scientists will conclude that their predictions are, for all practical purposes, good enough to warrant immediate large-scale action in the global community. If, or more probably when, this occurs, it should be quite clear that we must begin to coordinate our experience with economic reality based on an environmentally responsible economic theory. In the next chapter, we will consider some ways in which such a theory might be developed and some actions that could be taken during the period in which this effort is in progress.

CHAPTER 9

TOWARD A NEW THEORY OF ECONOMICS

The Costs of Doing Business in the Global Environment

> On the largest and most important questions facing the governments of the industrial countries the economics profession—I choose my words with care—is intellectually bankrupt. It might as well not exist.
>
> —John Kenneth Galbraith

I suspect that few mainstream economists actually believe that the choices made by economic actors are actually guided or determined by perfect knowledge of the consequences of their actions. Yet most do appear at least to believe that the natural laws of economics actually exist and this belief tends, in practice, to absolve economic actors in particular and market systems in general of any responsibility, moral or otherwise, for the state of the global environment. There may be some truth in the claim that neoclassical economics in practice tends to promote the development of democratic institutions, but it also denies in principle two fundamental precepts of democratic government—individuals are fully responsible for the consequences of their actions and free to coordinate their experience in ways that serve the common good. Because we cannot hope to develop and implement an environmentally responsible theory in the absence of these precepts, let us briefly consider why the creators of the narrative of mainstream economics came to deny their existence.

Adam Smith argued that people in previous generations were unable to perceive that there are lawful regularities in nature because they were blinded by various forms of gross superstition. This ignorance, said Smith, was eventually displaced by knowledge when more enlightened individuals realized that order in a mechanistic Newtonian universe results from the operations two sets of laws created by the absentee God of the Deists—the laws of physics and the natural laws of economics. But Smith could not offer any proof of the actual existence of the natural laws of economics and merely claimed that they must exist because no individual or group of individuals could possible direct activities in something as complex as a market system and sustain its orderly workings.

The creators of neoclassical economics, who were also convinced that order in economic reality could not be maintained by human agency, embraced Smith's view that the natural laws of economics are ontologically equivalent to the laws of physics. This explains why Jevons, Walras, Edgeworth, and Pareto were able to convince themselves that it was somehow appropriate to substitute economic variables for physical variables in the equations of a badly conceived and soon-to-be-outmoded mid-nineteenth century physics. But after substituting utility for energy in the physical equations, these economists were obliged to assume that utility is a force that acts causally and deterministically on atomized parts (economic actors and firms) to sustain general equilibrium in the whole (market system). And this required the imposition of the ad hoc assumption that the parts obey fixed decision-making rules that reflect their "perfect knowledge" of all possible outcomes for the economy.

This makes for a curious history. The inability to believe that human beings are capable of sustaining order in economic reality resulted in the creation of an altar to an unseen god and the proof of the existence of this god took the form of general equilibrium theory. According to this proof, economic actors are ultimately powerless over the motive force that obliges them to make economic decisions that reflect perfect knowledge of the consequences of their actions. Hence we are allegedly bound by the lawful manifestations of a force we perfectly understand, and yet our perfect knowledge of these manifestations merely testifies to the fact that our bondage is utterly complete.

In exchange for this perfect knowledge and this complete lack of freedom, the god promises to maintain the orderly workings of a stable and expanding whole (market system) in which the utility, or economic satisfaction and well-being, of parts (economic actors) will be perpetually enhanced. The god also alleges that it is both natural and good for economic actors to pursue selfishly their own economic interests because this serves, whether the actors know it or not, to sustain optimal conditions in the whole (closed market system). And because the outcomes of these self-ish actions are merely the manifestations of impersonal, amoral forces that govern the workings of a closed market system, the god absolves the actors of moral responsibility for the consequences of their economic behavior. Frank Hahn, widely viewed as one of the greatest neoclassical economists, made some comments in an interview that nicely illustrate how this process works: "There are many really difficult economic problems that we still need to tackle to understand how society works. And we (neoclassical economists) all recognize that from the economic point of view the environment is not a difficult intellectual problem. Yet, there are interesting aspects of the subject on a factual level, but otherwise they are elementary matters. In general it is an undergraduate exercise."[1]

In the formalism of neoclassical economic theory, the "environment is not a difficult problem" because it has value only as environmental resources that are subject to price mechanisms that operate within closed market systems. And dealing with environmental problems within the context of this theory is, in fact, an "elementary" exercise that any under-graduate major in neoclassical economics should be able to perform. In this exercise, one simply inserts numbers representing internalized costs of environmental resources into designated categories in standard equations and computes the results.

Later in the aforementioned interview Hahn says, "There is nothing in economic theory to suggest that the market could solve problems such as the environment." He explains why this must be the case: "The market can improve the situation, through policies such as taxation, licenses and so on. But it is the government that is making such policy decisions, not the market."[2] If the situation improves, this is not, implies Hahn, due to any actions taken within the market, because these actions are presumably governed by lawful or lawlike mechanisms which ensure that atomized economic actors maximize their utility based on available resources. Hence any improvements must result from policy decisions made outside the closed market system in another domain of reality where people are not subject to the mechanisms that govern economic behavior within the system.

Hahn's comments also suggest that actions taken to protect the environment by government are unnatural or artificial in economic terms because they are not subject to the natural laws of economics. He also clearly implies that these laws operate in a domain of reality in which the resources of nature exist only as capital and where capital as abstract value can be substituted for scarce resources. This suggests that the real value of these resources in economic terms is determined by mechanisms that disallow the prospect that an individual economic actor can freely confer a value other than that imposed by mechanisms. The problem here is not merely that there is nothing in neoclassical economic theory that can "solve problems in the global environment." It is also that there is no basis in this theory for accounting for these problems in economic terms or for recognizing or dealing with them in moral terms.

Milton Friedman is less sanguine than Hahn about the ability of government to deal with environmental problems and believes that the lawful mechanisms of market systems can, if left alone, resolve these problems:

> There is an appropriate regulatory institution, the market, in which prices are automatically adjusted to real costs; it's an automatic process which will place limits on itself, with full responsibility lying with population, and without anyone imposing limits from the outside. . . . All I know is that we have an institution that can stop us going too far: if we go too far the market will stop us through the price mechanism.[3]

In an effort to illustrate how this "automatic process" can impose limits on adverse environmental impacts of economic activities, Friedman says the following:

> Take oil, for example. Everyone says it's a limited resource: physically it may be, but economically we don't know. Economically there is more oil today than there was a hundred years ago. . . . When resources are really limited prices go up, but the price of oil has gone down and down. Suppose oil became scarce: the price would go up, and people would start using other energy sources. In a proper system the market can take care of the problem. . . . The price of oil has not been rising, so we're not living on the capital. When that is no longer true, the price system will give a signal and the price of oil will go up. As always happens with a truly limited resource.[4]

If the natural laws of economics actually existed and operated in the manner that Friedman describes, there would be no crisis in the global environment. But because these laws do not exist, the notion that "automatic" processes in the market system, which are nothing more than algorithms in the equations of neoclassical economics, will resolve environmental problems is clearly specious. Equally important for our purposes, Friedman also suggests that these automatic processes will resolve environmental problems in closed market systems even if economic actors are not aware of their existence and the external agency of government does nothing to resolve them.

Friedman's apparent belief in the real or actual existence of the invisible hand also explains why he is willing to make the claim that a physically limited resource, such as oil, is not really limited if prices for that resource do not reflect scarcity. For Friedman, the real amount of oil must be reflected in the market price of oil and lower prices indicate that this resource is abundant in spite of the fact that actual oil reserves will soon be exhausted. Similarly, he infers that the market price of oil is real because it is determined by the "automatic processes" of the closed market system and that any costs associated with damage done to the external environment by oil use is not, therefore, a real price.

Also consider some comments made in a recent interview by a more liberal mainstream economist—former U.S. Treasury Secretary Lawrence Summers. When asked if the "laws of economics" might be "changing or bending with the so-called new economy," Summers replied, "What has changed are the parameters of what's possible, of how rapidly we can expect our economy to grow. But what is always perilous is when governments believe they can repeal the laws of economics because they are inconvenient." Summers was then asked to comment on his thesis that the "Newtonian system of checks and balances in economics" is giving way to "a new Darwinism":

> What evolution teaches is that improvements in innovation come in many different forms. That evolution is an invisible process rather than a guiding hand process. . . . The essence of the Newtonian system was that you could predict where Saturn would be in a.d. 3800. The essence of a Darwinian system is that you can't make the same kind of predictions. And I think that imparts a certain humility to government as we make public policy. On the one hand, it inclines us toward deregulation, and on the other hand, it teaches us that the broadest environment is the best parameter in which evolution is allowed to operate. . . . The lesson for public policy is to pay attention to the overall framework in which the economy approaches its problems, but not to try to direct particular forms of it for which its evolution must follow.[5]

Summers, who is more flexible in his view of the dynamics of market systems than most neoclassical economists, is willing to admit that there is an element of indeterminacy in the operation of such systems. On the other hand, he clearly alleges that the laws of economics exist, that they will, if left alone, cause a market system to expand or grow, and that any attempt by government to "repeal the laws" could imperil the orderly workings of this system.

It is also interesting that Summers transforms the "invisible hand" of neoclassical economic theory into "a guiding hand process" in a "Darwinian system." One problem with this claim is that the dynamics of Darwinian evolution do not operate in complex human societies and have absolutely nothing to do with market economies. Another is that because the process of evolution includes random or chance mutations, the idea that this process could rationally determine the future of a humanly conceived and constructed market system makes no sense at all.

As we have seen, many neoclassical economists have abused scientific knowledge in an effort to "prove" that the natural laws of economics actually exist. It now seems clear, however, that those who believe in the existence of the god of the invisible hand must no longer be allowed to justify this belief in public debates about environmental problems by making appeals to scientific knowledge that have absolutely no basis in theory or in fact. If any of these individuals resist this conclusion, it is both reasonable and prudent to ask them to justify the real existence of the natural laws of economics in empirical terms without appealing to metaphysical assumptions or unfounded generalizations about the self-serving and self-aggrandizing behavior of human beings.

The intent here, however, is not to question the personal integrity of well-known and highly respected mainstream economists. It is to demonstrate that assumptions about part–whole relationships in neoclassical economic theory pervade the debate about economic solutions for environmental problems at the highest levels of public discourse and policymaking. The economists who appeal to these assumptions are not guilty of anything more than advancing the tenets of a theory that they presume to have substantive validity and their intent in doing so is to enhance the public good as they conceive it. Equally important, they did not invent these assumptions, and the fact that they are presumed to be scientific or quasi-scientific in the mathematical formalism of neoclassical economics would be perfectly meaningless in the absence of a large willingness among the public to believe that the assumptions represent fundamental truths.

Recognizing that the assumptions are arbitrarily conceived cultural products that constitute one of the greatest barriers to resolving the environmental crisis in economic terms may be the first critical step in the process of developing an environmentally responsible economic theory. But we cannot hope even to begin this development process, much less displace neoclassical economics with an environmentally responsible economic theory, in the absence of a political process in which large numbers of people realize that we are worshipping at the altar of a nonexistent deity. Mainstream economists may serve, unwittingly to be sure, as the priests in the temple that honors this god. But there would be no temple in absence of a large congregation of believers and many, perhaps most, of these people will mightily resist the conclusion that this god is dead.

ORDER IN ECONOMIC REALITY

To develop and implement an environmentally responsible economic theory, we must also recognize and appreciate a self-evident truth that is erased or displaced in the mathematical theories of neoclassical economics—the agency that creates incredible complex economic systems and manages them in ways that allow for a high level of coherence and stability is entirely human. This coherence and stability result from stochastic processes in human cognition that inform economic decisions, and it exists because large numbers of economic actors have assimilated narratives that describe roles, habits, and behavior in institutional frameworks and processes that deal in units of money. Because the institutional rules that govern monetary transactions are fairly stable and resistant to change, this also contributes in significant ways to the relative stability of markets.

Any unbiased examination of the dynamics of an actual or real economic process reveals that the only regularities involved are emergent from the cognitive processes of individuals who base decisions on a range of possible outcomes described in widely known and shared economic narratives. The narratives that inform these decisions may feature numerically based analyses that can be quite staggering in their complexity and very daunting in their abundance of details. But any order that emerges from this process has nothing to do with the operation of a transcendent godlike agency with a hand to spare. It results from cognitive processes in the minds of individuals that inform decisions to use available capital resources in transactions that are consistent with their perceptions of potential monetary gains or losses.

One can, of course, employ sophisticated mathematical techniques to describe emergent regularities in economic behavior within a range of probabilities and those descriptions can be useful in coordinating experience with market economies. But this clearly does not mean that the mathematical description discloses lawful dynamics in this behavior that point to the existence of "natural laws" that govern this behavior. It simply means that mathematical language is an effective means of modeling tendencies to occur in stochastic processes in which patterned behavior is a function of widely shared and mutually reinforced economic narratives. This becomes obvious when the conduct of normal or everyday life is disrupted by some disturbing event, which neoclassical economists conveniently label "nonmarket variables," and people express their fear, uncertainty, and confusion by deviating from scripts in the economic narratives. Nevertheless, people are, in fact, capable of sustaining a complex economic process in the absence of any assistance from the god of the invisible hand, and they do so with amazing regularity.

The developers of an environmentally responsible economic theory must also contend with another obvious fact of human existence that is ignored in neoclassical economic theory—there is no basis for accurately predicting the choices that large numbers of economic actors will make in response to any economic situation. Human cognition is an emergent phenomenon in the most complex structure in the known universe, the human brain, and there is no way to precisely predict how this cognition will inform economic decisions. Granted, a hungry person will in all probability choose to eat and a thirsty person will in all probability choose to drink. But if we exclude choices driven by biological functions, there is nothing more indeterminate in nature than the mental processes that inform human decisions in any domain of experience, including economic reality.

As the game theorists discovered, attempts to predict causally the choices that individual economic actors will make in response to even a limited number of well-defined variables result in outcomes that are neither fixed or determinant. And if we fully examined choices made by real people in real economic situations, this would require an infinite regress into the staggering complexities of language and culture. The fact that we cannot "in principle" predict with a high degree of certainty the choices that an individual economic actor will make in response to an economic situation in which there are a huge number of variables obliges us to draw the following conclusion. *There is no basis in economic reality for positing general laws or lawful regularities that would allow us to accurately predict the pattern of choices that will be made by economic actors.*

What this means for our purposes is that an environmentally responsible economic theory cannot be a science like the physical and biological sciences in its dealings with choices made by parts (economic actors and firms). Yet it must be a science like the physical and biological sciences to assess the impacts of the economic activities of the parts on the state of the whole (global ecosystem or biosphere). This new theory would obviously feature means and methods for understanding the bases on which economic actors make choices in terms of real or imagined needs and preferences and ability to pay. It would do so, however, based on a much more robust understanding of the multiple factors that inform these choices. And this should result in statistically more accurate assessments of consumer needs and preferences and more reliable proximate predictions of both short-term and long-term economic trends.

The developers of an environmentally responsible economic theory must also view the role of government as much more integral to the economic process than neoclassical economics allows. The notion that actions taken by government lie outside the closed market system and that these actions only impede the workings of market economies is absurd in principle and has never been the case in practice. Governments regulate market economies, manage institutions that facilitate the operation of these economies, enact and enforce laws that protect the interests of economic actors, protect the health and safety of consumers, and provide essential services that allow both local and global economies to function. The fundamental means of exchange in market systems, paper money, is issued and backed by governments, and the value of paper currencies is protected and maintained by governments. If we actually existed in a world where governments impose no taxes and serve no regulatory and oversight functions, the global economic system would immediately collapse.

The primary role of a democratic government is to serve and protect the "public good" and the term "public" typically refers to people who are citizens of a particular nation-state or who live within its boundaries. This conception of the character of geopolitical reality is imaged on a typical globe where countries are marked by dark boundaries and painted different colors. The stark difference between these geopolitical representations of life on earth and a scientific understanding of earth as a living system is immediately apparent when the representations are compared with satellite images that environmental scientists use to assess regional and global conditions.

In these images, it is clear that all aspects of the nonlinear system of life are interdependent and interactive and that the activities of all parts (organic and inorganic systems and processes) impact the condition of the whole (global ecosystem or biosphere). It is also obvious in these images that the impacts of economic activities on conditions in this whole are not circumscribed by or contained within national boundaries, and there are no overt indications that nation-states, as separate and discrete entities, even exist.

What this crude comparison between geopolitical maps and satellite images illustrates is the massive difference between two paradigms for constructing part–whole relationships on planet earth: (1) a geopolitical paradigm in which the whole is the sum of separate and discrete parts and the parts compete with other parts for domination or hegemony by extending territory and influence, and (2) a scientific paradigm in which the parts exist in embedded and interactive relationship to the whole, the whole is more than the sum of the parts, and the survival of parts is dependent upon conditions in the whole that are sustained and regulated by the interactions of the parts.

If government is to serve and protect the public good in environmental terms, the public must be defined as all people on planet earth and the good as the health and well- being of these individuals and their descendants. And because this public good cannot be served in the absence of a sustainable global environment, the fundamental challenge is to coordinate global economic activities in ways that can realize this goal. For obvious reasons, the only system of government that can accomplish this effectively is international, and there are no indications that such a system will emerge anytime soon. The United Nations has been hugely ineffectual in dealing with environmental problems in economic terms, and the only system in place with institutional frameworks and processes that are truly international in reach is the global economic system. As the environmental crisis becomes more acute, however, it is not unreasonable to assume that an international system of government based on the principles of democracy could eventually emerge and that one of its primary functions will be to coordinate global economic activities based on an environmentally responsible economic theory.

TOWARD AN ENVIRONMENTALLY RESPONSIBLE ECONOMIC THEORY

But given the present state of geopolitical reality, the best that we hope to accomplish in the near term is to forge an international agreement between nation-states that results in the creation a well-funded organization or agency charged with completing the following tasks:

- Develop scientifically valid means and methods for measuring the relationship between the economic activities of parts (major production and distribution systems) and the state of the whole (ecosystem or biosphere);
- Develop means and methods for translating these measures into price mechanisms that realistically reflect the costs of doing business in the global environment;
- Devise a plan that could lead to the creation of an international organization or agency that has the power and authority to ensure that these price mechanisms are universally applied in a fair and consistent manner throughout the global economic system.

Obviously, this would be an incredibly ambitious research project, and today we can only imagine what workable solutions might look like. I do not pretend to know what these solutions are, and the following description of a general framework within which an environmentally responsible economic theory could be developed is approximate and quite crude. The intent is merely to illustrate that there is at least one viable basis for developing such a theory. And the hope is that this discussion will serve as a catalyst for a public debate that could culminate in a willingness to create and adequately fund what could be the most vitally important research program in human history.

We can now represent with a reasonable degree of accuracy the economic activities of the parts (major production and distribution systems) based on the following measures:

- Amount of low-entropy materials consumed in major production and distribution
- Amount of high-entropy generated in the production of materials and goods and in the distribution of products

- Total amount of throughput in production and distribution measured in units of energy
- Amounts of greenhouse gases, pollutants, and toxic substances generated
- Amounts of consumption of nonrenewable resources
- Amounts of biological important nutrients removed from nutrient cycling in the biosphere
- Environmental impacts over the lifetimes of products
- Environmental impacts of product wastes
- Recycling of products
- Efficient use of energy resources

Measures of the state of the whole, which can also now be determined with a reasonable degree of accuracy, could include the following:

- Levels of greenhouse gases in the atmosphere
- Ozone levels in the atmosphere
- Percentage increases or decreases in global warming
- Conditions of rainforests, fisheries, arable lands, and rangelands
- Percentage increases or decreases in coral reefs
- Amounts of arable land, potable water, open water, and groundwater
- Extinction rates
- Loss of species diversity
- Percentage increases, or decreases, in human population growth

One of the most challenging problems faced by the developers of this theory will be to determine how to translate correlations between these part–whole relationships into units of money. Some have argued that this is not possible because we do not know how to define baseline measures for a sustainable global environment in scientific or empirical terms and, therefore, there is no basis upon which to confer a monetary value on this environment.[6] We are now in the process, however, of developing vastly more sophisticated computer models that can simulate the dynamics of nonlinear systems and a new generation of climate modeling computers that can handle the orders of magnitude increases in computation required by the models.

For example, Japan has spent more than $400 million on the development of a linked array of supercomputers that can calculate orders of magnitude faster than the best existing climate modeling systems. A typical array used for climate modeling in the United States can process about twenty gigaflops, or twenty billion floating operations per second, and the best European systems about one hundred gigaflops. The performance of the new Japanese system, appropriately called the Earth Simulator, is measured in teraflops, or thousands of gigaflops per second.[7] With the use of these new research tools, along with the vast amounts of improved data from satellites and ground-based observation systems, scientists are increasingly confident that they can reasonably determine baseline measures for sustainability in the global environment.

But because life on earth is an enormously complex nonlinear system in which indeterminacy is a macro-level phenomenon, the only way in which the baseline measures can ever be defined is within a range of probabilities. This means that those who develop the new economic theory must realize that measures for sustainability in the whole (global ecosystem or biosphere) can only be determined in these approximate terms and that the baseline measures of sustainability included in the economic theory must be based on the precautionary principle.

Those involved in this development project must also decide how to deal with a major dilemma that we have, thus far, been unable to resolve. How can we value a sustainable global environment in monetary terms when there is no basis for realistically doing so in the economic theory that serves almost universally as the basis for establishing the monetary value of all goods and commodities, including environmental resources? This dilemma has resulted in another Catch-22 situation for those who have attempted to confer a cost on natural resources by enlarging the framework of neoclassical economics in ways that would allow these resources to be valued as "natural capital."

For example, ecological economist Robert Costanza has recently developed a model in which global ecosystem services have a central value of $33 trillion per year with a range of $16 to $54 trillion per year.[8] Although this scheme confers a value on global environmental resources that is roughly one to three times global GNP, it cannot and will not work for a now familiar reason. The actual character of relationships between parts (organisms) and whole (global ecosystem or biosphere) is categorically different from and wholly incompatible with assumptions about the relationships between parts (economic actors and firms) and wholes (market systems) in neoclassical economic theory.

Because the theory obliges Costanza to represent the costs of environmental resources in terms of internalized market values, these costs may not be taken seriously by those who believe that "real" costs can only be determined by pricing mechanisms that operate within closed market systems. The neoclassical conception of value also forces Costanza to link the value of the natural capital of environmental resources to a volatile and unpredictable variable, global consumption of scarce resources based on market prices. Consequently, the resulting market value of the natural capital is related to the value of a sustainable environment only in the sense that the opportunity costs associated with the use of this capital are higher. For example, the scheme suggests that if the total value of environmental resources is at its maximum three times that of global GNP, there might be plenty of room to grow the global economy. The most fundamental problem with any such schemes, however, is that internalized market values of environmental resources, even if these values are recognized as the equivalent of market values, can never be equal to or the same as the value of a sustainable environment. For example, internalized market values necessarily exclude the costs of negative environmental impacts of nonmarket activities and cannot realistically account for the very large value in ecological terms of the global commons.

Perhaps the most reasonable way to resolve this dilemma in an environmentally responsible economic theory is to begin with the following assumptions:

- The absolute value is a sustainable global environment.
- The prime value is the goal of achieving this environment.
- All other values are a function of these values.

In this value theory, the absolute value would be represented in monetary terms by some robust measure of the activities of the whole of the global economy over a period of time. The measure used here is total flows of global capital for the previous ten years. There may, of course, be more suitable ways to determine how to represent this absolute value in monetary terms. However, it does seem clear that the amount must be large enough to clearly indicate that global economic activities have value only as a function of the absolute value of a sustainable environment.

The next major task of the developers of the new economic theory will be to define a sustainable global environment in terms of optimal values for the designated measures of the state of the whole in accordance with the precautionary principle. These optimal measures could be represented in an algorithm that describes in proximate terms a sustainable global environment, and this algorithm could be updated and refined on an annual basis to reflect advances in knowledge and improved observational data. This algorithm would allow the relative contributions of each of the optimal measures of sustainability to be broken down into percentage terms. The percentage assigned each measure could then be translated into dollar equivalents as that percentage of the value of the sustainable whole (global ecosystem or biosphere). Hence the dollar amount assigned each measure would represent its value as a percentage of the absolute value of the sustainable whole, and this amount could serve as the basis for calculating costs associated with the prime value of achieving the goal of a sustainable environment.

These costs could be calculated by first determining in percentage terms the extent to which specific measures of the global economic activities of a part (major system of production or distribution) in the previous year contributed to "decreases" in specific optimal values for sustainability in the whole. The percentage decrease for each value could then be translated into dollar equivalents as the percentage decrease in the value of the corresponding optimal measure.

One concern here is that the costs of doing business in the global environment in the initial phase of implementation of the new economic theory could be so high that they could easily cause a breakdown in the global economic system. For example, several recent scientific studies have indicated that in order to achieve the goal of a sustainable global environment, material flows in industrialized economies may have to be reduced by roughly 90 percent, or by a factor of ten.[9] This suggests that the developers of the new theory must devise a strategy for phasing in environmental costs that will not cause massive disruptions in the global economic system. At the same time, however, they must be certain that these costs are consistent with the prime value of achieving a sustainable environment. The translation of these costs into actual dollar amounts in very different economies, such as those in the first and third worlds, would obviously be a large problem. However, this problem could be resolved in equitable ways based on measures such as the Index for Sustainable Economic Welfare and the Human Development Index.

The index of optimal measures for sustainability in the whole (global ecosystem or biosphere) and the index of measures of the activities of parts (major production and distribution systems) could be perpetually reviewed, extended, and refined based on improved observational techniques and more advanced computer models. As the knowledge base expands, the new economic theory could be continually refined to include more physical variables and advances in scientific knowledge, such as an improved understanding of the dynamics of nonlinear systems.

Another major challenge that the developers of an environmentally responsible economic theory must meet is to develop a value theory that is not premised, like that of neoclassical economics, on a categorical distinction between market values and ecological values. Value theory in neoclassical economics merely reifies choices made by consumers by alleging that these choices are governed and directed by the god of the invisible hand. If the consumer is willing to pay, the god has spoken and there is nothing else than can be said about the matter. In the new economic theory, however, markets would not be viewed as separate in any sense from the global environment or even as subsystems of this environment. They would be viewed as collections of human activities embedded in and interactive with the real economy of the global environment. Hence the price paid for a sustainable environment in the new pricing mechanisms would be viewed as a cost of doing business in this environment and not as a tax on business activities.

This distinction between a cost and a tax is not a trivial matter. A tax is a compulsory levy on private individuals and organizations, including firms, made by government to raise revenue to finance public goods and services. A cost is a measure of what must be given up in order to obtain or acquire something in a purchase or exchange. In the new environmentally responsible economic theory, government would, of course, continue to levy taxes for all the usual reasons and that includes protecting the environment via oversight, regulation and research. But because economic activities in the new theory would be represented as parts that exist in embedded and interactive relationship to the whole of the global environment, the costs of goods and commodities would necessarily include the costs that represent this relationship. And because these costs would be understood as the costs of doing business in the global environment and no different in kind from any other costs, they would be represented as such in pricing mechanisms and systems of accounting. In other words, the column labeled taxes would not include these costs, and there would no tax advantage associated with paying this cost.

It is important to realize here that the greatest barrier to the implementation of such an economic theory would not be technical. We have the means to measure the inputs and outputs of major economic systems that are responsible for damage done to the global environment and the means to measure variables on the state of the whole. We now have, or will soon have, the means to establish baseline measures of sustainability in the whole (global ecosystem or biosphere), and the resulting environmental costs could be calculated with an algorithm running on a desktop computer. The greatest barrier to implementation is the assumption that a sustainable environment is an absolute value, that the prime value is the goal of achieving this environment, and that all other values in economic terms must be a function of this value.

In the absence of this assumption, it will probably not be possible to develop an environmentally economic theory that can displace neoclassical economic theory, and we may well continue along a path that could easily result in large-scale disruptions in the global environment. Keep in mind, however, that as the environmental crisis intensifies, the value of a sustainable whole could well be perceived as an ultimate value for a simple reason. It will soon become clear that the activities of human beings will have no ultimate value, economic or otherwise, in the absence of a sustainable whole.

If we do elect to develop an environmentally responsible economic theory, this effort could go forward during a period in which our scientific understanding of long-term environmental impacts significantly improves and large-scale disruptions in the global environment become increasingly more apparent. It is reasonable to assume that over the next ten years international concern about the deterioration of the global environment will become very acute, that national governments will be under enormous pressures to speak to the problem, and that many companies and corporations will realize that it is in their best interests to attempt to resolve the problem. Under these conditions, the need to develop an economic theory for the real economy of the global environment will be quite apparent.

If we elect to develop and implement an environmentally responsible economic theory, this could result in a global economic system in which the environmental impacts of major economic activities are reflected in units of money and monetary values are fundamentally ecological values. Because price mechanisms would constantly remind consumers of the intimate connection between economic activities and the state of the global environment, this should be reflected in the view of monetary values. And because these mechanisms would reflect on an ongoing basis an improved scientific understanding of the evolving relationship between parts and wholes in the global environment, ecological values should be closely wed to monetary values. It is also reasonable to assume that an enhanced understanding of these dynamics would make the overall scale of consumption more commensurate with basic needs than unlimited desires and that distribution of income and wealth would become more equitable than they are today.

One can also imagine a new global system of labeling laws that requires that a label be attached to all goods and commodities similar to the food-labeling system in the United States. This label would represent in easily understood graphic format the relationship between the environmental impacts associated with the production and distribution of a particular part (product or service) and the state of the whole (measures of optimal sustainability in the global environment).

ENVIRONMENTAL TAX REFORM

Given the short time frame where there will be an opportunity to reverse the damage to the global ecosystem, it is imperative that we do something more than elect to develop an environmentally responsible economic theory. One approach that could be implemented while the theory is under development is to make much more extensive use of a device that neoclassical economists view as external to closed market systems and, in most cases, as an impediment to economic growth—environmental tax reforms. The basic principle in these reforms, which have been enacted in Germany, the Netherlands, and the Scandinavian countries, is very simple—raise taxes on activities that should be discouraged and lower taxes on those that should be encouraged.

The large-scale imposition of environmental taxes would obviously retard growth in industries where production and distribution systems are large contributors to environmental damage. But it would also create new markets for products that have less adverse environmental impacts. Sales in the environmental protection industry in the United States, which employs about four million people, are already over $150 billion annually.[10] The market in green technologies in developed countries is now about $200 billion per annum and the growth of this market in developing countries is projected to be very dramatic in the coming decades. Based on a detailed account of existing green technologies and others that will soon be available, Paul Hawken, Amory Lovins, and Hunter Lovins have made a convincing case in *Natural Capitalism: Creating the Next Industrial Revolution* that companies that exploit these technologies could reap enormous financial gains.[11] Given that the widespread implementation of these technologies would be labor-intensive, they also argue that this would create large numbers of jobs and dramatically increase levels of employment internationally.

There is no question that environmental tax reform in highly industrialized first- world economies is critically important. There is, however, no prospect that reforms on this level alone can begin to reverse the damage that is now being done to the global environment by global economic activities. The only way we can hope to achieve this goal is to create an international system of environmental tax reform that is almost universally applied and very rigorously enforced. That recent attempts to establish international agreements that would result in a very modest decrease in the global emissions of greenhouse gases have failed miserably is not encouraging. Let us not forget, however, that those who were responsible for frustrating these agreements consistently appealed to assumptions about economic reality in neoclassical economics.

The following proposal is in accord with the basic principles of environmental tax reform, but it is far more ambitious and much broader in scope. The proposal is for an Ecosystem Restoration Tax that could be levied in the initial phase on the two hundred largest transnational or international corporations and administered by a new international agency. This agency, which should be independent of existing international agencies, such as the United Nations, World Bank, and International Monetary Fund, could be created during an international conference dedicated to this purpose. Participating nations should be required to eliminate tax breaks and subsidies for some corporations, like those in the fossil fuel industry, that artificially lower costs of low-entropy resources and encourage overconsumption.

The bases for determining the amount of this tax could be derived from extensions and refinements of measures already in use in Germany, the Netherlands, and the Scandinavian countries. The tax would serve as a large incentive to develop more energy efficient production techniques and processes as well as products that have longer lifetimes and fewer adverse environmental impacts. Because prices of goods and commodities would be highly sensitive to the amount of tax, consumers would have a large financial incentive to purchase products with lower environmental impacts. The amount of revenue generated by the tax, which could conceivably be as large as the GNP of the United States, could be used for some of the following purposes:

- Lease or purchase of environmentally sensitive areas, such as rain-forests, wetlands, and deserts, and furnish resources to manage them;
- Provide alternate economic opportunities for those who earn their livelihood in environmentally sensitive areas;
- Finance the development of green technologies, or products and processes with low environmental impact;
- Finance the dissemination and implementation of these green technologies;
- Create a worldwide educational system that focuses on problems in the global environment and that relies heavily on electronic media and computer-based distance learning;
- Fund ongoing research on the state of the global environment;
- Establish a more extensive network of centers for family planning within developing nations and provide some financial incentives to use birth control to couples that have two or more children;
- Establish an educational campaign in developed countries with heavy reliance on print and electronic media that encourages couples to have no more than two children;
- Promote the use of trade barriers, boycotts and bans on products produced by nations that refuse to implement the Ecosystem Maintenance Tax.

Granted, it would not be difficult to compile an impressively long list of reasons why these or other similar proposals will not be enacted, but this list will grow progressively shorter as large-scale disruptions in the global environment become increasingly more apparent.

There is, however, another source of resistance that will be much more difficult to overcome—the enormous emotional appeal of the neoclassical economic paradigm. Part of this appeal can be explained in terms of the absurd expectation that the lawful mechanisms of market systems will, if left alone, result in the emergence of a global economic system in which all material needs and desires are endlessly gratified. But materialism as a utopian ideal is merely the alleged earthly reward for believing in the existence of an unseen god whose metaphysical or religious appeal derives from a large promise that has nothing to do with the reward per se. The promise is that the part (self) in economic reality is a meaningful aspect of an ordered whole (market system) and that the actions taken by this self in its own best interests will contribute to the maintenance of this whole.

Self as an atomized entity acted upon by the wholly deterministic and impersonal forces of natural laws may be consistent with the implications of classical physics. It should now be clear, however, that this view of self makes no sense at all from the perspective of modern biology and physics. In the next chapter, I will argue that we have arrived at a place in human history where we can no longer afford to ignore the human implications of our most advanced scientific knowledge in the conduct of our lives. This knowledge not only lends emotional force to the necessity of developing an environmentally responsible economic theory, but it could also serve as the basis for the emergence of a new global ethos, or an "ecology of mind," that could massively contribute to the timely resolution of the environmental crisis.

CHAPTER 10

THE CEREMONY OF INNOCENCE
Science, Ethics, and the Environmental Crisis

> Nor shall you scare us with talk of the death of the race.
> How should we dream of this place without us?—
> The sun mere fire, the leaves untroubled about us,
> A stone look on the stone's face?
>
> —Richard Wilbur, "Advice to a Prophet"

This book began with a reminiscence about the awe and wonder I felt, as did so many millions of others, in 1969 when we first saw a televised picture of the whole earth taken by cameras on the Apollo 11 spacecraft. For a time, this image seemed to be pervasive in American culture—it appeared on posters, on the covers of popular magazines, in films and movies, and in an impressive number of ads in both print and electronic media. Like any visual image repeated with great frequency in a variety of different contexts, the whole earth image seemed to lose, in a matter of months, much of its original significance and emotive power. But for some of us, myself included, the image still serves as sign and symbol of two astonishing facts—life evolved on this planet to a level of incredible beauty and complexity, and only one species eventually became, against all odds, fully conscious of its own being and becoming.

The chemical compounds from which the first self-replicating molecules of life emerged on this planet are present in the universe at large and particularly prevalent in our own galaxy. Some of the necessary ingredients, such as amino acids, can spontaneously emerge under suitable conditions, and this process has been duplicated in the laboratory. In order for life to arise from these compounds on other planets, however, a delicate balance between many other factors, such as temperatures, atmospheric pressures, and water content, would be required. But because galaxies number in the billions and an average galaxy contains hundreds of billions of stars, many planets with conditions suitable for life could circle their own sun in our galaxy or in neighboring galaxies. And if life has arisen on millions of these planets, it is conceivable that intelligent or conscious life forms have evolved elsewhere in the universe and developed their own advanced civilizations.

The most ardent promoters of this thesis tend to be physicists and molecular biologists, and public acceptance of their views resulted in the creation of the Search for Extraterrestrial Intelligence (SETI) project. The intent of those involved in this project, as many Americans learned for the first time after seeing the movie based on the late Carl Sagan's novel *Cosmos*, is to intercept intragalactic or intergalactic communications between advanced civilizations on other planets. What the book and movie failed to mention, however, is that an impressive group of scientists, most of whom are evolutionary biologists, are convinced that the odds that advanced civilizations exist anywhere in the cosmos are slim to none. Some members in this group, like Ernst Mayr, have made a rather convincing case that SETI was a deplorable waste of taxpayers' money.[1]

These skeptics point out that even if we assume that life has emerged numerous times elsewhere, we must then imagine an evolutionary pathway that results in a species like our own that has the capacity to acquire and use complex language systems. Because evolution at the level of mutations is a completely random process and its future cannot in principle be predicted, the skeptics claim that there is no basis for assuming that life on other planets would necessarily result in the emergence of an intelligent life form. During billions of years of evolution on this planet, 99 percent of existing species became extinct, and only a small portion of mammals, the anthropoid apes, emerged via innumerable indeterminate branch points with an intelligence that surpasses that of other mammals. During the twenty-five million years in which these apes have existed, there were probably hundreds of branching points and independently evolving lines and only one became the lineage that evolved into modern humans.

Many evolutionary biologists have concluded that the evolution of consciousness in this single lineage was itself highly improbable and this conclusion has been considerably reinforced by recent studies on the preadaptive changes that eventually allowed modern humans to acquire and use the complex symbol systems of ordinary language. Until quite recently, very little was known about the evolution of those aspects of the human brain associated with language use, and virtually nothing was known about the neural mechanisms involved in language processing. What has changed this situation dramatically over the past two decades is advances in neuroscience made possible by new computer-based brain imaging systems such as positron emission tomography (PET) and functional magnetic resonance imaging (fMRI). These systems essentially allow researchers to observe which areas in the brains of conscious subjects are active while performing cognitive tasks.

Research based on these technologies has revealed that language processing is staggeringly complex and places incredible demands on memory and learning. Language functions extend, for example, into all major lobes of the neocortex—auditory input is associated with the temporal area, tactile with the parietal area, and attention, working memory, and planning with the frontal cortex of the left or dominant hemisphere. The left prefrontal region is associated with verb- and noun-production tasks and in the retrieval of words representing action. Broca's area, adjacent to the mouth-tongue region of the motor cortex, is associated with vocalization in word formation, and Wernicke's area, adjacent to the auditory cortex, is associated with sound analysis in the sequencing of words.

Lower brain regions like the cerebellum have also evolved in our species to assist in language processing. Until recently, the cerebellum was thought to be exclusively involved with automatic or preprogrammed movements such as throwing a ball, jumping over a high hurdle, or playing well-practiced notes on a musical instrument. Imaging studies in neuroscience indicate, however, that the cerebellum is activated during speaking and most activated when the subject is making difficult word associations. It is now thought that the cerebellum plays a role in association by providing access to automatic word sequences and by augmenting rapid shifts in attention.

The midbrain and brain stem, situated on top of the spinal cord, coordinate input and output systems in the head and play a crucial role in communication functions. Vocalization has a special association with the midbrain, which coordinates the interaction of the oral and respiratory tracks necessary to make speech sounds. Because human vocalization requires synchronous activity between oral, vocal, and respiratory muscles, these functions probably connect to a central site. This site appears to be the central gray area of the brain. The central gray area links the reticular nuclei and brain stem motor nuclei to comprise a distributed network for sound production. Although human speech is dependent on structures in the cerebral cortex and rapid movement of the oral and vocal muscles, this is not true for vocalization in other mammals.[2]

When we consider the wayward evolutionary pathway by which modern humans emerged with a brain capable of imaging and manipulating a world in the symbolic space of mind, it is not difficult to appreciate why many evolutionary biologists are skeptical about the prospect that intelligent life exists on other planets. From their perspective, it could well be that earth is the only planet on which fully conscious beings exist. But if conscious life forms have emerged on other planets, we can safely assume that this would be an equally improbable event in which the evolution of progressively more complex mutually interdependent interactions between parts (organisms) and whole (ecosystem or biosphere) eventually allowed for this remarkable result.

THE HOMELESS MIND

After the bodies and brains of members of our species evolved the capacity to acquire and use complex language systems, our ancestors were able to construct a symbolic universe in which an actor called self became aware of its own awareness. The price paid for entering this symbolic universe was an acute sense of the existence of a self that is separate from world and a corresponding loss of any immediate and unmediated sense of connection to world. This explains why one of the most profound human impulses is now and has always been to bridge the gap between self and world in themes and narratives that are progressively more inclusive, extended, and refined.

The meta-narrative or frame tales in the symbolic universes of modern humans that allowed the categorical oppositions and terms of relation between self and world to be legitimized, rationalized, and explained have consistently been those of religious thought. In the seventeenth century, Newtonian or classical physics provided an alternate basis for understanding this relationship in a meta-narrative or frame tale called science that also allowed constructs in our symbolic universes to be constructed in terms of origins, primary oppositions and underlying causes. The two meta-narratives were perceived as providing competing and often categorically different explanations for phenomena in the same domains of reality, and the conflict and tension between them was immediate and ongoing.

The first scientific revolution of the seventeenth century freed Western civilization from the paralyzing and demeaning forces of superstition, laid the foundations for rational understanding and control of the processes of nature, and ushered in an era of technological innovation and progress that provided untold benefits for humanity. But as classical physics progressively dissolved the distinction between heaven and earth and united the universe in a shared and communicable frame of knowledge, it presented us with a view of physical reality that was totally alien from the world of everyday life.

Nature in classical physics was viewed as a vast machine in which forces act between mass points in the abstract background of space and time and collections of mass points interact as isolated and isolatable systems. The knowing self was separate, discrete, atomized, and achieved its knowledge of physical reality from the "outside" of physical systems without disturbing the system under study. As physicist Henry Stapp puts it, "Classical physics not only fails to demand the mental, it fails to even provide a rational place for the mental. And if the mental is introduced ad hoc, then it must remain totally ineffectual, in absolute contradiction to our deepest experience."[3]

René Descartes, the father of modern philosophy, realized that there was nothing in this view of nature that could provide a foundation for the mental, or for all that we know from direct experience as distinctly human. In classical physics, external reality consisted of inert and inanimate matter moving in accordance with deterministic physical laws, and collections of discrete atomized parts constituted wholes. Because physical reality, or that which actually exists external to self, in this physics was only that which could be represented in terms of mathematical and geometrical relationships, Descartes concluded that there was no privileged place or function for mind and that the separation between mind and matter is absolute. Even living organisms, according to Descartes, were machines that could be completely analyzed and understood in terms of component parts. He was also convinced, however, that the immaterial essences that gave form and structure to physical reality were coded in geometrical and mathematical ideas and this insight led him to invent algebraic geometry.

A scientific understanding of these ideas could be derived, said Descartes, with the aid of precise deduction and the contours of physical reality could be laid out in three-dimensional coordinates. Following the publication of Newton's *Principia Mathematica* in 1687, reductionism and mathematical modeling became the most powerful tools of modern science. The dream that the entire physical world could be known and mastered through the extension and refinement of mathematical theory became the central feature and guiding principle of scientific knowledge. Scientists used increasingly more complex mathematical theories to situate natural processes in the three-dimensional Cartesian space and linear time. The success of this enterprise suggested that the map was the landscape and that other unknown territories could be discovered and charted by simply following the map.

The radical separation between mind and nature formalized by Descartes allowed scientists to concentrate on developing mathematical descriptions of matter as pure mechanisms in the absence of any concerns about its spiritual dimensions or ontological foundations. Meanwhile, attempts to rationalize, reconcile, or eliminate Descartes's stark division between mind and matter became the most central feature of Western intellectual life, and this, as many have argued, became the source of much of our disillusionment, anguish, and angst.

The Enlightenment idea of deism, which imaged the universe as a clockwork and God as the clockmaker, provided grounds for believing in divine agency at the moment of creation. It also implied, however, that all the creative forces of the universe were exhausted at origins, that self was merely a cog in a giant machine linked to other parts of the machine in only the most mundane material terms, and that all events in the cosmos are utterly preordained. The French moral philosophers who influenced the creators of classical economics embraced these views and constructed a relationship between self and world consistent with the classical paradigm in physics. As a result, they posited the existence of a set of natural laws analogous to the laws of Newtonian physics that allegedly govern the interaction and behavior of separate, discrete, and atomized human minds. From this perspective, Smith, Malthus, and Ricardo were merely extending the program begun by the moral philosophers by attempting to bridge the gap between mind and world in economic reality with an appeal to the natural laws of economics.

In the nineteenth century, Cartesian dualism remained the central preoccupation of mainstream philosophers, in spite of challenges from the romantics, and seemed completely compatible with mid-nineteenth century physics, in spite of its deviations from Newtonian physics. But when the neoclassical economists introduced their new form of this dualism into mathematical theories derived from mid-nineteenth century physics, the freedom associated with the domain of mind was immeasurably compromised. The single mind that Descartes imagined as free within its own domain to assert its existence without constraint became two minds. This second mind, which slavishly obeyed mechanical decision-making rules in accordance with the deterministic force of the invisible hand, was not free. It was bound to its possessor by what Smith termed the "chains" of the invisible hand, and this bondage was made to appear utterly complete and inexorable in the mathematical theories of the neoclassical economists.

The widespread acceptance of the absurd and indefensible claim that the neoclassical economists had transformed economics into a science not only served to erase all associations with the God of the Deists. It also legitimated the view that self in economic reality is an atomized entity governed and controlled by the inexorable forces of natural laws in a soulless and brute automatism called the market system. One compensation for this obeisance to a power over which one has no control is the anxiety-reducing awareness that the lawful or lawlike mechanisms of the system are universal and maintain order in the absence of any conscious intervention or control by fallible human beings. Another is that the machinations will preserve the whole (market system) by perpetually enhancing the economic well-being of all the parts (economic actors and firms).

When a society systematically engages in activities based on a broadly disseminated and reinforced set of dogmatic beliefs that seem to bridge the gap between mind and world even though they are not true, anthropologists refer to this phenomenon as a "useful myth." Neoclassical economics can fairly be described as a useful myth that has outlived its usefulness, and those of us who realize that this is the case must seek to dismantle it with all deliberate speed. Part of what is required to accomplish this formidable task is the ability to systematically demonstrate that the invisible hand is nothing more than a metaphysical construct. But because the useful myth of neoclassical economics is a product of the Western metaphysical tradition and rests on metaphysical foundations, it is at base level a religious system. The large problem here is that a religious system is rarely, if ever, abandoned simply because it is unscientific. It must be displaced by an alternate useful myth that provides a more compelling sense of the meaningful interdependence and interconnection between self and world.

The useful myth that could displace that of neoclassical economics is a new understanding of the relationship between part (self or mind) and whole (nature or cosmos) that is consistent with the radical new understanding of part–whole relationships that has emerged in contemporary physics and biology. Those who are not inclined, for whatever reasons, to explore the extrascientific philosophical and religious implications of scientific knowledge may dismiss some of this discussion out of hand. But an interest in such matters is not required to appreciate the manner in which our most advanced scientific knowledge of part–whole relationships in physical reality could contribute to the resolution of the environmental crisis.

A NEW PHILOSOPHY OF MIND

On the most primary level, the cosmos is a dynamic sea of energy manifesting itself in entangled quanta and in seamlessly interconnected events. This dynamic process eventually allowed for the emergence of new wholes in organic molecules that display novel properties that are more than the sum of their parts and that do not exist in inorganic molecules. The embedded interaction of these parts allowed for the emergence of a whole (ecosystem or biosphere) that was more than the sum of its parts and that displayed emergent properties, such as those that regulate global temperature and the relative abundance of atmospheric gases, that sustain the whole.

Much of the ambiguity in attempts to explain the character of wholes in both physics and biology derives from the assumption that order exists "between" parts. But order in the relationship between difference and sameness in any physical event is never external to that event—the connections are immanent in the event. Each of the systems we attempt to isolate in the study of nature is in some sense a whole in that each system represents the whole in the activity of being the part. But no single system, with the exception of the entire universe, can fully realize the cosmic order of the totality due to the partial and subordinate character of differentiated systems. No part can sustain itself in its own right because difference is only one aspect of its being—the other aspect requires participation in the sameness of the cosmic order. All differentiated systems in nature require, in theory and in fact, supplementation by other systems, and this now appears to be as true in biology as it is in physics.

In these terms, consciousness, or mind, can be viewed as an emergent phenomenon in the seamless evolution of the cosmos at the highest levels of complexity in biological reality. If consciousness manifests or emerges in the later stages and has been progressively unfolding from the beginning stages, we can logically conclude, as opposed to scientifically prove, that the universe could be conscious. In the grand interplay of quanta and field in whatever stage of complexity, including the very activities of our brain, there is literally "no thing" that can be presumed isolated or discrete. From this perspective, consciousness may enfold within itself progressive stages of emergent complex order throughout the history of the universe.[4]

I do not wish to suggest that this consciousness is in any sense anthropomorphic. Our present understanding of nature neither supports nor refutes any conceptions of design, meaning, purpose, intent, or plan associated with any mytho-religious or cultural heritage. As Werner Heisenberg put it, such words are "taken from the realm of human experience" and are "metaphors at best."[5] What I mean by conscious universe is, however, consistent with the totality of scientific facts and is anthropocentric only to the extent that it answers to a very basic human need. The need is to feel that a profound awareness of unity with the whole is commensurate with our scientific worldview, and this awareness cannot be discounted or undermined with an appeal to scientific knowledge.

A NEW BASIS FOR DIALOGUE BETWEEN SCIENCE AND RELIGION

Much has been written about the manner in which the "useful myth" of mainstream economics was clothed in the garb of theological justification by Calvinism, Puritanism, and, in a more curious fashion, the radical individualism of the European and American romanticism. But in spite of this infusion of religious ideas, the understanding of the relationship between part and whole in neoclassical economics is categorically different from that in mainstream religious traditions. The part in mainstream economics is an atomized economic actor whose only relationships to other such entities are prescribed and governed by fixed decision-making rules. This atomized part (self) exists in a closed universe (market system) in which the perpetual enhancement of the economic well-being of all atomized parts is the single organizing principle and motive force and all other bases for identification with human beings do not exist.

215

In bold contrast, the part (self) in all mainstream religious traditions of both East and West is a contingent and transient manifestation of a whole (God or Ground of Being) whose relationships to other parts is defined in terms of a sense of unity with the whole. The terms of this relationship reduce to the maxim that "self is other," and the idea that self is separate from the whole is viewed as a fundamental source of disillusionment and spiritual and moral decay. The collection of parts in these terms is necessarily greater than their sum, and the welfare of the whole is inseparably connected to the behavior of the parts.

For those who are so inclined, there is a new basis for meaningful dialogue between science and religion that could play a large role in the resolution of the environmental crisis. Yet anyone who enters this dialogue will obviously have to overcome a rather large obstacle. Scientific knowledge can no longer be viewed as obviating in any sense the most profound religious impulse—the apprehension of the single significant whole. But that fact is likely to be lost on those who insist that scientific truths must legitimate anthropomorphic versions of religious truths. The assumption that one must make to enter this dialogue, which may be impossible for many, is that Being assumes the anthropomorphic guise of our particular conceptions of beings in a cultural context. Religious truth, like scientific truth, must be viewed as metaphor for that which we cannot fully describe. Yet there is, of course, more involved here than a stubborn refusal to reexamine the character of belief from the perspective of our evolving knowledge.

As Immanuel Kant pointed out, we use two kinds of reason in coming to terms with reality—"theoretical reason" and "practical reason." Theoretical reason in science may have disclosed that the life of the cosmos is marvelously whole or unified. But practical reason, which we employ to coordinate experience in everyday life, still obliges us to act "as if" we are discrete entities moving through the separate dimensions of space and time. It is, however, demonstrably true that theoretical reason does over time refashion the terms of construction of human reality and thereby alters the dynamics of practical reason.

If theoretical reason in modern physics and biology does eventually refashion the terms of constructing our symbolic universe to the extent that it impacts practical reason, conceiving of a human being, as Einstein put it, as "part of the whole" is the leap of faith that would prove most critical. It is only in making this leap that we can begin to free ourselves of the "optical illusions" of our present conception of self as a "part limited in space and time," and to widen "our circle of compassion to embrace all living creatures and the whole of nature in its beauty."[6]

Yet one cannot, of course, merely reason or argue oneself into an acceptance of this proposition. One must also have the capacity for what Einstein termed "cosmic religious feeling," and the hope is that many of those who have this capacity will be able to communicate this awareness to others in metaphoric representations in ordinary language with enormous emotional appeal. The task that lies before the poets of this new reality has been nicely described by Jonas Salk:

> Man has come to the threshold of a state of consciousness regarding his nature and his relationship to the Cosmos, in terms that reflect "reality." By using the processes of Nature as metaphor, to describe the forces by which it operates upon and within Man, we come as close to describing "reality" as we can within the limits of our comprehension. Men will be very uneven in their capacity for such understanding, which, naturally, differs for different ages and cultures, and develops and changes over the course of time. For these reasons it will always be necessary to use metaphor and myth to provide "comprehensible" guides to living. In this way, Man's imagination and intellect play vital roles in his survival and evolution.[7]

THE EMERGENCE OF THE ECOLOGICAL PARADIGM

The most potent and immediate threat to human survival over the last fifty years has been the threat of nuclear holocaust. While progress in solving the nuclear dilemma has typically involved a limited number of decision makers in positions of authority, progress in solving the environmental crisis must involve a great deal more than the mutual consent and cooperation of a small group of global economic planners. One of the great virtues of free market economies in practice, which does not actually exist in the theories of neoclassical economics, is that individuals are free to use their purchasing power to acquire goods and commodities and to shape economic reality through their actions. And this, as noted earlier, is an aspect of economic reality we should try very hard to preserve.

This means that literally billions of people living in very diverse economic, political, and social realities must become far more aware of environmental problems and the manner in which they can use their purchasing power to address these problems. Yet understanding, much less dealing with, these problems requires an awareness of an ecological situation in which the whole is embedded in the parts and the actions of all parts are inextricably related to the welfare of the whole. Let us also not forget that if we fail to deal with these problems before large-scale effects massively disrupt conditions of life in environmentally sensitive regions, democratic governance, along with the fragile peace that exists between nations in these regions, could easily be threatened.

There are, however, many who believe that the implications of the vision of reality contained in modern physics and biology is already occasioning a massive restructuring of the terms of constructing our symbolic universe. The phrase that is most often used to describe this alleged revolution in thought, invented by Thomas Kuhn, is paradigm shift. Because the word "paradigm" has taken on many diverse meanings, the term as it is used here is defined as follows: A paradigm is a constellation of values, beliefs, practices, and perceptions shared by a community, which governs the manner in which the community organizes itself.

Fritjof Capra has made the case that one of the indications that this paradigm shift is in progress is the emergence of what he terms an "ecological worldview."[8] On the most fundamental level, says Capra, ecological awareness is a deeply religious awareness in which the individual feels connected with the whole. The ecological worldview, or social paradigm, is distinguishable, he suggests, in terms of five related "shifts" in emphasis which are entirely consistent with the understanding of physical reality revealed in modern physics:

1. Shift from the Part to the Whole—The properties of the parts must be understood as dynamics of the whole.
2. Shift from Structure to Process—Every structure is a manifestation of an underlying process, and the entire web of relationships is understood to be fundamentally dynamic.
3. Shift from Objective to "Epistemic" Science—Descriptions can no longer viewed as objective and independent of the human observer and the process of knowledge, and this process must be included explicitly in the description.
4. Shift from "Building" to "Network" as Metaphor of Knowledge—Phenomena exist by virtue of their mutually consistent relationships, and knowledge must be viewed as an interconnected network

of relationships founded on self-consistency and general agreement with facts.

5. Shift from Truth to Approximate Descriptions—The true description of any object is a web of relationships associated with concepts and models, and the whole which constitutes the entire web of relationships cannot be represented in this necessarily approximate description.

Although one could extend and refine this list, these shifts, or new terms for the construction of human knowledge, are entirely consistent with our new understanding of nature in physics and biology. They are not arbitrary in the least. If thoughtful people reexamine the character of human knowledge and belief in terms of this understanding, they will draw remarkably similar conclusions.

This understanding can, of course, be achieved by those who have no interest in spiritual reality or feel that the vision of physical reality disclosed in modern biology and physics has nothing to do with spiritual reality. Nothing prevents those who have no interest in such matters from appealing to the implications of our modern scientific worldview to arrive at an improved understanding of better ways to coordinate human experience in the interest of survival. And threats to this survival could be eliminated based on a pragmatic acceptance of the actual conditions and terms for sustaining and protecting human life.

Capra, however, has consistently argued that a global revolution in thought may be prerequisite to human survival and that this revolution may not occur unless intellectual understanding of the character of physical reality is wedded to profound religious or spiritual awareness. In practical or operational terms, this must, in my view, be the case because the "timely" adjustments needed to deal with the ecological crisis will require some very tangible personal sacrifices, particularly on the part of members of economically privileged cultures. It also seems clear that a willingness to sacrifice oneself for the good of the other, or for the good of the whole, has rarely occurred in the course of human history as the direct result of a pragmatic intellectual understanding of the "necessity" to make such sacrifices.

Sacrifice on this order requires a profound sense of identification with the "other" that operates at the deepest levels of our emotional lives. This sense of identification has always been one of the primary challenges and goals of religious thought and practice. Yet one clearly does not arrive at a belief in the existence of a spiritual reality, which has typically been the only way in which human beings have achieved a truly profound sense of identification with the "other," based on the "practical" necessity of doing so. Such a belief requires, as Kierkegaard pointed out, a "leap of faith."

A NEW PROGRAM FOR SCIENTIFIC EDUCATION

If those who have the capacity for this awareness are to become the poets and philosophers of this new reality, they will obviously need something more than a passing acquaintance with modern physics and biology. The study of science could now be vital to the human future not merely because it provides greater levels of mastery and control over natural processes and the bases for building new technologies, but also because it could play a vital and central role in developing a spiritual pattern for the entire global community and an ethics that can serve as a basis for dealing with the environmental crisis. Yet it also seems clear that this will not occur in the absence of some dramatic improvements in the manner in which we "teach" science.

The study of science I have in mind is not the pallid and dispirited version normally taught in public schools and, often enough, in college or university classrooms. It is a science self-reflexively aware of its origins, its transformations, and its inherent limits. This science is not a meaningless number-crunching and equation-solving activity. It continuously emphasizes the essential wonder and beauty of the universe, is aware of its creators and their dreams and struggles, and consistently advertises, as the best scientists have always done, that it is the most communal of all our ways of knowing. Most important, it remains aware in the analysis of "parts" of the greatest and most startling of scientific facts—the ceaseless interconnectedness and interdependence between parts and wholes. This science will never compromise its truths out of deference to the anthropomorphic truths of religion. But it must also be aware that it should not, or rather cannot, legislate over the character of the most profound religious truth for a simple reason—ontological questions no longer lie within the province of science.

Religion, in turn, could enter the dialogue with the recognition that science neither wants nor needs to challenge its authority. If religious thinkers elect to challenge the truths of science within its own domain, they must either withdraw from the dialogue or engage science on its own terms. Applying metaphysics where there is no metaphysics, or attempting to rewrite or rework scientific truths and/or facts in the effort to prove metaphysical assumptions, merely displays a profound misunderstanding of science and an apparent unwillingness to recognize its successes. Yet it is also true that the study of science could serve profoundly religious truths while not claiming to legislate over the ultimate character of these truths.

If the dialogue between the truths of science and religion were as open and honest as it could and should be, we might begin to discover a spiritual pattern that could function as the basis for a global human ethos. Central to this vision would be a cosmos rippling with tension evolving out of itself endless examples of the awe and wonder of its seamlessly interconnected life. And central to the cultivation and practice of the spiritual pattern of the community would be a profound acceptance of the astonishing fact of our being.

Assuming that the dross of anthropomorphism can be eliminated in a renewed dialogue between science and religion, the era in which we were obliged to conceive of the truths of each way of knowing as two truths, and therefore as providing no truth at all, could be over. Science in our new situation in no way argues against the existence of God, or Being, and can profoundly augment the sense of the cosmos as a single significant whole. That the ultimate no longer appears to be clothed in the arbitrarily derived terms of our previous understanding simply means that the mystery that evades all human understanding remains. The study of physical reality should only take us perpetually closer to that horizon of knowledge where the sum of beings is not and cannot be Being and will never be able to comprehend or explain this mystery in its own terms. As William Blake suggested in the age of Newton, the "bounded is loathed by its possessor," and what loathing we would surely feel if we had discovered that the meaning of meaning was only ourselves.

Physicist Wolfgang Pauli, who also thought long and hard about the ethical good that could be occasioned by a renewed dialogue between science and religion, made the following optimistic forecast:

Contrary to the strict division of the activity of the human spirit into separate departments—a division prevailing since the nineteenth century—I consider the ambition of overcoming opposites, including also a synthesis embracing both rational understanding and the mystical experience of unity, to be the mythos, spoken and unspoken, of our present day and age.[9]

This is a project that will demand a strong sense of intellectual community, a large capacity for spiritual awareness, a profound commitment to the proposition that knowledge coordinates experience in the interest of survival, and an unwavering belief that we are free to elect the best means of our survival. The essential truth revealed by science that the religious imagination should now begin to explore with the intent of enhancing its ethical dimensions was described by Erwin Schrödinger: "Hence this life of yours which you are living is not merely a piece of the entire existence, but is, in a certain sense, the whole; only this whole is not so constituted that it can be surveyed in one single glance."[10]

The history of religious thought reveals a progression in virtually all religious traditions toward the conception of spiritual reality as a unified essence in which the self is manifested, or mirrored, in intimate connection with the whole. This suggests that the evolution of human consciousness in both scientific and religious thought is toward the affirmation of the existence of the single significant whole, and that these two versions of the ultimate truth exist in complementary relation. It is also important to stress, however, that the scientific worldview, as Schrödinger also appreciated, simply cannot in itself satisfy our need to understand the character of ultimate truth: "The scientific picture of the real world around me is very deficient. It gives me a lot of factual information, puts all our experience in a magnificently consistent order, but it is ghastly silent about all and sundry that is really dear to our heart, that really matters to us."[11]

At this critical point in human history, the time has clearly come for the religious imagination and the religious experience to engage the truths of science in filling that silence with meaning. One is, however, free to recognize a new basis for a dialogue between science and religion for the same reason that one is free to deny that this basis exists—there is nothing in our current scientific worldview that can prove the existence of God or Being and nothing that legitimates any anthropomorphic conceptions of the nature of God or Being. The question of belief in God or Being remains what it has always been, a question, and the physical universe on the most basic level remains what it has always been, a riddle. And the ultimate answer to the question and the ultimate meaning of the riddle are, and probably always will be, a matter of personal choice and conviction.

There is, however, another conclusion to be drawn here that is not a matter of personal faith or conviction—there is no basis in the scientific description of nature for believing in the radical Cartesian division between mind and world sanctioned by classical physics and incorporated into mainstream economic theory. This radical separation between mind and world was an illusion fostered by limited awareness of the actual character of physical reality and by the extension of mathematical idealizations in classical physics much beyond the realm of their applicability.

If there were world enough and time enough, we could continue to coordinate our experience with economic reality on spaceship earth based on the mathematical idealizations of market systems in neoclassical economics. But as the ecological crisis teaches us in no uncertain terms, the "world enough" capable of sustaining the economic activities of our growing numbers and the "time enough" that remains to reduce and reverse the damage that these activities are inflicting on this planet are rapidly diminishing. Let us therefore get on with the business of displacing neoclassical economics with an environmentally responsible economic theory before large-scale disruptions in the conditions of life on this fragile planet are inevitable.

1. SPACESHIP EARTH: *HOMO ECONOMICUS* AND THE ENVIRONMENTAL CRISIS

1. U Thant, quoted in Lorraine Glennon, ed., *Our Times: The Illustrated History of the Twentieth Century* (Atlanta: Turner Publishing, 1995), p. 513.

2. Robert Heilbroner, *The Worldly Philosophers: The Lives, Times and Ideas of the Great Economic Thinkers* (New York: Simon & Schuster, 1992).

3. K. J. Arrow and F. H. Hahn, *General Competitive Analysis* (San Francisco: Holden Day, 1971), p. 1.

4. Adam Smith, *An Inquiry into the Nature and Causes of the Wealth of Nations*, ed. R. H. Campbell, A. S. Skinner, and W. B. Todd (Oxford: Oxford University Press, 1976), book 4, chapter 2.

5. Philip Mirowski, *Against Mechanism: Protecting Economics from Science* (Lanham, Md.: Rowman & Littlefield, 1988); Bruno Ingrao and Giorgio Israel, *The Invisible Hand: Economic Equilibrium in the History of Science* (Cambridge, Mass.: MIT Press, 1990).

6. Edward O. Wilson, *Consilience: The Unity of Knowledge* (New York: Knopf, 1998), p. 277.

7. Wilson, *Consilience*, p. 280.

8. See Joel E. Cohen, *How Many People Can the Earth Support?* (New York: Norton, 1995).

9. Paul H. Ehrlich and John P. Holdren, "Impact of Population Growth," *Science* 171 (1971): 1212–1217.

10. Wilson, *Consilience*, p. 282.

11. William E. Ross and Mathis Wackernagel, "Ecological Footprints and Appropriated Carrying Capacity," in AnnMari Jansson et al., eds., *Investing in Natural Capital: The Ecological Economics Approach to Sustainability* (Washington, D.C.: Island Press, 1994), pp. 362–390.

12. The most comprehensive summaries of data on the global environment are provided by the World Watch Institute in Washington. See *State of the World and Vital Signs: Trends That Are Shaping Our Future* (New York: Norton, 1997).

13. Philip P. Pan, "Scientists Issue Dire Prediction on Warming," *Washington Post*, 22 January 2001; Craig S. Smith, "150 Nations Start Groundwork for Global Warming Projects," *New York Times*, 18 January 2001.

14. Reed F. Noss and Robert L. Peters, *Endangered Species: A Status Report of America's Vanishing Habitat and Wildlife* (Washington, D.C.: Defenders of Wildlife, 1995); Reed F. Noss, Edward T. LaRoe III, and Michael Scott, *Endangered Species of the United States:*

A Preliminary Assessment of Loss and Degradation (Washington, D.C.: U.S. Department of the Interior, National Biological Service, 1995).

15. E. O. Wilson, *The Future of Life* (New York: Knopf, 2002), pp. 98–99.

16. "The Least Developed Countries Report 2002," in *Escaping the Poverty Trap* (New York: United Nations, 2002).

2. THE NOT SO WORLDLY PHILOSOPHERS: METAPHYSICS, NEWTONIAN PHYSICS, AND CLASSICAL ECONOMICS

1. R. Aron, *Les étapes de la pensée sociologique* (Paris: Gallimard, 1967), p. 40.

2. F. Quesnay, "Analyse de la formule arithmétique du tableau économique de la distribution des dépenses annuelles d'une nation agricole," *Journal de l'Agriculture du Commerce et des Finances* 5, no. 3 (Juin 1766), p. 921.

3. Quesnay, "Analyse de la formule arithmétique," p. 921.

4. Bruno Ingrao and Giorgio Israel, *The Invisible Hand: Economic Equilibrium in the History of Science* (Cambridge, Mass.: MIT Press, 1990), p. 44.

5. A. R. J. Turgot, "Reflections on the Formation and Distribution of Riches," in R. L. Meek, ed., *Turgot on Progress, Sociology and Economics* (Cambridge: Cambridge University Press, 1973), pp. 83–84.

6. Marquis de Condorcet, "Discours prononcé dans l'Académie française le jeudi 21 févier 1792 a la réception de M. le marquis de Condorcet," in A. Condorcet-O'Connor and F. Arago, eds., *Oeuvres de Condorcet* (Paris, 1847), vol. 1, pp. 390ff.

7. Ingrao and Israel, *The Invisible Hand*, pp. 50–51.

8. Robert Heilbroner, *The Worldly Philosophers: The Lives, Times and Ideas of the Great Economic Thinkers* (New York: Simon & Schuster, 1992), pp. 42–43.

9. Heilbroner, *The Worldly Philosophers*, pp. 33–50.

10. Adam Smith, *An Inquiry into the Nature and Causes of the Wealth of Nations*, ed. R. H. Campbell, A. S. Skinner, and W. B. Todd (Oxford: Oxford University Press, 1976), Astronomy Intro. 1,7, II, 2.

11. Smith, *Wealth of Nations*, III, 2.

12. Smith, *Wealth of Nations*, III, 2.

13. Smith, *Wealth of Nations*, Astronomy, II, 12, III, 3.

14. Smith, *Wealth of Nations*, Astronomy, II, 12, III, 3.

15. Smith, *Wealth of Nations*, IV.ix.51.

16. Smith, *Wealth of Nations*, V.i.f.28.

17. Smith, *Wealth of Nations*, Physics 9.

18. Smith, *Wealth of Nations*, Physics 9.

19. Adam Smith, *The Theory of Moral Sentiments*, ed. D. D. Raphael and A. L. Macfie (Oxford: Oxford University Press, 1976), IV.1.10.

20. Smith, *Theory of Moral Sentiments*, IV.1.10.

21. Smith, *Wealth of Nations*, Astronomy IV, 19.

22. Peter Minowitz, *Profits, Priests, and Princes: Adam Smith's Emancipation of Economics from Politics and Religion* (Stanford: Stanford University Press, 1993), p. 131.
23. Smith, *Theory of Moral Sentiments*, VII.ii.1.20.
24. Smith, *Theory of Moral Sentiments*, I.i.4.2.
25. Smith, *Wealth of Nations*, VI.i.11–12.
26. Smith, *Wealth of Nations*, VI.i.13.
27. Smith, *Theory of Moral Sentiments*, IV.I.10.
28. William Godwin, quoted in James Bonar, *Malthus and His Work* (New York: Augustus M. Kelley, 1967), p. 15.
29. Thomas Robert Malthus, *An Essay on the Principle of Population*, ed. Philip Appleman (New York: Norton, 1976), pp. 15ff.
30. Malthus, *Essay on Population*, pp. 15ff.
31. Bonar, *Malthus and His Work*, pp. 1–2.
32. Heilbroner, *The Worldly Philosophers*, p. 95.
33. David Ricardo, *On the Principles of Political Economy and Taxation* (New York: Cambridge University Press, 1951), p. 52.
34. Ricardo, *Principles of Political Economy*, p. 55.

3. THE EMPEROR HAS NO CLOTHES: THE NEOCLASSICAL ECONOMISTS AND MID-NINETEENTH CENTURY PHYSICS

1. Philip Mirowski, *Against Mechanism* (Lanham, Md.: Rowman and Littlefield, 1988); Mirowski, *More Heat Than Light* (New York: Cambridge University Press, 1989).
2. Bruno Ingrao and Giorgio Israel, *The Invisible Hand: Economic Equilibrium in the History of Science* (Cambridge, Mass.: MIT Press, 1990).
3. Mirowski, *Against Mechanism*, pp. 19–20.

For readers interested in a detailed discussion of the manner in which the creators of neoclassical economics abused mid-nineteenth century physics, the best available source is Mirowski's *Against Mechanism*. The following is a less robust treatment that illustrates how these economists appropriated the mathematics of this physics and redefined energy as the equivalent of utility.

Assume a mass point is displaced from point A to B in a three-dimensional plane by force vector F and that the force vector is decomposed into its perpendicular components, $F = iF_x + jF_y + kF_z$, where the notation i,j,k represents unit vectors along the three spatial axes. In the same manner, assume that the vector of displacement dq can also be decomposed into its perpendicular components, $dq = idx + jdy + kdz$. Hence the work accomplished, or the product of the force and the infinitesimal displacements, is defined as the integral of the force times the displacement:

$$T = \int_A^B (F_x dx + F_y dy + F_z dz) = \frac{1}{2}\, mv^2 \Big|_B - \frac{1}{2}\, mv^2 \Big|_A$$

The mid-nineteenth century physicists redefined the change in *mv* as the change in the kinetic energy of the particle and represented this as a single value vector function with *T* representing the change in kinetic energy. Assume that $(F_x dx + F_y dy + F_z dz)$ is an exact differential and that there exists a uniquely identified scalar function $U(x,y,z)$ such that:

$$F_x = -\partial U/\partial x;\ F_y = -\partial U/\partial y;\ F_z = -\partial U/\partial z$$

The scalar function *U* was viewed as the unobserved potential energy of the particle and the total energy of the particle, which is presumably conserved through any motion, was represented as $T + U$. William Hamilton had earlier defined the action integral over time of the path of the particle as

$$\int_{t_1,A}^{t_2,B} (T - U)dt.$$

The Hamiltonian principle of least action asserts that the actual path of the particle from *A* to *B* will be the one that makes the action interval stationary and that this path can be calculated by finding the constrained extrema using either Lagrangean constrained maximization/minimization techniques or the calculus of variations. In a conservative system where $T + U = $ a constant, action is only a function of position. Walras borrowed these equations and made *F* the vector of the prices of a set of traded goods and *q* the vector of the quantities of those goods purchased. He then defined the integral $\int F\,dq = T$ as the total expenditure on these goods, integrated the expression as an exact differential, and defined the scalar function of the goods *x* and *y* as $U = U(x,y,z)$. Amazingly enough, he concluded that the resulting scalar function represents or describes the "utilities" of those goods.

Walras assumed that these utilities, like the concept of potential energy in the physics, are unobservable, and that their existence can only be "inferred" through linkage with observable variables. He then argued that relative prices are equal to the ratios of the marginal utilities of goods by defining the "potential field" of utility as the locus of the set of constrained extrema. Although the other creators of neoclassical economic theory treated utility as a derived phenomenon by viewing the utility field as the exogenous data to which market transactions adjusted, they used the same mathematics. The assumption that this "market system" is reversible and without history did not seem totally unreasonable because the second law of thermodynamics, the entropy law, had not been formulated.

4. William Stanley Jevons, *The Principles of Science*, 2d ed. (London: Macmillan, 1905), pp. 735–736.

5. William Stanley Jevons, *Investigations in Currency and Finance* (London: Macmillan, 1884).

6. R. D. C. Black, ed., *The Papers and Correspondence of W. S. Jevons* (London: Macmillan, 1981), vol. 4, pp. 299–300.

7. W. S. Jevons, *The Theory of Political Economy* (New York: Penguin, 1970), pp. 18–19.

8. Jevons, *Theory of Political Economy*, pp. 18–19.

9. Ingrao and Israel, *The Invisible Hand*, p. 97.

10. Leon Walras, "Letter to Louis Ruchonnet," in W. Jaffe, ed., *Correspondence of Leon Walras and Related Papers* (Amsterdam: North-Holland, 1965), vol. 1, p. 201.

11. Leon Walras, *Elements of Pure Economics* (New York: Kelly Watson, 1960), p. 61.

12. Walras, *Elements of Pure Economics*, p. 63.

13. Walras, *Elements of Pure Economics*, p. 69.

14. Walras, *Elements of Pure Economics*, p. 40.

15. Walras, *Elements of Pure Economics*, p, 224.

16. Leon Walras, "Economique et mécanique," *Metroeconomica* 12 (1965).

17. Walras, "Economique et mécanique," p. 3-11.

18. Leon Walras, quoted in Philip C. Newman, Arthus D. Gayer, and Milton H. Spencer, eds., *Source Readings in Economic Thought* (New York: Norton, 1954) pp. 466–467.

19. Newman, Gayer, and Spencer, *Source Readings in Economic Thought*, pp. 466–467.

20. Walras, *Elements of Pure Economics*, p. 305.

21. Mirowski, *More Heat Than Light*, pp. 193–275.

22. Francis Ysidro Edgeworth, *Mathematical Physics* (London: Routledge, 1881), pp. 9, 12.

23. Vilfredo Pareto, *Manual of Political Economy* (New York: Augustus M. Kelley, 1971), pp. 36, 113.

24. Alfred Marshall, *Principles of Economics*, 8th ed. (London: Macmillan, 1920), p. xiv.

25. Marshall, *Principles of Economics*, pp. xvi–xvii.

26. John Maynard Keynes, letter to George Bernard Shaw, quoted in Roy Harrod, *The Life of John Maynard Keynes* (New York: Augustus M. Kelley, 1969), p. 462.

27. John Keynes, quoted in Robert Clower, "Reflections on the Keynesian Perplex," *Zeitschrift für National Ökonomie* 35 (1975): 5.

28. John von Neumann in conversation with Oskar Morgenstern, in Oskar Morgenstern, "The Collaboration between O. Morgenstern and J. von Neumann on the Theory of Games," *Journal of Economic Literature* 12 (1976): 805–816.

29. Oskar Morgenstern, "Professor Hicks on Value and Capital," *Journal of Political Economy* 29, no. 3 (1949): 361–393.

30. Oskar Morgenstern in A. Schotter, ed., *Selected Economic Writings of Oskar Morgenstern* (New York: New York University Press, 1976), p. 390.

31. Paul A. Samuelson, *Foundations of Economic Analysis* (Cambridge, Mass.: Harvard University Press, 1947), p. 3.

32. Samuelson, *Foundations of Economic Analysis*, p. 4.

33. Samuelson, *Foundations of Economic Analysis*, p. 258.

34. Paul A. Samuelson, "Economic Theory and Mathematics: An Appraisal," *American Economic Review* 42, no. 2 (1952): 55–56.

35. Gerard Debreu, *Theory of Value: An Axiomatic Analysis of Economic Equilibrium* (New Haven: Yale University Press, 1959).

36. Debreu, *Theory of Value*, p. x.

37. Debreu, *Theory of Value*, p. x.

38. Gerard Debreu, *Mathematical Economics: Twenty Papers of Gerard Debreu* (Cambridge: Cambridge University Press, 1983), p. 5.

39. Kenneth J. Arrow and Gerard Debreu, "Existence of an Equilibrium for a Competitive Economy," *Econometrica* 22 (1954): 265–290.

40. Martin Shubik, *Game Theory in the Social Sciences* (Cambridge, Mass.: MIT Press, 1982), p. 300.

41. Shubik, *Game Theory in the Social Sciences*, p. 10.

42. Martin Shubik, *The Theory of Money and Financial Institutions* (Cambridge, Mass.: MIT Press, 1999), vol. 1, p. 3.

43. Shubik, *Theory of Money*, vol. 1, p. 4.

44. Shubik, *Theory of Money*, vol. 1, p. 4.

45. Shubik, *Theory of Money*, vol. 1, pp. 4–5.

46. Shubik, *Theory of Money*, vol. 1, pp. 4–5.

47. Shubik, *Theory of Money*, vol. 2, p. 333.

48. Shubik, *Theory of Money*, vol. 2, pp. 334–337.

49. R. Sugden, "Rational Choice: A Survey of Contributions from Economics and Philosophy," *Economic Journal* 101 (4 July 1991): 783.

50. Wassily Leontief, letter in *Science* 217 (9 July 1981), pp. 104–107.

51. Jean-Pierre Aubin, *Optima and Equilibria: An Introduction to Nonlinear Analysis* (New York: Springer-Verlag, 1998).

52. Lawrence Summers, interviews with Jeffrey Sachs and Lawrence Summers, World Bank, *World Bank Development Report, 1991* (New York: Oxford University Press, 1991), p. 20.

53. Friedrich A. Hayek, *The Road to Serfdom* (Chicago: University of Chicago Press, 1994).

54. Morrison Halcrow, *Keith Joseph: A Single Mind* (London: Macmillan, 1989), p. 152.

55. Richard Cockett, *Thinking the Unthinkable: Think-tanks and the Economic Counter Revolution, 1931–1983* (London: HarperCollins, 1994), p. 174.

56. Margaret Thatcher, *The Path to Power* (New York: HarperCollins, 1995), p. 26.

57. Morrison Halcrow, *Keith Joseph: A Single Mind* (London: Macmillan, 1989), pp. 136–138.

58. John Vickers and George Yarrow, *Privatization: An Economic Analysis* (Cambridge, Mass.: MIT Press, 1993), p. 127.

59. Jon Sopel, *Tony Blair: The Modernizer* (London: Bantam, 1995), p. 35.

60. Herbert Stein, *Presidential Economics: The Making of Economic Policy from Roosevelt to Reagan and Beyond* (New York: Touchstone, 1985), pp. 135–136.

61. William R. Neikirk, *Volcker: A Portrait of the Money Man* (New York: Congdon & Weed, 1987), pp. 137–138.

62. Milton Friedman, *Capitalism and Freedom* (Chicago: University of Chicago Press, 1982).

63. Milton Friedman, *Free to Choose* (New York: Harcourt Brace Jovanovich, 1980).

64. William A. Niskanen, *Reaganomics: An Insider's Account of the Policies and the People* (New York: Oxford University Press, 1988).

65. Paul Ruscavage, *Income Inequality in America* (Armonk, N.Y.: M. E. Sharpe, 1999).

66. Congressional Budget Office, "Economic and Budget Outlook: Fiscal Years 1998–2005," January 1997.

67. Al Gore, *Earth in the Balance: Ecology and the Human Spirit* (New York: Penguin, 1993).

4. NO FREE LUNCH: MAINSTREAM ECONOMICS AND GLOBALIZATION

1. Holly Sklar, ed., *Trilateralism: The Trilateral Commission and Elite Planning for World Management* (Boston: South End Press, 1980).

2. Sklar, *Trilateralism.*

3. David C. Korten, "The Failures of Bretton Woods," in Jerry Mander and Edward Goldsmith, eds., *The Case against the Global Economy* (San Francisco: Sierra Club Books, 1966), pp. 20–21.

4. Ralph Nader and Lori Wallach, "GATT, NAFTA, and the Subversion of the Democratic Process," in Mander and Goldsmith, eds., *The Case against the Global Economy*, pp. 92–107.

5. Tony Clarke, "Mechanisms of Corporate Rule," in Mander and Goldsmith, eds., *The Case against the Global Economy*, p. 298.

6. Herman E. Daly, *Beyond Growth: The Economics of Sustainable Development* (Boston: Beacon Press, 1996), p. 28.

7. Kurt Eichenwald, "Audacious Climb to Success Ended in a Dizzying Plunge," *New York Times*, 13 January 2002.

8. Eichenwald, "Audacious Climb."

9. John Schwartz and Richard A. Oppel, Jr., "Foundation Gives Way on Chief's Big Dream," *New York Times*, 29 November 2001.

10. Eichenwald, "Audacious Climb."

11. Leslie Wayne, "Enron, Preaching Deregulation, Worked the Statehouse Circuit," *New York Times*, 9 February 2002.

12. Joe Stevens, "Hard Money, Strong Arms and 'Matrix': How Enron Dealt with Congress, Bureaucracy," *Washington Post*, 10 February 2002.

13. Gretchen Morgenson, "How 287 Turned into 7: Lessons in Fuzzy Math," *New York Times*, 20 January 2002.

14. Michael Grunwald, "How Enron Sought to Tap the Everglades: Water Unit Lobbied Jeb Bush on Privatization Bid, But Access Led Nowhere," *Washington Post*, 8 February 2002.

15. Quoted in Grunwald, "How Enron Sought to Tap the Everglades."

16. Steven Pearlstein, "Debating the Enron Effect: Business World Divided on Problems and Solutions," *Washington Post*, 17 February 2002.

17. Quoted in William D. Ruckelshaus, "Toward a Sustainable World," *Scientific American* (September 1989): 166–174.

18. Christine Todd Whitman, quoted in Erin Pianin, "U.S. Rebuffs Europeans Urging Change of Mind on Kyoto Treaty," *Washington Post*, 4 April 2001.

19. George W. Bush, quoted in Edmund L. Andrews, "Bush Angers Europe by Eroding Pact on Warming," *New York Times*, 1 April 2001.

20. Romano Prodi, quoted in Andrews, "Bush Angers Europe."

21. Anthony DePalma, "Talks Tie Trade in the Americas to Democracy," *New York Times*, 23 April 2001.

22. David E. Sanger, "Bush Links Trade with Democracy at Quebec Talks," *New York Times*, 22 April 2001.

23. Sanger, "Bush Links Trade with Democracy."

24. Associated Press, "U.S. Criticized on Climate Change," *New York Times*, 22 April 2001.

25. Eric Pianin, "160 Nations Agree to Warming Pact," *Washington Post*, 10 November 2001.

26. Jon Ponk, quoted in Eric Pianin, "Warming Pact a Win for European Leaders," *Washington Post*, 11 November 2001.

27. Paul Blustein, "WTO Cautions Against 'Protectionism,' " *Washington Post*, 10 November 2001.

28. Paul Blustein, "142 Nations Reach Pact on Trade Negotiations," *Washington Post*, 15 November 2001.

29. George W. Bush, quoted in Eric Pianin, "Bush Touts Greenhouse Gas Plan," *Washington Post*, 14 February 2002.

30. Pianin, "Bush Touts Greenhouse Gas Plan."

31. Paul Krugman, "Ersatz Climate Policy," *New York Times*, 15 February 2002.

32. Herman E. Daly, "Sustainable Growth? No Thank You," in Mander and Goldsmith, eds., *The Case against the Global Economy*, p. 193.

33. Daly, "Sustainable Growth?" p. 193.

34. Thomas Prugh et al., *Natural Capital and Human Economic Survival*, 2d ed. (Washington, D.C.: Lewis Publishers, 1999), p. 38.

35. R. Heuting, *New Scarcity and Economic Growth* (New York: Oxford University Press, 1980).

36. *Economist*, 25 April 1992, p. 48.

37. UN Environment Programme, cited in Herman Prager, *Global Marine Environment* (Lanham, Md.: University Press of America), pp. 61–62.

38. Peter Freund and George Martin, *The Ecology of the Automobile* (Montreal: Black Rose Books, 1993).

39. James J. MacKenzie and Michael P. Walsh, *Driving Forces: Motor Vehicle Trends and Their Implications for Global Warming* (Washington, D.C.: World Resources Institute, 1990); and "A Billion Cars," *World Watch*, January–February 1996.

40. J. R. McNeill, *Something New under the Sun: An Environmental History of the Twentieth Century* (New York: Norton, 2000), p. 311.

41. Michel Meybeck, Deborah Chaplin, and Richard Helmer, eds., *Global Freshwater Quality: A First Assessment* (Oxford: Blackwell Scientific, 1989).

42. *Changing the Earth's Climate for Business* (Washington, D.C.: Institute for Policy Studies, 1997).

43. Barry Naughton, "The Chinese Economy: Fifty Years into the Transformation," in Tyrene White, ed., *China Briefing 2000: The Continuing Transformation* (Armonk, N.Y.: M. E. Sharpe, 2000), pp. 49–70.

44. Naughton, "The Chinese Economy."

45. Richard Baum, *Burying Mao: Chinese Politics in the Age of Deng Xiaoping* (Princeton: Princeton University Press, 1994), p. 344.

46. Anders Aslund, *How Russia Became a Market Economy* (Washington, D.C.: Brookings Institution Press, 1995), pp. 64–71.

47. Chrystia Freeland, *Sale of the Century: Russia's Wild Ride from Communism to Capitalism* (New York: Crown Business, 2000), pp. 72–81.

48. Freeland, *Sale of the Century*, pp. 172–176.

49. Lilia Shevtsova, *Yeltsin's Russia: Myths and Reality* (Washington, D.C.: Carnegie Endowment for International Peace, 1999), p. 175.

50. Boris Yeltsin, quoted in *Financial Times*, 29 May 1997, p. 21.

51. Kenneth E. Boulding, "The Economics of the Coming Spaceship Earth," in Henry Jarrett, ed., *Environmental Quality in a Growing Economy* (Baltimore: Johns Hopkins University Press, 1966), pp. 3–14.

5. A GREEN THUMB ON THE INVISIBLE HAND:
ENVIRONMENTAL ECONOMICS

1. Nick Hanley, Jason F. Shogren, and Ben White, *Environmental Economics in Theory and Practice* (New York: Oxford University Press, 1997), p. 358.

2. Hanley, Shogren, and White, *Environmental Economics*, p. 22.

3. A. C. Pigou, *The Economics of Welfare*, 4th ed. (London: Macmillan, 1932), p. 183.

4. Pigou, *Economics of Welfare*, p. xii.

5. R. H. Coase, "The Problem of Law and Economics," *Journal of Law and Economics* (October 1960): 1–44.

6. Nathaniel O. Keohane, Richard L. Revesz, and Robert N. Stavins, "The Choice of Regulatory Instruments in Environmental Policy," in Robert N. Stavins, ed., *Economics of the Environment*, 4th ed. (New York: Norton, 2000), p. 563.

7. Keohane, Revesz, and Stavins, "Choice of Regulatory Instruments," p. 563.

8. Office of Technology Assessment, Technical Assessment Board of the 103d Congress, *Environmental Policy Tools: A User's Guide* (Washington, D.C.: U.S. Government Printing Office, 1995).

9. William D. Norhaus, "Reflections on the Economics of Climate Change," *Journal of Economic Perspectives* 7, no. 4 (Fall 1993): 14.

10. Robert N. Stavins, ed., *Economics of the Environment*, 4th ed. (New York: Norton, 2000).

11. W. Michael Hanneman, "Valuing the Environment through Contingent Value," *Journal of Economic Perspectives* 8, no. 4 (Fall 1994): 19.

12. A. M. Freeman III, "The Measurement of Environmental Resource and Values: Theory and Methods," *Resources for the Future* (Washington, D.C.: U.S. Government Printing Office, 1993).

13. J. W. Fletcher, W. Adamowicz, and T. Graham-Tomasi, "The Travel Cost Model of Recreation Demand," *Leisure Studies* 12 (1990): 119–147.

14. Mark Sagoff, "Some Problems with Environmental Economics," *Environmental Ethics* 10 (Spring 1988): 55.

15. Paul J. Portney, "The Contingency Valuation Debate: Why Economists Should Care," *Journal of Economic Perspectives* 8, no. 4 (Fall 1994): 3.

16. Richard T. Carson et al., *A Bibliography of Contingent Valuation Studies and Papers* (La Jolla, Calif.: Natural Resource Damage Assessment, 1994).

17. Hanneman, "Valuing the Environment," pp. 19–43.

18. J. A. Hausman, ed., *Contingent Valuation: A Critical Assessment* (New York: North-Holland, 1993).

19. Richard W. Olschavsky and Donald H. Granbois, "Consumer Decision Making—Fact or Fiction?" *Journal of Consumer Research* 6 (September 1977): 93–100.

20. J. R. Bettman and M. A. Zins, "Constructive Processes in Consumer Choice, *Journal of Consumer Research* 4 (September 1977): 75–78.

21. Robert C. Mitchell and Richard T. Carson, "Valuing Drinking Water Risk Reduction Using the Contingent Valuation Methods: A Methodological Study of Risks from THM and *Giardia*," paper prepared for Resources for the Future, Washington, D.C., 1986.

22. George Tolley et al., "Establishing and Valuing the Effects of Improved Visibility in Eastern United States," paper prepared for the Environmental Protection Agency, Washington, D.C., 1986.

23. James Bowker and John R. Stoll, "Use of Dichotomous Choice Nonmarket Methods to Value the Whooping Crane Resource," *American Journal of Agricultural Economy* 23, no. 5 (May 1987): 372–381.

24. Kevin J. Boyle and Richard C. Bishop, "Valuing Wildlife in Benefit-Cost Analyses: A Case Study Involving Endangered Species," *Water Resources Research* 23, no. 5 (May 1987): 943–950.

25. Debraj Ray, *Development Economics* (Princeton: Princeton University Press, 1998), p. xiv.

26. Irma Adelman, "Fallacies in Development Theory and Their Implications for Policy," in Gerald M. Meier and Joseph E. Stiglitz, eds., *Frontiers of Development Economics* (New York: Oxford University Press, 2001), pp. 106–107.

27. Anne Krueger, *Trade and Employment in Developing Countries* (Chicago: University of Chicago Press, 1983).

28. Anne Krueger, "Government Failures in Development," *Journal of Economic Perspectives* 4, no. 3 (Summer 1990): 9–23.

29. Kavi Kanbur and Lyn Squire, "The Evolution of Thinking about Poverty," in Meier and Stiglitz, eds., *Frontiers of Development Economics*, p. 203.

30. Vinod Thomas and Jan Wang, "Education, Trade and Investment Returns," Economic Development Institute, World Bank, Washington, D.C., 1997.

31. Sagrario Floro and Pan Yotopoulus, *Informal Credit Markets and the New Institutional Economics* (Boulder, Colo.: Westview, 1991); and Karla Hoff, Avishay Beaverman, and Joseph E. Stiglitz, eds., *The Economics of Rural Organization: Theory, Practice and Policy* (New York: Oxford University Press, 1993).

32. Vito Tanzi and Hamid Davoodi, "Corruption, Public Investment, and Growth," IMF Working Paper WP/97 139; Shang-Jin Wei, "How Taxing Is Corruption on International Investors?" NBER Working Paper 6030, National Bureau of Economic Research, Cambridge, Mass.; and Cheryl W. Gray and Daniel Kaufmann, "Corruption and Development," *Finance and Development* 36, no. 1 (1998): 7–10.

33. *World Development Report 1997: The State of a Changing World* (New York: Oxford University Press, 1997).

34. Sir Hans Singer, "Pioneers Revisited," in Meier and Stiglitz, eds., *Frontiers of Development Economics*, pp. 517–519.

35. Amartya Sen, "The Concept of Development," in Hollis Chenery and T. N. Srinivasan, eds., *Handbook of Developmental Economics* (Amsterdam: North-Holland, 1988); James D. Wolfensohn, "The Other Crisis," address to the annual meeting of the World Bank and the International Monetary Fund, Washington, D.C., 6 October 1998; and Joseph E. Stiglitz, "Some Lessons from the East Asian Miracle," *World Bank Research Observer* 11, no. 2 (August 1996): 151–177.

36. John Newman, Steen Jorgensen, and Menno Pradhan, "How Did Workers Benefit From Bolivia's Emergency Social Fund?" *World Bank Economics Review* 5, no. 2 (1991): 367–393; Lyn Squire, "Introduction: Poverty and Adjustment in the 1980," *World Bank Economics Review* 5, no. 2 (1991): 177–185; and Partha Dasgupta, "The Economics of Poverty in Poor Countries," *Scandinavian Journal of Economics* 100, no. 1 (1998): 41–68.

37. Karla Hoff and Joseph E. Stiglitz, "Modern Economic Theory and Development," in Meier and Stiglitz, eds., *Frontiers of Development Economics*, pp. 395–396.

38. Arnold C. Herberger, "The View from the Trenches: Development Processes as Seen by a Working Professional," in Meier and Stiglitz, eds., *Frontiers of Development Economics*, pp. 227–268.

39. Alfred S. Eichner, ed., *Why Economics Is Not Yet a Science* (New York: M. E. Sharpe, 1983), p. 238.

40. Robert M. Solow, "Economic History and Economics," *American Economic Review* 75, no. 2 (May 1985): 330.

6. SCHISMS, HERESIES, AND KEEPING THE FAITH: ECOLOGICAL ECONOMICS

1. Erwin Schrödinger, *What Is Life?* (Cambridge: Cambridge University Press, 1967), p. 79.

2. Nicholas Georgescu-Roegen, *The Entropy Law and the Economic Process* (Cambridge, Mass.: Harvard University Press, 1971), pp. 20–21.

3. Herman E. Daly and Kenneth N. Townsend, eds., *Valuing the Earth: Economics, Ecology, Ethics* (Cambridge, Mass.: MIT Press, 1993), p. 21.

4. Herman E. Daly, "Allocation, Distribution, and Scale: Toward an Economics That Is Efficient, Just, and Sustainable," *Ecological Economics* 6 (December 1992): 186.

5. Daly, "Allocation, Distribution, and Scale," pp. 190–191.

6. Robert Costanza, "Embodied Energy and Economic Valuation," *Science* 210 (12 December 1980): 1219–1224.

7. Garrett Hardin, "The Tragedy of the Commons," *Science* 162 (13 December 1968): 1243–1248.

8. H. S. Gordon, "The Economic Theory of a Common-Property Resource: The Fishery," *Journal of Political Economy* 62 (1954): 124–142.

9. Colin W. Clark, "Economic Biases against Sustainable Development," in Robert Costanza, ed., *Ecological Economics: The Science of Management and Sustainability* (New York: Columbia University Press, 1991), p. 323.

10. Richard B. Norgaard and Richard B. Howarth, in John M. Hollander, ed., *The Environmental Connection* (Washington, D.C.: Island Press, 1992), pp. 347–363.

11. Richard Norgaard, "Three Dilemmas of Environmental Accounting," *Ecological Economics* 1 (December 1989): 303–314.

12. Richard Norgaard, "Economic Indicators of Resource Scarcity," *Journal of Environmental Economics and Resource Management* 19 (July 1990): 19–25.

13. Herman E. Daly and John B. Cobb Jr., "Appendix: The Index of Sustainable Development," in *For the Common Good: Redirecting the Economy toward Community, the Environment and a Sustainable Future* (Boston: Beacon Press, 1989), pp. 443–507.

14. Robert Repetto et al., *Wasting Assets: Natural Resources in the National Income Accounts* (Washington, D.C.: World Resources Institute, 1989); Wilfrido Cruz and Robert Repetto, *The Environmental Effects of Stabilization and Structural Adjustment Programs: The Philippines Case* (Washington, D.C.: World Resources Institute, 1992); Maria Concepción Cruz et al., *Population Growth, Poverty and Environmental Stress: Frontier Migration in the Philippines and Costa Rica* (Washington, D.C.: World Resources Institute, 1992).

15. Kirk Hamilton, "Monitoring Environmental Progress" and "Green Adjustments to GDP," World Bank Environment Discussion Papers, 1994.

16. Mark Sagoff, "Some Problems with Environmental Economics," *Environmental Ethics* 3 (Spring 1988): 55–74.

17. Silvio O. Funtowicz and Jerome R. Ravetz, "The Worth of a Songbird: Ecological Economics As a Post-Normal Science," *Environmental Economics* 10 (August 1994): 197–207.

18. Bruce Hannon, "Measures of Economic and Ecological Health," in Robert Costanza, Brian Norton, and Benjamin Haskell, eds., *Ecosystem Health: New Goals for Environmental Management* (Washington, D.C.: Island Press, 1992).

19. F. Hinterberger, "Another Plea for Pluralism in Ecological Economics," *ESEE Newsletter* (November 1997): 3-7.

20. Andreas Renner, "Some Methodological Reflections: A Plea for a Constitutional Ecological Economics," in Jörg Kohn et al., eds., *Sustainability in Question: The Search for a Conceptual Framework* (Northampton, Mass.: Edward Elgar, 1999), p. 320.

21. Charles Perrins, "Reserved Rationality and the Precautionary Principle: Technological Change, Time, and Uncertainty in Environmental Decision Making," in Costanza, ed., *Ecological Economics*, p. 157.

7. THE REAL ECONOMY IN BIOLOGY: EMERGENCE AND A NEW VIEW OF ORDER

1. P. J. Vorzimmer, *Charles Darwin: The Years of Controversy; The Origins of Species and Its Critics, 1859–1852* (Philadelphia: Temple University Press, 1977).

2. L. B. Jones, "Schumpeter versus Darwin: In re: Malthus," *Southern Economic Journal* 56, no. 2 (October 1989): 410–422.

3. Stephen J. Gould, *Ever Since Darwin: Reflections in Natural History* (London: Burnett Books, 1979), p. 22.

4. Charles Darwin, "The Linnean Society Papers," in *Darwin: A Norton Critical Edition*, ed. Philip Appleman (New York: Norton, 1970), p. 83.

5. Charles Darwin, *The Origin of Species* (New York: Mentor, 1958), p. 75.

6. Darwin, *Origin of Species*, p. 120.

7. Geoffrey M. Hodgson, "Hayek, Evolution, and Spontaneous Order," in Philip Mirowski, ed., *Natural Images in Economic Thought* (New York: Cambridge University Press, 1994), pp. 408–447.

8. Lynn Margulis and Dorion Sagan, *Microcosmos: Four Billion Years from Our Microbial Ancestors* (New York: Simon & Schuster, 1986), p. 16.

9. Margulis and Sagan, *Microcosmos*, p. 18.

10. Margulis and Sagan, *Microcosmos*, p. 18.

11. Margulis and Sagan, *Microcosmos*, p. 19.

12. J. Shaxel, *Grundriss der Theorienbildung in der Biologie* (Jena: Fisher, 1922), p. 308.

13. Ludwig von Bertalanffy, *Modern Theories of Development: An Introduction to Theoretical Biology*, trans. J. H. Woodger (New York: Harper, 1960), p. 31.

14. Ernst Mayr, *The Growth of Biological Thought: Diversity, Evolution and Inheritance* (Cambridge, Mass.: Harvard University Press, 1982), p. 63.

15. P. B. Medawar and J. S. Medawar, *The Life Sciences: Current Ideas in Biology* (New York: Harper & Row, 1977), p. 165.

16. Margulis and Sagan, *Microcosmos*, p. 265.

17. Darwin, *Origin of Species*, p. 83.

18. Darwin, *Origin of Species*, 77.

19. Darwin, *Origin of Species*, p. 75.

20. Darwin, *Origin of Species*, p. 76.
21. Darwin, *Origin of Species*, pp. 78–79.
22. Richard M. Laws, "Experiences in the Study of Large Animals," in Charles Fowler and Tim Smith, eds., *Dynamics of Large Mammal Populations* (New York: Wiley, 1981), p. 27.
23. Charles Fowler, "Comparative Population Dynamics in Large Animals," in Fowler and Smith, eds., *Dynamics*, pp. 444–445.
24. Charles Elton, *Animal Ecology* (London: Methuen, 1968), p. 119.
25. David Lack, *The Natural Regulation of Animal Numbers* (Oxford: Oxford University Press, 1954), pp. 29–30, 46.
26. James L. Gould, *Ethology: Mechanisms and Evolution of Behavior* (New York: Norton, 1982), p. 467.
27. Paul Colinvaux, *Why Big Fierce Animals Are Rare: An Ecologist's Perspective* (Princeton: Princeton University Press, 1978), p. 145.
28. Colinvaux, *Why Big Fierce Animals Are Rare*, p. 146.
29. Peter Farb, *The Forest* (New York: Time-Life, 1969), p. 116.
30. P. Klopfer, *Habitats and Territories* (New York: Basic Books, 1969), p. 9.
31. Lynn Margulis, *Symbiosis in Cell Evolution* (San Francisco: Freeman, 1981), p. 163.

8. THE REAL ECONOMY IN PHYSICS: COSMIC CONNECTIONS

1. Philip Mirowski, *More Heat Than Light* (New York: Cambridge University Press, 1989), pp. 354–401.
2. Werner Heisenberg, quoted in James B. Conant, *Modern Science and Modern Man* (New York: Columbia University Press, 1953), p. 40.
3. Max Planck, *Where Is Science Going?* (London: G. Allen and Unwin, 1933), p. 24.
4. Albert Einstein, "Autobiographical Notes," in P. A. Schlipp, ed., *Albert Einstein: Philosopher-Scientist* (New York: Harper & Row, 1959), p. 3.
5. Albert Einstein, quoted in *New York Post*, 28 November 1972.
6. Richard Feynman, *The Character of Physical Law* (Cambridge, Mass.: MIT Press, 1967), p. 130.
7. Steven Weinberg, quoted in Heinz Pagels, *The Cosmic Code* (New York: Bantam Books, 1983), p. 239.
8. Milic Capek, "New Concepts in Space and Time," in Ken Wilbur, ed., *Quantum Questions* (Boulder, Colo.: New Science Library, 1988), p. 99.
9. Henry Stapp, "Quantum Theory and the Physicist's Conception of Nature: Philosophical Implications of Bell's Theorem," in Richard D. Kitchener, ed., *Bell's Theorem, Quantum Theory and Conceptions of the Universe* (Albany: SUNY Press, 1988), p. 54.
10. Werner Heisenberg, *Physics and Philosophy* (London: Faber, 1959), p. 96.
11. A. Aspect, P. Grangier, and G. Roger, *Physical Review Letters* 49 (1982): 91, 1804.

12. W. Tittle, J. Brendel, H. Zbinden, and N. Gisin, "Violation of Bell's Inequalities More Than 10km Apart," *Physical Review Letters* 81 (1988): 3563–3566.

13. See Bernard d'Espagnat, *In Search of Reality* (New York: Springer-Verlag, 1981), pp. 43–48.

14. N. David Mermin, "Extreme Quantum Entanglement in a Superposition of Macroscopically Distinct States," *Physical Review Letters* 85, no. 15 (1990): 1838–1840.

15. Robert Nadeau and Menas Kafatos, *The Non-Local Universe: The New Physics and Matters of the Mind* (New York: Oxford University Press, 1999).

16. Ilya Prigogine and Isabelle Stengers, *Order out of Chaos* (Bantam: New York, 1984), p. 292.

17. James Glanz, "Droughts Might Speed Climate Changes," *New York Times*, 11 January 2001.

9. TOWARD A NEW THEORY OF ECONOMICS: THE COSTS OF DOING BUSINESS IN THE GLOBAL ENVIRONMENT

1. Frank H. Hahn in Carla Raviola, ed., *Economists and the Environment* (New Jersey: Zed Books, 1995), p. 23.

2. Raviola, ed., *Economists and the Environment*, p. 37.

3. Milton Friedman in Raviola, ed., *Economists and the Environment*, p. 63–74.

4. Raviola, ed., *Economists and the Environment*, p. 33.

5. Lawrence Summers in Peter D. Henig, "Charles Darwin Meets Adam Smith," *Red Herring*, 3 February 2001.

6. D. A. Underwood and P. G. King, "On the Ideological Foundations of Environmental Policy," *Ecological Economics* 1 (1989). 315–334; and J. M. Gowdy and C. N. McDaniel, "One World, One Experiment: Addressing the Biodiversity-Economics Conflict," *Ecological Economics* 15 (1996): 181–192.

7. Andrew C. Revkin, "U.S. Losing Status As a World Leader in Climate," *New York Times*, 6 June 2001.

8. Robert Costanza et al., "The Value of the World's Ecosystem Services and Natural Capital," *Nature* 387 (15 May 1997): 253–260.

9. J. Spangenberg, ed., *Toward Sustainable Europe* (Brussels: Friends of the Earth, 1995); R. A. Waterings and J. B. Spschoor, "The Ecocapacity As a Challenge to Technological Development," Publication RNMO 74a, Advisory Council for Research on Nature and Environment, Rijswijk, 1992.

10. *The Net Impact of Economic Protection on Jobs and the Economy*, Management Information Services, Washington, D.C., 1993. Results summarized in R. Bezdex, "Environment and the Economy: What's the Bottom Line?" *Environment* 35, no. 7 (1993): 7–11.

11. Paul Hawken, Amory Lovins, and L. Hunter Lovins, *Natural Capitalism: Creating the Next Industrial Revolution* (New York: Little, Brown, 1999).

10. THE CEREMONY OF INNOCENCE: SCIENCE, ETHICS, AND THE ENVIRONMENTAL CRISIS

1. Ernst Mayr, *Toward a New Philosophy of Biology* (Cambridge, Mass.: Harvard University Press, 1988), pp. 66–74.

2. Robert Nadeau and Menas Kafatos, *The Non-Local Universe: The New Physics and Matters of the Mind* (New York: Oxford University Press, 1999), pp. 125–146.

3. Henry P. Stapp, "Quantum Theory and the Physicist's Conception of Nature: Philosophical Implications of Bell's Theorem," in Richard E. Kitchener, ed., *The World View of Contemporary Physics* (Albany: SUNY Press, 1988), p. 54.

4. Errol E. Harris, in Kitchener, ed., *World View of Contemporary Physics*, p. 159.

5. Werner Heisenberg, in Ken Wilbur, ed., *Quantum Questions* (Boulder, Colo.: New Science Library, 1984), p. 96.

6. Albert Einstein, quoted in *New York Post*, 28 November 1972.

7. Jonas Salk, *Survival of the Wisest* (New York: Harper & Row, 1973), p. 82.

8. Fritjof Capra, "The Role of Physics in the Current Changes of Paradigms," in Kitchener, ed., *World View of Contemporary Physics*, p. 151.

9. Wolfgang Pauli, in Wilbur, ed., *Quantum Questions*, p. 163.

10. Erwin Schrödinger, in Wilbur, ed., *Quantum Questions*, p. 97.

11. Erwin Schrödinger, in Wilbur, ed., *Quantum Questions*, p. 81.